Lisa Goldberg
Merelyn Frank Chalmers
Natanya Eskin
Jacqui Israel

Photography *by* Alan Benson
Styling *by* David Morgan
Design *by* Evi-O.Studio

Monday Morning Cooking Club

Now for Something Sweet

HarperCollins*Publishers*

Contents

Introduction

There's something about the Jewish community and cake.

- -

We are always
dreaming of soft, airy, pale chiffon cake
thinking about chocolate-swirled, glossy yeasted babke
imagining flaky, chewy, jammy strudel
baking almond-studded, citrus-glazed Dutch buns
frying golden, syrup-drenched coiled fishuelas
biting into hot, sugared jam-filled doughnuts
eating crisp-shelled, marshmallowy vanilla-flecked meringues
feasting on sticky, steaming, sweet butterscotch pudding
and sharing it all with abundance and love

- -

We've been on a mission – a quest, a non-stop search – to uncover, to persistently test and tweak, and to preserve the many sweet recipes entrusted to us over our years of collecting. And here we have it: our conscientiously curated selection of sweet recipes we love the most, from Jewish homes across Australia and around the world. This is not an encyclopaedic collection; these are simply the recipes we are most excited to share. And the ones you'll catch us eating straight from the tray/tin/bowl/jar in the corner of the kitchen, again and again.

We formed our sisterhood, the Monday Morning Cooking Club, in 2006 to collect the recipes and stories from the best cooks we could find in Sydney's Jewish community. This adventure culminated in our first cookbook, *Monday Morning Cooking Club: The food, the stories, the sisterhood*, in 2011.

We journeyed Australia-wide to deliver our next book, *The Feast Goes On*, in 2014, and the trilogy was completed in 2017 with *It's Always About the Food*, a culturally interesting collection from across the world.

We've searched for Sydney's best, looked for Australia's heirloom masterpieces and explored the dishes of the global Jewish diaspora. (And we've fried more onions than we can count.)

It has become our custom, our trademark and our greatest pride to tell honest, heartwarming and poignant stories alongside the recipes: tales of old lands and new beginnings, accounts of trauma and sorrow, lessons of love and joy. Stories of cooking from memory to rekindle the warmth of a time gone by, memoirs telling of kitchen secrets learnt at a grandmother's side, discovering the joy of feeding and nurturing a young family. And each and every story reveals the universal connection to, and honouring of, tradition.

Over the years we've mastered *challah* with egg and onion, and chicken soup with matzo balls. We've explored Sephardi chicken curry and Ashkenazi *cholent*. We've slow-cooked Hungarian goulash and Roman lamb. We devoured Israeli *shakshouka* and Algerian couscous.

And now, it's time for something sweet.

These are the sweet recipes we will make and remake. The biscuits we package up and give to a friend in need. The cakes we need to eat, sliver after sliver after sliver. The warm buns we gently cradle like newborn babies to inhale the intoxicating yeasty aroma. These are the desserts we truly long for after we've eaten the last spoonful. And at the end, there's one completely irresistible savoury chapter for some salty relief.

With this book, we continue to weave the tapestry of a culturally diverse, uniquely food-obsessed community that loves to cook, and, most importantly, to nurture those we love through food. We give you, with our collective heart and soul, recipes to pass on to the next generation, and stories to tell as we slice just one more piece of cake. And all with much love and deliciousness, from our kitchen to yours,

Lisa, Merelyn, Natanya & Jacqui

Monday Morning Cooking Club

The Sisterhood

MERELYN CHALMERS

I pinch myself to think I've been sharing my Mondays with this special group of women for 14 years. I love sharing cooking tips and techniques, teaching unconfident cooks that cooking can be fun and talking about food till forever. I have a pedantic respect for punctuation and well-measured ingredients, and I just adore the precision of my digital scales and a freshly sharpened cook's knife. I have inherited my mother's passion for searching out elusive ingredients, believing I can cure any of my family's ills with food, and endless cups of tea.

LISA GOLDBERG *Chief Pot Stirrer*

I embrace the part of Jewish culture that embodies the saying 'it's always about the food'. I am a *fresser* (one who eats with joy and abandon) with an unbridled passion for eating, cooking and nurturing those around me with food. My legal background has given me a great foundation to help guide – and work side by side with – this truly amazing bunch of kind, funny and enlightening women to produce and publish four extraordinary cookbooks. I feel incredibly grateful to have had (and to continue to have) the opportunity to spend so much of my time dedicated to, and fully immersed in, such a delicious, inspiring and worthwhile project.

NATANYA ESKIN

I have always been happiest in my kitchen, cooking and baking for my family, and have developed a strong passion for uncovering and preserving recipes. I could talk sweet recipes all day long, especially those that come from the older generations from whom I have learnt so much. And even after so many years in the Monday Morning Cooking Club kitchen with the girls – our sisterhood – I love nothing more than a good debate on a Monday morning about what or how to cook. Through much laughter, lots of sharing and many hours, we work hard as a team to create something special for generations to come.

JACQUI ISRAEL

I joined Monday Morning Cooking Club for a 'one-year project' in 2006 and I'm still here. I brought my schoolteacher-perfect handwriting, my need to colour-code pretty much everything and an organisational determination that I still try to insist on. When I think back to how I felt in those early years, with little cooking confidence, it was unfathomable that I would be part of a group producing the most beautiful cookbooks sold around the world. I am so pleased and proud to be involved in a project such as this, to discover the incredibly diverse traditions in people's kitchens and to unearth a cooking heritage that I had never taken the time to explore.

Kitchen Notes

We have tested and retested these recipes to make sure they can be replicated in your kitchen, and suggest you read these notes before you start as they contain lots of helpful hints and tips to ensure you get the best results possible.

First and foremost, buy the best quality and freshest ingredients you can. This is particularly important when it comes to chocolate, oil and nuts.

MEASUREMENTS

We use standard Australian metric measurements.

For cake, biscuit and pastry recipes, precision is essential and we recommend weighing ingredients using a digital scale.

1 cup = 250 ml = 8½ fl oz

1 tablespoon = 20 ml = ¾ fl oz = 4 teaspoons

1 teaspoon = 5 ml

If you are using a U.S. (non-metric) 15 ml tablespoon, add an extra teaspoon for each tablespoon specified.

OVENS AND EQUIPMENT

Our recipes are tested in a domestic oven on conventional heat settings. Oven temperatures can vary and you may need to adjust the cooking time or temperature according to your oven.

To beat using an electric mixer means to use the paddle attachment or K beater.

To whisk using an electric mixer means to use the whisk attachment.

To knead using an electric mixer means to use the dough hook.

A handheld mixer can be used for any beating and whisking.

CAKE TINS

Many recipes call for 'lined' tins or trays, which means you need to grease the surfaces lightly with butter, oil or cooking spray (a very good use for it!) and then press baking paper onto the surfaces. You will need to tear or cut the baking paper to fit the particular tin.

Cake tins and other dishes are measured by the diameter of the base rather than the top rim. If your baking tins have no markings, we find it helpful to write the measurement on the base with a permanent marker.

INGREDIENT NOTES

Butter: We always use unsalted butter for cooking so that you can better control the saltiness of the dish. If you have only salted butter in the fridge, go ahead and use it but leave out the salt listed in the recipe.

1 stick of butter = 113.5 g = 8 (U.S.) tablespoons = 4 oz

A recipe in this book may call for butter in one of four ways:

1. **Room temperature** – soft enough to be easily beaten

2. **Softened** – really soft but not melted, for example when adding to brioche dough. If your kitchen is warm, your butter may be 'softened' at room temperature. If it is a cold day, you will need to put it in a warm place to soften further.

3. **Melted** – slowly melt the butter in the microwave or in a saucepan.

4. **Cold** – straight from the fridge. Best to chop the butter as the recipe indicates and then return it to the fridge while you get the other ingredients ready.

Eggs: The eggs we use are free-range and extra large (with a minimum weight of 67 g/2⅓ oz).

Some recipes in this book contain raw eggs. Always use the freshest eggs for these recipes. If you are at increased risk of the effects of salmonella poisoning, and for food to be served to children, the elderly or pregnant women, please consult your medical professional before eating. It is recommended that any dish containing raw eggs be stored in the fridge below 5°C (41°F) and consumed within 24 hours.

Flour: We mostly use two types of flour in our recipes, plain (all-purpose) and self-raising (self-rising). You can substitute cake flour for plain flour when making cakes, biscuits and pastry.

To make self-raising flour, sift 2 teaspoons baking powder with 150 g (1 cup/5⅓ oz) plain (all-purpose) flour.

Remember to always have a little extra plain flour on hand, as it is often needed for rolling out dough or flouring cake tins. This is what we mean when we write 'plus extra'.

Lemons: 1 lemon, juiced = 50 ml (2½ tablespoons) juice

Matzo meal: This is an ingredient used (often instead of flour or breadcrumbs) in Passover recipes. It can be found in supermarkets or stores that sell kosher items and in Australia is available in three types: coarse (perfect for matzo balls), fine (perfect for biscuits and savoury dishes where breadcrumbs would be used) and superfine (sometimes called matzo flour, or cake meal, most similar to flour and perfect for cakes).

Nuts: All nuts in our recipes are shelled (out of the shell).

If a recipe calls for toasted or roasted nuts you can sometimes buy them already roasted, or you can toast them yourself in a dry frying pan over medium heat, tossing frequently, or roast in a 160°C (325°F/Gas 3) oven. The cooking time is usually 10–20 minutes, but will depend on the type of nut.

Almond meal in any recipe can be replaced with ground almonds. Packaged almond meal is usually made from ground blanched almonds (no skin). Ground almonds can be made from raw (with skin), blanched (no skin) or roasted almonds, depending on the recipe. If you wish to grind your own almonds, pulse in the food processor until they have reached the desired consistency.

Oil: When a recipe calls for oil, use any unflavoured oil such as grapeseed, canola or sunflower. In chiffon cakes, Merelyn's preference is light olive oil.

Salt: We use two types of salt: fine or medium-grained best-quality salt for most cooking and baking needs and flaky salt for seasoning during and after cooking.

Sugar: We prefer baking with caster (superfine) sugar, which appears in many of the recipes. If you are unable to buy it where you are, substitute white (granulated) sugar.

Yeast: We have used active dried yeast for the recipes in this book. If you prefer to use fresh yeast, use double the weight we've specified in the recipe.

1 sachet (envelope) active dried yeast = 7 g = 2¼ teaspoons = 15 g fresh yeast

HOW TO MELT CHOCOLATE

We like to use the best-quality chocolate we can, and sometimes specify percentage of cocoa in recipes where the flavour of the chocolate is particularly important.

Melt the chocolate either in the microwave or on the stove. To use the microwave, put the chocolate (broken into pieces or chopped) in a heatproof bowl, and heat on a medium–high power, checking and stirring at 30-second intervals to avoid burning. If there are still a few bits of unmelted chocolate left, stir until melted rather than cooking longer in the microwave. To melt on the stove, use the double boiler method. Bring a small saucepan with about 2.5 cm (1 inch) of water to the boil. Place the chocolate in a heatproof bowl that will fit snugly on top of the saucepan without touching the water. Turn the water down to a simmer, place the bowl on top of the saucepan and allow the chocolate to melt, stirring from time to time.

FOLDING INTO A MIXTURE

To fold means to gently mix in a circular motion, pushing the spoon down the side of the mixture to the bottom and then back over the top, turning the bowl and repeating. This technique helps to ensure air stays in the mixture and it remains as light as possible.

BISCUITS

Most of the biscuit doughs and mixtures can be prepared ahead of time and frozen, then thawed, rolled out and shaped when needed for baking. For some of them, you can shape the uncooked dough and then freeze, ready to pull out of the freezer and bake at another time. All the biscuits should be stored in airtight containers at room temperature and most will be good for up to one week.

LANGUAGE

Our books use standard British spelling and grammar, irrespective of where the recipe or contributor originates.

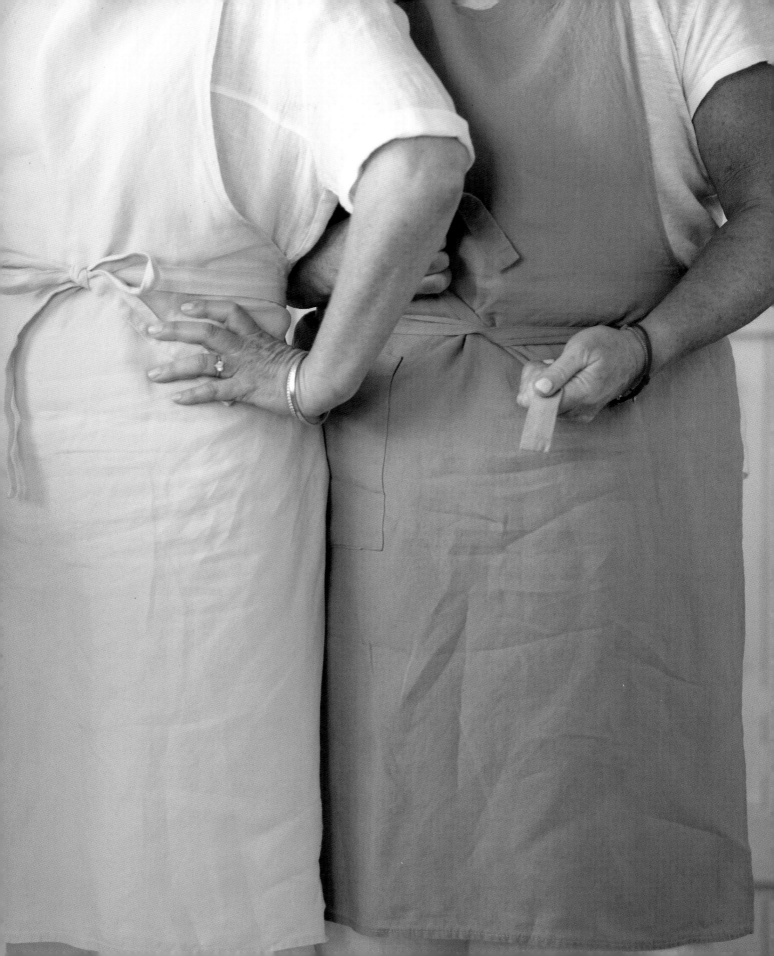

A quiet moment on your own, a quick cup of tea shared with a friend, the biscuit tin delivers at the pop of a lid. We are always inspired by the grannies and bubbas who filled leaning towers of biscuit tins with love, to be opened the moment someone dropped in. Heaven forbid there was nothing to offer. These are the biscuits we want in our pantries, from the one-bowl/one-spoon mix to those made patiently with many hands. From European one-bite morsels to the unique flavours of the Americas, these are the biscuits we will make over and over (and over) again.

When Lisa first met her late mother-in-law, **TALIA GOLDBERG**, she would sneak into Talia's kitchen and eat handfuls of her tiny bagel-shaped almond biscuits. Literally handfuls. Lisa tells evocative stories of the incredible food that came out of Talia's kitchen. Her family remember her as a wonderful and passionate home cook, as well as a strong and cultured Israeli *sabra*. Talia immigrated to the remote and foreign shores of Australia after she met and married her husband, a Griffith-born doctor, also with roots in Israel. She loved reading, classical concerts, learning Italian and teaching Hebrew and, above all, feeding her family.

Melbourne was a drawcard for third-generation Dubliner and trained chef **MISH ARNDT**. She visited Australia as a backpacker in the 1990s, fell in love with its warm and welcoming culture and never left. Like so many of us, Mish learnt to cook at her mother's side, *fressing* (eating with abandon) the first fritter from the pan and licking any bowl ready to be licked. She now runs Mish's Dishes cooking school, but loves nothing more than having her two daughters by her side, teaching them traditional dishes and relishing in their joy at each Jewish festival as they wait expectantly for their perennial favourites to appear.

MIRIAM MILLINGEN thrives on feeding her family. Her Polish mum would regularly bake for WIZO charity events and Miriam would ask for a piece of whatever cake she had just baked. Always eager to feed her family, Miriam's mother would actually say, 'Yes,' then quickly bake another one to give away. Miriam's parents settled in the rusty red town of Whyalla after the war, and she was born in this rural outpost of South Australia where her father practised medicine. The family eventually moved to Adelaide and became part of its small Jewish community. With only a thousand people in the community, Miriam participated in everything on offer and became particularly involved with WIZO. Like many of her peers, she followed her children to Melbourne where they now live.

ANNE DIBOWITZ'S kitchen was stacked floor to ceiling with biscuit tins filled with beautiful sweet biscuits and slices she had lovingly baked for her precious grandchildren. Anne, granny of past Monday Morning Cooking Club author Lynn Niselow, lived in Cape Town and, inspired by her Lithuanian mother's passion for bagels and *teiglach* (golden syrup pastries), loved to cook. Everywhere she went she was armed with pen and paper to note down recipes she enjoyed and to share her own recipes with anyone who was interested. She relished time alone in the kitchen, preparing feasts for her family to enjoy when they arrived from Johannesburg for the school holidays. And as Jewish festivals approached, she gathered her friends together and a production line was set up in the garage so they could prepare the traditional dishes, side by side.

It's a beautiful thing to witness the influence of grandmothers. **SILVIA NACAMULLI'S** passion for food began as a young girl in Rome, cooking for Jewish festivals with her mother and grandmothers as she absorbed the smells, tastes and flavours of the oldest Jewish community in the Western world. Silvia, who we first came across while collecting recipes for *It's Always About the Food*, now lives in London and spreads the joy of Italian–Jewish cuisine through Cooking for the Soul (her cooking school and catering business) and her magazine columns, cookbooks and tours of Italy. You can take the girl out of Italy, but you can never take Italy out of the girl.

Sydney local and good friend of Monday Morning Cooking Club, **LAINIE CADRY** contributed to *It's Always About the Food* when she was only a teenager. She is now a paediatric nurse as well as an accomplished cook. She connects with her cooking, like her Judaism, straight from the heart. Lainie learnt the traditional dishes of both her European and Persian grandparents, and now her cooking is not bound by any one style, but is layered and nuanced with exotic ingredients and depth of flavour. She continues to astound and delight her family and friends (and us!) with the incredible feasts she produces.

JANICE LAVINE'S cooking leans towards Jewish culture with her regular *Shabbat* (Sabbath) dinners thanks to the standard 'Friday-night menu' (yes, we all relate!), festival celebrations with traditional food and the continuation of her mother's legendary *Chanukah* party. We first spotted Los Angeles-based Janice in the pages of a second-hand 1990s kindergarten cookbook and – with the help of Google, a friend of Lisa's in L.A. and some Monday Morning Cooking Club persistence – we found her. Inspired and encouraged by her own food intolerances and those of her young daughter, Janice created the Breakaway Bakery in 2010. For eight years it was a dedicated kosher, organic and gluten-, soy-, dairy-*and* nut-free bakery. So amazing! How lucky for all who needed what she had to offer.

Another cook from the younger generation, Lisa's daughter, **JESSIE GOLDBERG**, has a reputation for delivering cellophane bags of deliciousness to friends. Now totally consumed with life as a young doctor in Sydney, as well as playing football on weekends and volunteering for the community, it's a wonder she is able to fit in anything else. She manages to find time to make her excellent shortcut *shakshouka* for weekend breakfasts with friends, and her Choc Oat Cookies have become legendary. Lisa is hopeful that Jessie has inherited her love of food and her love of nurturing friends and family with food. From biscuit tin to biscuit tin, from generation to generation.

CAROLYN LEVITT

Honey Snaps

A snappy honey biscuit for Jewish New Year or any time of year. These are the most delightful biscuits – simple to make, great to gift and, best of all, easy to eat.

450 g (3 cups/1 lb) plain (all-purpose) flour, plus extra
1½ teaspoons bicarb soda (baking soda)
1 teaspoon ground ginger
½ teaspoon ground mixed spice
½ teaspoon ground cinnamon
½ teaspoon salt
185 g (6½ oz) unsalted butter, at room temperature, chopped
220 g (1 cup, firmly packed/7¾ oz) brown sugar
1 egg
90 g (¼ cup/3¼ oz) honey

Sift the flour, bicarb, ginger, mixed spice, cinnamon and salt together, then set aside. Beat the butter until creamy then add the sugar and beat until the mixture is light and fluffy. Add the egg and the honey and beat until well combined.

Fold in the dry ingredients and mix gently to form a soft dough. Wrap the dough tightly in plastic wrap and refrigerate for at least 1 hour.

When ready to bake, preheat the oven to 180°C (350°F/ Gas 4). Line 2 large baking trays.

Divide the dough in 2 and, on a lightly floured benchtop, roll out the first half to a thickness of 2–3 mm (⅛ of an inch), lightly flouring the dough and the rolling pin as needed. Using a 6 cm (2½ inch) round (or other shaped) cookie cutter, cut out biscuits and place on the prepared trays, leaving a small space between them. Collect any scraps, combine them to form a ball and then set aside to rest while you roll out the other half of the dough. Repeat until all the dough has been used.

Bake for 10 minutes, or until they are just starting to brown and feel firm at the edges. Allow to cool on the trays.

Makes 90

JANICE LAVINE

Molasses Cookies

This recipe came from Janice's dear friend Priscilla Kromnick, a wonderful baker. As happened when we all had young children, they met when their daughters were in preschool. They'd spend afternoons at each other's houses – the girls playing, the mums chatting and Priscilla always supplying something delicious to eat. These cookies were one of the all-time favourites and one of the first recipes Janice converted to gluten-free for her Los Angeles bakery.

170 g (6 oz) unsalted butter, at room temperature, chopped
230 g (1 cup/8 oz) caster (superfine) sugar
1 egg, lightly beaten
85 g (¼ cup/3 oz) molasses or golden syrup (light treacle)
335 g (2¼ cups/12 oz) plain (all-purpose) flour
2 teaspoons bicarb soda (baking soda)
½ teaspoon salt
1 teaspoon ground ginger
1 teaspoon ground cinnamon
¼ teaspoon ground cloves
70 g (⅓ cup/2½ oz) white (granulated) sugar, for rolling

Preheat the oven to 175°C (350°F/Gas 4). Line 2 baking trays.

In a large bowl, beat together the butter and caster sugar until creamy. Mix in the egg and molasses until well combined.

Sift together the flour, bicarb, salt, ginger, cinnamon and cloves and fold into the butter mixture. With a teaspoon and your hands, shape the dough into walnut-sized balls.

Roll each ball in the white sugar and place on the trays, leaving a little space between them. Bake for 10 minutes or until golden brown. Allow to cool for a few minutes before removing to a wire rack to cool completely. Store in an airtight container.

Makes 45

TALIA GOLDBERG

Almond Butter Biscuits

These are the simple almond butter biscuits we always have (and now you will too) in a huge glass jar right next to the kettle. And you don't need to be shy – Lisa set the standard over 30 years ago, eating them by the handful in her mother-in-law's kitchen.

60 g (2 oz) raw almonds
225 g (1½ cups/8 oz) plain (all-purpose) flour
60 g (¼ cup/2 oz) caster (superfine) sugar
¼ teaspoon salt
120 g (4¼ oz) unsalted butter, softened
1 egg yolk
40 ml (2 tablespoons/1¼ fl oz) oil

Preheat the oven to 160°C (325°F/Gas 3). Line a large baking tray.

In a food processor, coarsely chop the almonds, then remove from the bowl and set aside. Put the flour, sugar and salt into the food processor and process to combine. Add the butter and pulse until crumbs are formed, then add the chopped almonds and pulse again to combine. In a cup, mix together the egg and oil, then add to the mixture in the food processor. Pulse a few times, just until a rough dough forms, then tip the dough onto the bench.

Take a small walnut-sized piece of dough, lightly knead it in your hand and roll it into a small sausage shape, about 7 cm (2¾ inches) in length. If it cracks, knead it a little more. Make a small loop, overlapping the ends and pressing to close. Place on the prepared tray, and repeat with the remaining dough. Bake for 20 minutes or until light golden underneath. They should remain pale on the top.

Makes 60

LAINIE CADRY

Persian Shortbread

These pay homage to Lainie's rich Persian heritage. Her *omi* (grandmother) passed down the secrets of her kitchen to Lainie's mum, who then shared her knowledge with Lainie. If rose petals aren't your thing, leave them out.

230 g (2 sticks/8 oz) unsalted butter, at room
   temperature, chopped
80 g (½ cup/2¾ oz) pure icing (confectioners') sugar, sifted
1 teaspoon vanilla extract
1 teaspoon food-grade rose water
200 g (1⅓ cups/7 oz) plain (all-purpose) flour
60 g (2 oz) cornflour (corn starch)
1 teaspoon ground cardamom
pinch of salt
125 g (¾ cup/4½ oz) shelled pistachios, roughly chopped
3 teaspoons dried food-grade rose petals (optional, see note)

Using an electric mixer, beat the butter until smooth, then add the icing sugar, vanilla and rose water, and beat until pale and creamy. Sift together the flour, cornflour, cardamom and salt, and add to the butter mixture, beating on a low speed until just incorporated. Add the pistachios and rose petals to the dough, and gently mix through on low speed.

Halve the dough and roll each half into a smooth log, approximately 4 cm (1½ inches) in diameter. Wrap each log in plastic wrap and refrigerate for at least 2 hours or until firm.

When ready to bake, preheat the oven to 160°C (325°F/Gas 3). Line 2 baking trays. Remove the plastic wrap from the first log and slice it into rounds of 5 mm (¼ inch) thickness. Place these on the prepared trays and then repeat with the second log.

Bake for 20 minutes or until the edges turn golden brown and the shortbreads are cooked through.

Allow to cool on the tray for 5 minutes then transfer to a wire rack to cool completely.

Makes 60

Note — You can find edible rose petals and rose water in specialty and Middle Eastern food stores.

Romany Creams

FELICIA KAHN

This wonderful heirloom recipe from Felicia's mother is cherished so deeply for the memories it creates, and the comfort it brings Felicia. In Australia, these biscuits remind us of Arnott's Kingstons. In South Africa, however, everyone grew up eating the real deal: Romany Creams. Eating these transports us back to childhood days spent working our way through packets of Arnott's Assorted Creams.

3 teaspoons unsweetened Dutch cocoa powder
60 ml (¼ cup/2 fl oz) boiling water
250 g (9 oz) unsalted butter, at room temperature, chopped
230 g (1 cup/8 oz) caster (superfine) sugar
185 g (2¼ cups/6½ oz) desiccated coconut
300 g (2 cups/10½ oz) plain (all-purpose) flour
1 teaspoon baking powder
150 g (5⅓ oz) milk chocolate, roughly chopped

Preheat the oven to 180°C (350°F/Gas 4). Line 2 large baking trays.

Combine the cocoa powder and boiling water and set aside. Beat the butter and sugar until pale and creamy. Add the cocoa mixture and beat to combine. Fold in the coconut, then sift together the flour and baking powder, and fold into the mixture until well combined.

Roll large teaspoonfuls of the mixture into balls and arrange on the prepared trays. You should end up with around 60 biscuits. Lightly press the tines of a fork on to the top of each ball. Bake for 15 minutes or until golden, then allow to cool.

Melt the chocolate in the microwave or over a double boiler until just melted and still thick. Use the melted chocolate to sandwich the flat sides of the cookies together.

Makes 30

ANNE DIBOWITZ

Chocolate Sugar Biscuits

Who doesn't love a sugary, buttery chocolate biscuit that takes ten minutes to make and ten to cook? The dough freezes beautifully if you want to put half away for a rainy day.

100 g (3½ oz) dark chocolate (70%), roughly chopped
175 g (6 oz) unsalted butter, at room temperature, chopped
150 g (⅔ cup/5⅓ oz) caster (superfine) sugar
250 g (1⅔ cups/9 oz) plain (all-purpose) flour, plus extra
30 g (¼ cup/1 oz) unsweetened Dutch cocoa powder
½ teaspoon bicarb soda (baking soda)
¼ teaspoon salt
75 g (⅓ cup) caster (superfine) sugar, for coating

Preheat the oven to 180°C (350°F/Gas 4). Line several large baking trays.

Melt the chocolate in the microwave or in a double boiler (see Kitchen Notes page 11). Set aside to cool.

Using an electric mixer, beat the butter and sugar until pale and creamy. Add the melted chocolate then beat well to combine.

Sift together the flour, cocoa powder, bicarb and salt, and add to the chocolate mixture. Beat on low until just combined.

On lightly floured baking paper, roll out the dough until it's about 3 mm (⅛ inch) thick. Cut out circles with a 4 cm (1½ inch) round cookie cutter and place the biscuits on the prepared trays, allowing a little space between them. Repeat with the rest of the dough then bake each batch for 10 minutes or until slightly firm to the touch. Remove from the oven and cool slightly. When cool enough to touch, gently press the tops of the biscuits into the caster sugar to coat.

Makes 120

MISH ARNDT

Brown Sugar Nutties

Simple, flourless nutty treats. The taste of the walnuts is so important here, so make sure they are the best quality, and from a store with high turnover.

150 g (1½ cups/5⅓ oz) walnuts, coarsely chopped
125 g (⅔ cup, lightly packed/4½ oz) brown sugar
20 g (¾ oz) unsalted butter, chopped
1 egg white, lightly beaten

Preheat the oven to 160°C (325°F/Gas 3). Line 2 baking trays.

Place the nuts, sugar, butter and egg white in a medium saucepan and cook, stirring constantly, over low heat until the butter has melted and the mixture is combined. Remove from the heat and allow to cool.

Place heaped teaspoons of the mixture onto the prepared trays, allowing enough space for them to spread.

Bake for 15 minutes or until golden brown and just firm to the touch. Allow to cool for 10 minutes on the baking tray before transferring to a wire rack.

Makes 30

Horseshoes

Lisa can still remember devouring the entire piled-high-plate of horseshoe biscuits that Elza delivered to the Goldberg family when Lisa's mother-in-law passed away. Originally known as elbow biscuits, this recipe came from the late Milly Pogorelsky, who shared the recipe with Elza, her WIZO friend. Milly used to make these at night when her hands were cool, and would pack them in neat sugary layers – each separated by baking paper. Milly brought them to WIZO meetings and events, and sold them at her corner store. Elza is now known for baking a huge batch for WIZO's Melbourne Cup event, and the memory of Milly lives on.

150 g (5⅓ oz) unsalted butter, at room temperature, chopped
60 g (¼ cup/2 oz) caster (superfine) sugar
60 g (⅔ cup/2 oz) almond meal
180 g (1 cup + 2½ tablespoons/6⅓ oz) plain (all-purpose) flour, sifted
115 g (½ cup/4 oz) caster (superfine) sugar, for coating

Using an electric mixer, beat the butter and sugar until pale and fluffy. Add the almond meal and mix well. Fold in the flour and mix gently until a dough forms. Wrap the dough tightly with plastic wrap and refrigerate for at least 2 hours.

When ready to bake, preheat the oven to 180°C (350°F/ Gas 4). Line 2 large baking trays.

Roll the dough into thumb-sized pieces and bend these into horseshoe shapes. Place on the prepared trays and bake for 15 minutes or until light golden.

Allow to cool slightly and then roll them in the caster sugar. When completely cool, store in an airtight container with any excess caster sugar tipped on top of the biscuits.

Makes 40

Choc Coconut Macaroons

Some of us grew up in a time when Passover (*Pesach* — the festival celebrating freedom) meant sweet biscuits from the *Manischewitz* (an iconic kosher brand) tin. They were soft, and surprisingly delicious, chewy coconut macaroons. A few years ago, we decided we wanted to create our own version, with all the things we love in a macaroon. Cook them a little longer if you prefer them crisp, or for a little less if you prefer them chewy.

120 g (4½ oz) dark chocolate (70%), chopped
230 g (1 cup/8 oz) caster (superfine) sugar
100 g (1 cup/3½ oz) almond meal
240 g (3 cups/8½ oz) shredded coconut
2 teaspoons unsweetened Dutch cocoa powder
¼ teaspoon salt
3 egg whites, lightly whisked

Preheat the oven to 175°C (350°F/Gas 4). Line 2 baking trays.

Melt the chocolate in the microwave or in a double boiler (see Kitchen Notes page 11). Set aside to cool.

In a large bowl, combine the sugar, almond meal, coconut, cocoa powder and salt. Using a whisk, mix the ingredients together to combine and remove any lumps. Using a wooden spoon, add the egg whites and stir to combine, then add the melted chocolate and stir again until well combined.

Using a teaspoon, place small walnut-sized balls onto the prepared trays – do not compress them too much. Bake in batches for 15 minutes or until they are crisp on the outside and a little soft in the centre. Allow to cool on a wire rack. Store in an airtight container and keep for up to 1 week.

Makes 60

Choc Sugar Biscuits
p. 24

Brown Sugar Nutties p. 24

Horseshoes
p. 25

Choc Coconut
Macaroons
p. 25

Choc Oat Cookies

JESSIE GOLDBERG

Jessie has been making these just-soft, slightly chewy, super-chocolatey and oat-crammed biscuits for over a decade (and she's only 25). She came across the original recipe (minus the oats) in Bill Granger's iconic cookbook, *Bills Sydney Food*. Her friends know and expect that whether they are celebrating a birthday, having a hard time with their new job or mourning the loss of a grandparent, Jessie will be there, personally delivering a cellophane bag tied with kitchen string, packed full of love and bursting with biscuits.

125 g (4½ oz) unsalted butter,
   at room temperature
230 g (1¼ cups, lightly packed/8 oz)
   brown sugar
1 egg
1 teaspoon vanilla extract
225 g (1½ cups/8 oz) plain
   (all-purpose) flour, sifted
½ teaspoon baking powder
pinch of salt
150 g (5⅓ oz) dark chocolate (70%),
   roughly chopped
80 g (¾ cup/2¾ oz) rolled
   (porridge) oats

Preheat the oven to 180°C (350°F/Gas 4). Line a large baking tray.

Using an electric mixer, beat the butter and sugar until pale and creamy. Add the egg and vanilla and beat until well combined. Sift together the flour, baking powder and salt, and then beat these into the mixture. Fold through the chocolate and oats with a wooden spoon.

With a spoon, place walnut-sized mounds of dough on the prepared tray, allowing enough room to spread – there's no need to flatten. Bake for 11 minutes or until golden around the edges then allow to cool on a wire rack.

Makes 35

Recipe credit — Adapted from the recipe Chocolate Chip Cookies and printed with permission of the author, from *Bills Sydney Food* by Bill Granger, published by Murdoch Books, 2001.

Viennese *Ishla* Biscuits

MIRIAM MILLINGEN

In their small community, where participation was the norm rather than the exception, Miriam and her late mother helped as part of the Ladies' Guild in the Adelaide Hebrew Congregation kitchen. A Hungarian lady shared this wonderful recipe at the time of Miriam's son's Bar Mitzvah (a boy's coming of age when he turns 13), and Miriam has been making them ever since.

250 g (1⅔ cups/9 oz) roasted
   hazelnuts, skins removed
   (see page 75)
180 g (6⅓ oz) unsalted butter,
   at room temperature, chopped
75 g (⅓ cup/2⅔ oz) caster
   (superfine) sugar
185 g (1¼ cups/6½ oz) plain
   (all-purpose) flour, plus extra
¼ teaspoon salt
175 g (½ cup/6 oz) apricot jam (jelly)

CHOCOLATE GANACHE

85 g (3 oz) dark chocolate (70%),
   roughly chopped
1 tablespoon unsalted butter

ALSO NEEDED

20 roasted hazelnuts, halved

Place the hazelnuts in a food processor and pulse until finely ground. Using an electric mixer, beat the butter and sugar until smooth and pale. Combine the ground hazelnuts, flour and salt, and then fold this mixture into the butter mixture with a wooden spoon until a dough forms.

Wrap the dough tightly in plastic wrap and refrigerate for at least 1 hour.

When ready to bake, preheat the oven to 170°C (340°F/Gas 3). Line 2 baking trays.

On a lightly floured board, roll out the dough to a thickness of 5 mm (¼ inch). Use a 4 cm (1½ inch) round cookie cutter to cut out circles. Re-roll any scraps and cut out more circles until all the dough is used. Place these onto the prepared tray. You should have around 80 biscuits.

Bake for 12 minutes or until lightly golden underneath. Once the biscuits are completely cool, take 2 biscuits and spread ¼–½ teaspoon of jam on the flat side of one, then place the flat side of another biscuit on top, sandwiching the jam between them.

To make the ganache, melt the chocolate in a microwave or double boiler (see Kitchen Notes page 11), then add the butter and stir until smooth. Top the biscuit pairs with the ganache and the hazelnut halve, and allow to set.

Makes 40

Alfajores

SANDRA SUCHIN KOFMAN

These sandwich biscuits (cookies) filled with *dulce de leche* (milk caramel) are a national treat in Argentina. Sandra tells us that this traditional caramel is eaten with absolutely everything, and can be found in every fridge; she compares it to ketchup – nobody makes it from scratch. We have found a shortcut *dulce de leche* recipe that is just perfect. Sandra's *alfajores* recipe is based on one first published in the 1930s from Doña Petrona, who Sandra describes as the Julia Child of Argentina.

320 g (2½ cups/11⅓ oz) cornflour (corn starch)
100 g (⅔ cup/3½ oz) plain (all-purpose) flour, plus extra
1 teaspoon baking powder
200 g (heaped ¾ cup/7 oz) caster (superfine) sugar
grated zest of ½ lemon
150 g (5⅓ oz) unsalted butter, at room temperature, chopped
1 egg
2 egg yolks
1 teaspoon vanilla extract
125 ml (½ cup/4¼ fl oz) *Dulce de Leche* (see recipe below)
85 g (1 cup/3 oz) desiccated coconut, for rolling

Sift the cornflour, flour and baking powder together and set aside. With a mortar and pestle (or a small bowl and the end of a rolling pin), pound the sugar with the lemon zest until fragrant. Using an electric mixer, beat the butter with the sugar until pale and creamy. Add the egg, the yolks and the vanilla, and beat to combine.

Gradually add the dry ingredients to the butter mixture, folding them together gently with a spatula until a dough forms. Wrap tightly with plastic wrap and place in the fridge for 2 hours.

When ready to bake, preheat the oven to 180°C (350°F/Gas 4). Line 2 large baking trays.

On a lightly floured benchtop, roll out the dough to a 5 mm (¼ inch) thickness. Using a 4 cm (1½ inch) round cookie cutter, cut the pastry into circles. Place these on the prepared trays, leaving some space between them. Bake for 10 minutes then remove the trays from the oven (the biscuits will be very soft) and allow them to cool completely on the trays.

Sandwich the flat sides of 2 biscuits together using ½ teaspoon of *dulce de leche*, and gently press to seal. Roll the edge of the biscuit sandwiches in the coconut so it sticks to the *dulce de leche* between them.

Makes 30

OVEN-BAKED *DULCE DE LECHE*

2 x 395 g (14 oz) tins sweetened condensed milk

Preheat the oven to 180°C (350°F/Gas 4). Pour the condensed milk into a 1 litre (4 cup/1 quart) baking dish and cover with foil. Sit the baking dish in a larger dish and pour enough boiling water to come halfway up the sides of the smaller dish, creating a bain marie. Cook in the oven, topping up with boiling water to maintain the level, for 2 hours or until the condensed milk is a deep toffee colour – this may take up to 3 hours. Carefully remove the baking dishes from the oven and stir while still warm. Set aside to cool completely. Transfer the *dulce de leche* to a very clean, dry glass jar. It will keep in the fridge for 2–3 weeks.

Makes 550 g (2 cups/1 lb 3 oz)

Dulce de leche recipe credit — Adapted and printed with permission of author (Ross Dobson) and the publisher from *The Food of Argentina* by Ross Dobson and Rachel Tolosa Paz, published by Smith Street Books, 2018.

Pizza Ebraica

SILVIA NACAMULLI

Natanya and Lisa have both visited Rome's famous Boccione bakery in the former Jewish ghetto, where people line up for pretty much one thing and one thing only – their slightly burnt raisin-and-almond-filled brick-like biscuits – *Pizza Ebraica*. They are made from a centuries-old family recipe, which the bakery has never shared. And yes, we did ask! Also known as *Pizza di Piazza* and *Pizza di Beridde*, it is a traditional fruit cake that the Roman–Jewish community enjoys for family celebrations. In Silvia's family, the baking of these biscuits (which they know as *Pizza Romana*) is a women-only affair; they are always made with her mother, sister, aunts and a few of her mother's friends for their large celebrations.

150 g raisins (⅔ cup/5⅓ oz)
    or sultanas (golden raisins)
150 g (1 cup/5⅓ oz) raw almonds
100 g (⅔ cup/3½ oz) pine nuts
100 g (½ cup/3½ oz) glacé cherries,
    quartered
100 g (½ cup/3½ oz) candied peel
100 ml (⅓ cup + 1 tablespoon/
    3½ fl oz) Marsala or sweet wine
1 teaspoon vanilla extract
230 ml (1 scant cup/8 fl oz) oil
500 g (3⅓ cups/1 lb 2 oz) plain
    (all-purpose or 00) flour, sifted
170 g (¾ cup/6 oz) caster (superfine)
    sugar
½ teaspoon salt

Preheat the oven to 240°C (475°F/Gas 9). Line a large baking tray.

Place the raisins, almonds, pine nuts, glacé cherries and candied peel in a bowl. Add the Marsala and the vanilla, and leave to soak for 15 minutes.

Heat the oil in a saucepan until warm, but not hot. Whisk together the flour, sugar and salt in a separate large bowl. Pour the warm oil into the bowl and mix well. Add the soaked nuts and fruit and mix until everything is well combined – it will be a little crumbly.

Divide the mixture into 4 equal pieces. Gently, without compressing the dough, mould one piece into a long, chunky rectangular block about 20 x 7 x 3 cm (8 x 2¾ x 1¼ inches). Using a sharp knife, cut each block into 5 equal pieces and lay these on the tray, side by side, just touching.

Bake for 20 minutes or until golden and slightly burnt underneath and around the edges.

Makes 20 large biscuits

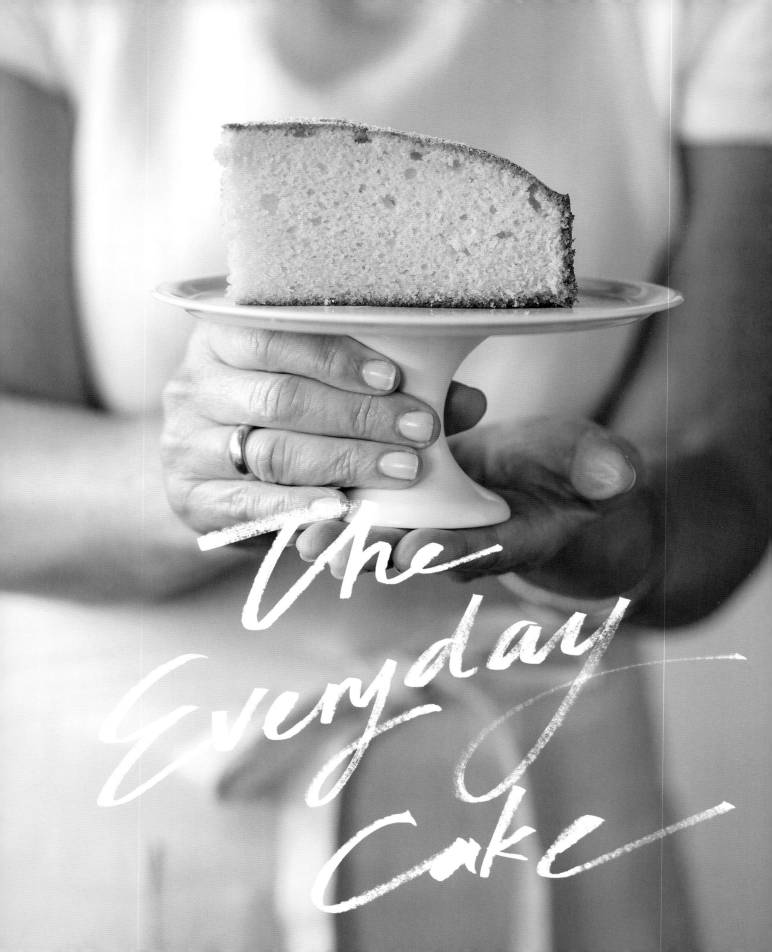

Someone's dropping over, the kids are on their way home from school, you just feel like making a cake and it happens to be one of those very busy weeks — sometimes we need a quick, no-fuss recipe that only requires a short time in the kitchen and no additional supermarket trips. Ingredients at the ready, we're arming you with a chapter of simple-to-make and totally fabulous all-day, everyday, any-day and rainy-day cakes. Make yourself a cup of tea, get the measuring cups out and let's get baking. Have a look at How to Basic Cake on page 40 if you need to brush up on your skills.

LEAH KOENIG dreams that the jammy depths of a spiralled *rugelach*, the briny snap of a pickle and the sputtering crackle of her grandma's just-fried latkes will evoke the same unexplainable feelings of love and connection in her young children as they do for her. Born in Chicago with a diverse heritage of Ashkenazi Jewish and German Christian, the bedrock of Leah's cooking philosophy stems from her mother. She was the champion of the home-cooked family dinner, using fresh produce and quality ingredients from the farmers' market long before it was fashionable. Now based in Brooklyn, Leah is a highly respected food writer with a focus on global Jewish cuisine. She treasures the family food rituals that are emerging in her own family – experiences that are becoming a part of the tapestry of their Jewish and food life.

MERRYLIN GOODMAN was part of a Sydney community that came together to share their recipes and stories; while preparing for celebrations, they became family. Growing up, weekends were spent helping her industrious mother set up *kiddushes* (small meals after services) for the Strathfield synagogue. Merrylin taught at several Sydney TAFEs and then set up a cooking school, which taught many of our generation the secrets of her kitchen. She now teaches teenagers food technology and hospitality. Her traditional salt beef appeared in our first book, and since then she has become a very involved grandmother sharing her kitchen wisdom with the next generation.

Thanks to a diverse Dutch–Indonesian heritage, **ANGELIQUE LAZARUS** shares stories of growing up with sambal oelek, peanut butter and cucumber sandwiches for school lunches. She is now a *balaboosta* (excellent homemaker) who credits her mother-in-law with teaching her everything there is to know about Jewish life (and food) and traditional Lithuanian fare. Many of those dishes have become staples in her own home, and Angelique is now known for her freshly baked *challah* (traditional plaited bread) every Friday as well as her legendary carrot cake, which appeared in *The food, the stories, the sisterhood*. Her time living all over the world, together with the Jewish–South African influence of her husband's family, has helped her create a wonderful warm kitchen and home in Sydney.

Seventh-generation Australian, Melbourne-born **KAREN GUTMAN** gave us the now-iconic Monday Morning Cooking Club Honey Cake for *The food, the stories, the sisterhood*. Karen's cooking was greatly influenced and inspired by her Polish grandmother, Mama Elke, whose kitchen was the true heart of her home. When it came to *Shabbat* (Friday night) dinners, Elke used to alternate between each of her three daughter's homes. But no matter what, she would prepare and deliver a complete meal to the other two daughters and their families. Karen's gorgeous kitchen in Sydney is now the heart of her home, and cooking is a huge part of her life, albeit in a more contemporary and healthy way.

YOLAN FRANK in *The Chiffon Cake* (page 109)

For **SUZIE GOLDBACH**, food is a huge part of life. She attributes this to her mother and her late grandmother, both exceptional cooks, and to her transformative time in Italy studying gastronomy. For Suzie, food is about discovering culture, learning history and understanding people. She lives in Budapest in a close-knit family, running a supper club sharing authentic Hungarian cuisine and hospitality with visitors to the city. Her most vivid childhood memories include picking raspberries with her uncle in the countryside, making *palinka* (brandy) from homegrown plums and decorating gingerbread with her cousins, something she still does today.

HELEN NIGHTINGALE channelled memories of growing up in Birmingham, UK, and devouring her German grandmother's butter biscuits on Saturday afternoons to become the great cake baker she is today. After one unforgettable meal when Helen used a whole head of garlic instead of one clove, she decided her calling was sweet baking. Armed with an Evelyn Rose cookbook, she never looked back. Her family were so enamoured with the sweet goodness coming out of the kitchen, they encouraged her to start her own business. And now, in addition to her work supporting children with special needs, Helen's Heavenly Desserts supplies many in Sydney's eastern suburbs with the most sought-after cakes, tortes and desserts.

In Paris in 1942, **SUZANNE RESS'S** mother, Marie, showed enormous courage, saving her family from the Vel' d'Hiv round-up, a Nazi-led mass arrest of Jewish citizens. They escaped to a small Loire valley village, where they remained hidden until the liberation. After the war, Suzanne followed her brother to Melbourne, and soon after met her husband, hotelier Leon. Their wedding, at Leon's hotel, reminded Suzanne of Paris life, and she suggested they get a licence to put tables, chairs and umbrellas on the pavement. And so, in 1957, Melbourne's first outdoor café was created at the newly coined 'Paris end of Collins Street'. Suzanne's passion for French baking led to the 'cake trolley' being presented to each of the café's 20 tables. She was inspired by Marie, who blended traditional Jewish family recipes with French style, setting an example for a life of entertaining.

MAY STEIN'S spectacular *kugelhopf* (sour cream chocolate marble cake) featured in *The food, the stories, the sisterhood*, and we all remember her warmth and kindness whenever we bumped into her in Sydney. Growing up in Iraq, May's family really celebrated Judaism – making their own matzo at Pesach in a wood-burning mud oven and enthusiastically dressing up for the synagogue during *chagim* (festivals). Life for Jewish Iraqis was fraught with difficulty, and so in 1948 the family fled to London. May then moved to Israel before settling in Australia and starting a family with husband Fred. May lives on in our hearts and in our kitchens.

How to Basic Cake

This will guide you through the basic steps of making any cake that starts by beating butter and sugar together until creamy.

1. Place the room temperature, chopped butter and sugar in the bowl of a stand mixer (or a large bowl, if using a handheld mixer).

2. Using the paddle beater (or the beaters on your handheld mixer), beat on medium speed until pale and creamy.

3. Add the eggs, one at a time, beating well after each addition, ensuring the mixture is well combined. You may need to scrape down the sides of the bowl with the spatula to reincorporate all the mixture. Don't worry if it curdles at this stage – it will come back together.

4. While continuing to beat on low speed, alternate the wet ingredients (milk, juice, etc.) with the dry ingredients (flour, cocoa powder, baking powder, etc.) in about 3 lots, and beat until just combined.

5. Stop beating from time to time to scrape down the sides of the bowl. Remove any remaining batter from the beater with a spatula.

6. Pour or spoon the batter into the prepared tin, smooth the surface with a spatula and bake according to the recipe.

Basic Butter Cake

MERRYLIN GOODMAN

Mummy's All-round Basic Cake – since 1941 and still going strong! Merrylin's recipe from her mother is a perfect basic cake, waiting for a handful of sultanas thrown into the batter before it goes into the tin, just a sprinkle of icing sugar or a vanilla or orange icing on top. It also will become your go-to cupcake mixture, just add two tablespoons of flour to the mix and bake for about 23 minutes (makes 18 cupcakes). Merrylin also makes this cake successfully with margarine when she wants a dairy-free cake.

250 g (9 oz) unsalted butter, at room temperature, chopped
345 g (1½ cups/12¼ oz) caster (superfine) sugar
4 eggs
125 ml (½ cup/4¼ fl oz) milk or orange juice
2 teaspoons vanilla extract
350 g (2⅓ cups/12⅓ oz) self-raising (self-rising) flour
finely grated zest of 1 orange (if using juice instead of milk)
2 tablespoons boiling water

Preheat the oven to 170°C (340°F/Gas 3). Line a 26 cm (10½ inch) springform cake tin.

Using an electric mixer, beat the butter and sugar together until very pale and creamy. Add the eggs one at a time, beating well after each addition, then add the vanilla and zest (if using). Stop the mixer and scrape the sides down from time to time.

Using a spatula, fold in the flour, alternating with the milk (or juice), until just combined. Add the boiling water and stir gently to combine. Pour into the prepared tin and bake for 50 minutes or until a skewer inserted into the centre comes out clean.

Allow to cool completely before removing from the tin.

Serves about 12

Lemon Syrup Cake

HELEN NIGHTINGALE

This is a cake with heritage. Helen found the Luscious Lemon Cake almost 30 years ago in a recipe book by Evelyn Rose MBE, the leading Anglo–Jewish cookery writer of her generation. It first appeared in print in 1967 when Evelyn was cookery writer and editor at the *Jewish Chronicle* in London, after she brought the concept of a lemon-scented pound cake infused with fresh lemon syrup home from the U.S. It became an instant hit with her readers, became her signature recipe and eventually entered mainstream consciousness as the Lemon Drizzle Cake. Evelyn's magnum opus on Jewish cuisine, *The Complete International Jewish Cookbook*, was first published in 1976. Helen has doubled the original recipe.

250 g (9 oz) unsalted butter, at room temperature, chopped
350 g (1½ cups/12⅓ oz) caster (superfine) sugar
4 eggs
350 g (2⅓ cups/12⅓ oz) self-raising (self-rising) flour
pinch of salt
finely grated zest of 2 lemons
125 ml (½ cup/4¼ fl oz) milk, at room temperature

LEMON SYRUP

160 g (1 cup/5⅔ oz) icing (confectioners') sugar
juice of 3 lemons

LEMON ICING

320 g (2 cups/11⅓ oz) pure icing (confectioners') sugar
juice of 1 lemon

ALSO NEEDED

50 g (½ cup) slivered almonds, toasted and roughly chopped

Preheat the oven to 180°C (350°F/Gas 4). Grease and line the base of a 25 cm (10 inch) round cake tin.

Using an electric mixer, beat the butter with the caster sugar until pale and creamy. Add the eggs one at a time, beating well after each addition. Combine the flour, salt and lemon zest. Add to the egg mixture, alternating with the milk in 3 batches until just combined. Spoon the batter into the prepared tin and spread evenly. Bake for 1 hour or until a skewer inserted into the centre comes out clean.

While the cake is baking, make the lemon syrup. In a small saucepan over medium heat combine the icing sugar and lemon juice, and stir until dissolved. Gently heat without boiling the syrup.

Prick the cake all over with a skewer, gently pour over the warm syrup and leave to cool completely.

To make the icing, whisk together the icing sugar and just enough of the lemon juice to form a thick icing. Turn the cake out of the tin and place it on a serving plate right-way up or with the flat side on top, whichever you prefer. Pour the icing over the top of the cake, letting it drip down the sides. Sprinkle with the almonds.

Serves about 12

Recipe credit — Adapted and printed with permission of the author, from *The New Complete International Jewish Cookbook* by Evelyn Rose with Judi Rose, published by Pavilion Books, revised and updated in 2011.

Orange and Coconut Cake

Suzanne and her London-based sister, Simone Hylander, are now well into their 80s, and still have the reputation of being so French, so extremely stylish and such fabulous entertainers. This simple cake of Simone's became one of Suzanne's go-to cakes, which she often baked to cheer up a friend. And it most certainly cheered us up. It's a delicious cake you can whip up with ten minutes of prep and a mere 45 minutes in the oven.

125 g (4½ oz) unsalted butter, at room temperature, chopped
175 g (¾ cup/6 oz) caster (superfine) sugar
2 eggs
finely grated zest of 1 orange
225 g (1½ cups/8 oz) self-raising (self-rising) flour, sifted
45 g (½ cup/1½ oz) shredded or desiccated coconut
250 ml (1 cup/8½ fl oz) milk

ORANGE BUTTER ICING

45 g (1½ oz) unsalted butter, at room temperature
320 g (2 cups/11⅓ oz) icing (confectioners') sugar
2 tablespoons orange juice
finely grated zest of 1 orange

ALSO NEEDED

2 tablespoons flaked coconut

Preheat the oven to 180°C (350°F/Gas 4). Line a 20 cm (8 inch) springform cake tin or a medium (23 x 13 cm/9 x 5 inch) loaf (bar) tin.

Using an electric mixer, beat the butter with the caster sugar until pale and creamy. Add the eggs one at a time, beating well after each addition. Add the orange zest. Combine the flour and coconut in a small bowl and add to the mixture, alternating with the milk, beating on low speed until just combined.

Pour the batter into the prepared tin. Bake for 45 minutes or until a skewer inserted into the centre comes out clean. Remove from the oven and allow to cool for 10 minutes, then remove the cake from the tin and allow to cool completely on a wire rack before icing.

Make the icing using an electric mixer, and beat the butter, icing sugar, orange juice and zest until the mixture is smooth and fluffy. Spread on top of the cake, then sprinkle with the flaked coconut.

Serves about 8

Orange & Coconut Cake
p. 46

Spiced Honey Cake
p. 48

Carrot Loaf Cake
p. 49

Spiced Honey Cake

KAREN GUTMAN
AND MMCC

Another of our truly iconic festival cakes is the honey cake, first shared by Karen Gutman in *The food, the stories, the sisterhood*. The hilariously named Gina's Hair Raising Honey Cake (long story, with thanks to Gina Swart!) is pretty much the best honey cake we've come across. This time round we've updated the recipe with spices and tea and it's half the size. (You're welcome.) It's great eaten on the day it's made, but this cake is at its sticky peak two or three days after baking.

DRY MIXTURE

110 g (¾ cup/3¾ oz) plain
    (all-purpose) flour
110 g (¾ cup/3¾ oz) self-raising
    (self-rising) flour
¾ teaspoon bicarb soda (baking soda)
½ teaspoon ground ginger
¼ teaspoon ground allspice
½ teaspoon ground cinnamon
⅛ teaspoon ground nutmeg
pinch of salt

WET MIXTURE

2 eggs
175 g (¾ cup/6 oz) caster (superfine)
    sugar
100 ml (⅓ cup + 1 tablespoon/3½ fl oz)
    vegetable oil
250 g (¾ cup/9 oz) honey
½ teaspoon vanilla extract

ALSO NEEDED

185 ml (¾ cup/6 fl oz) freshly brewed
    black tea

Preheat the oven to 180°C (350°F/Gas 4).

Line a large (25 x 13 cm/10 x 5 inch) loaf (bar) tin.

Sift the ingredients for the dry mixture together into a bowl. In a separate large bowl, using an electric mixer, beat the ingredients for the wet mixture together until well combined. Beat the dry mixture into the wet mixture in 3 batches, alternating with the hot tea.

Pour the batter into the prepared tin. Bake for 25 minutes and then turn the oven down to 160°C (320°F/Gas 3) for a further 25 minutes or until a skewer inserted into the cake comes out clean. Allow the cake to cool before removing from the tin.

Serves about 10

Carrot Loaf Cake

ANGELIQUE LAZARUS
AND MMCC

Nachas is the inexplicable joy one gets from something, often one's children. Well, that's how we felt when, in 2016, the *Sydney Morning Herald* judged Angelique Lazarus's carrot cake, featured in our first book, the best in Australia. We've modified the best carrot cake ever to become the best carrot loaf cake ever, something to slowly slice away, day by day, till every crumb is gone.

DRY INGREDIENTS

190 g (1¼ cups/6¾ oz) plain
   (all-purpose) flour
1 teaspoon baking powder
¾ teaspoon bicarb soda (baking soda)
1 teaspoon ground cinnamon
¼ teaspoon ground nutmeg
¼ teaspoon allspice
1 teaspoon salt

WET INGREDIENTS

170 g (¾ cup/6 oz) caster (superfine)
   sugar
180 ml (¾ cup/6 fl oz) oil
2 eggs

FRUIT

250 g (1½ cups/9 oz) coarsely
   grated carrot
70 g (¼ cup/2½ oz) drained tinned
   crushed pineapple
100 g (¾ cup/3½ oz) chopped pecans

GLAZE

1 tablespoon oil
55 g (¼ cup, firmly packed/2 oz)
   brown sugar
1 tablespoon milk
20 g (¾ oz) chopped pecans

CREAM CHEESE ICING

250 g (9 oz) cream cheese, at room
   temperature, chopped
125 g (½ cup/4½ oz) sour cream
100 g (⅔ cup/3½ oz) icing
   (confectioners') sugar
½ teaspoon vanilla extract

Preheat the oven to 180°C (350°F/Gas 4).

Grease a large (25 x 13 cm/10 x 5 inch) loaf (bar) tin.

Sift the dry ingredients together into a bowl. In a separate bowl, beat the wet ingredients together until frothy. Mix together the dry, wet and fruit ingredients. Pour the mixture into the prepared tin and bake for 35 minutes.

While the cake is baking, mix the glaze ingredients together in a small saucepan over medium heat until just combined.

Remove the cake from the oven and pour the glaze over the top while it is still hot. Return to the oven for a further 15 minutes or until a skewer inserted into the cake comes out clean.

To make the icing, using an electric mixer, beat the cream cheese, sour cream, icing sugar and vanilla. When the cake is completely cool, turn it out of the tin and set it on a serving plate, glazed side up. Spread the icing generously over the cake.

Serves about 10

Date, Walnut and Brandy Cake

May's family will always remember her as their baking matriarch. Over the last few years, a steady stream of her cake recipes have landed in our inbox from family and friends who have been lucky enough to taste or bake her wonderful cakes. It warms the cockles of our hearts that we can continue to honour her memory.

500 g (3⅓ cups/1 lb 2 oz) pitted dried
  dates, chopped
250 ml (1 cup/8½ fl oz) black tea
1 teaspoon bicarb soda (baking soda)
300 g (10½ oz) unsalted butter
  at room temperature, chopped,
  plus extra for greasing
230 g (1 cup/8 oz) caster (superfine)
  sugar
4 eggs
½ teaspoon vanilla extract
2 tablespoons brandy
2 tablespoons sherry
225 g (1½ cups/8 oz) self-raising
  (self-rising) flour, plus extra for
  flouring
300 g (3 cups/10½ oz) walnut halves,
  chopped

Preheat the oven to 180°C (350°F/Gas 4). Generously butter and lightly flour an 8-cup bundt (fluted tube) tin.

In a small saucepan, combine the dates and tea, then add the bicarb and bring to a boil over medium heat. Simmer for 3 minutes or until the dates are soft and the liquid has evaporated. Set aside to cool.

Using an electric mixer, beat the butter and sugar until pale and creamy. Add the eggs one at a time, beating well after each addition. Add the vanilla, brandy and sherry and beat to combine. In 3 batches, fold in the flour, alternating with the date mixture, until just combined. It will be quite a wet mixture. Fold in the walnut pieces.

Spoon the batter into the prepared tin. Bake for 1 hour or until a skewer inserted in the middle of the cake comes out clean.

Serves about 12

Flourless Poppy Seed Cake

SUZIE GOLDBACH

Merelyn tasted this moist gluten-free cake at Eat and Meet in Budapest, a pop-up dinner party where tourists eat traditional homemade Hungarian delicacies while Suzie explains the local cuisine. Funny story, while explaining the poppy seed ingredient to one group, a perturbed French woman asked if she was going to be drugged. Suzie quickly understood her concern and reassured her that edible poppy seeds do not contain any opium.

300 g (3⅓ cups/10½ oz) finely ground poppy seed
170 g (¾ cup/6 oz) caster (superfine) sugar
75 g (¾ cup/2 ⅔ oz) almond meal
45 g (⅓ cup/1½ oz) cornflour (corn starch)
230 g (2 sticks/8 oz) unsalted butter, at room temperature, chopped
135 g (¾ cup + 1 tablespoon/4¾ oz) icing (confectioners') sugar
pinch of salt
1 teaspoon vanilla extract
finely grated zest of 1 lemon
9 eggs, separated
icing (confectioners') sugar, for sprinkling

Preheat the oven to 180°C (350°F/Gas 4). Line a 26 cm (10½ inch) round springform cake tin.

In a bowl, combine the ground poppy seed with half of the caster sugar, the almond meal and the cornflour. Set aside. Using an electric mixer, beat the butter and the icing sugar until pale and creamy. Add the salt, vanilla and zest, and continue to beat until combined. Add the egg yolks one by one, beating between each addition. Continue to beat until the mixture is smooth and fluffy.

In a separate bowl, whisk the egg whites until soft peaks form, then add the remaining caster sugar and continue to whisk until the egg whites are stiff, but not dry. In 3 batches, gently fold in the poppy seed mixture, alternating with the egg whites. Try to keep as much air as possible in the batter.

Pour the batter into the prepared tin and bake for 45 minutes or until a skewer inserted in the centre comes out clean. Cover the cake with foil if it is browning too quickly.

Place on a wire rack to cool for 10 minutes, then remove from the tin and return to the wire rack to cool completely. Sprinkle with icing sugar to serve.

Serves about 12

Apple and Jam Oil Cake

YOLAN FRANK

Merelyn's mother, Yolan, seemed to make an apple cake every week. This was her regular when Merelyn was young, but it was later superseded by her apple pie, featured in *The Feast Goes On*. Dairy free, rustic and easy to make, it works equally well with stone fruit in summer or firm pears in winter.

3 eggs
345 g (1½ cups/12¼ oz) caster (superfine) sugar
250 ml (1 cup/8½ fl oz) oil
1 teaspoon vanilla extract
300 g (2 cups/10½ oz) self-raising (self-rising) flour, sifted
60 ml (¼ cup/12 fl oz) strawberry jam (jelly)
3 large granny smith apples, peeled and sliced
1 tablespoon cinnamon sugar (see note)
1 tablespoon caster (superfine) sugar, for sprinkling

Preheat the oven to 180°C (350°F/Gas 4). Line a 24 cm (9½ inch) round springform cake tin.

Using an electric mixer, beat the eggs and caster sugar until pale and creamy. Add the oil and vanilla and beat until just combined. Using a spatula, gently fold in the flour.

Pour half of the batter into the prepared tin, then dot with the strawberry jam and cover with half of the sliced apple. Sprinkle with the cinnamon sugar. Top with the remaining batter then the remaining apple slices. Finally, sprinkle over the tablespoon of caster sugar.

Bake for 1 hour then reduce the temperature to 160°C (325°F/Gas 3) and bake for a further 30 minutes or until deep golden and a skewer inserted into the centre comes out clean.

Serves about 10

Note — To make cinnamon sugar, combine 230 g (1 cup/8 oz) caster sugar with 2 tablespoons of ground cinnamon. Store in an airtight jar and use as needed.

Passover Pear Cake

LEAH KOENIG

One of the best Passover cakes we've tasted. Ever. One of those 'I can't believe it's a *Pesach* cake' cakes. We've tried it with plums and almonds, and figs and hazelnuts, and it is just so great! You can replace the matzo meal with plain (all-purpose) flour for a cake any time of the year. In her book *Modern Jewish Cooking*, Leah explains that she isn't a fan of baking with matzo meal, but in this cake it's very well hidden.

60 g (½ cup/2 oz) pecans, chopped

110 g (½ cup, firmly packed/3¾ oz) brown sugar

2 teaspoons ground cinnamon

½ teaspoon ground nutmeg

4 eggs

230 g (1 cup/8 oz) caster (superfine) sugar

125 ml (½ cup/4¼ fl oz) oil

1 teaspoon vanilla extract

140 g (1 cup/5 oz) superfine matzo meal (cake meal) (see Kitchen Notes page 11)

4 medium pears, unpeeled, sliced

Preheat the oven to 180°C (350°F/Gas 4). Line a 20 cm (8 inch) square baking tin. Mix together the pecans, brown sugar, cinnamon and nutmeg in a small bowl.

Using an electric mixer, whisk the eggs until creamy and light. Add the caster sugar, 2 spoons at a time, whisking until the mixture is thick and billowy. Add the oil in a steady stream, followed by the vanilla, and whisk until just combined. Add the matzo meal and mix on low speed until just combined.

Pour half the batter into the prepared tin. Sprinkle with half the pecan mixture and arrange half the sliced pears on top. Pour over the remaining batter, smoothing the top with a spatula. Top with the remaining pears, followed by the remaining pecan mixture.

Bake for 60 minutes or until a skewer inserted into the centre comes out clean. Transfer to a wire rack and allow to cool completely before removing from the tin.

Serves about 10

Recipe credit — Adapted and printed with permission of the publisher, from *Modern Jewish Cooking: Recipes and customs for today's kitchen* by Leah Koenig, published by Chronicle Books, 2015.

Everyone loves chocolate. Everyone loves cake. The combination of the two is simply irresistible. We'll often find Natanya standing quietly in the corner of the kitchen, mixing bowl in one hand, chocolatey spatula in the other and a smile on her face. Our generous community has shared their best chocolate cake recipes, and we have curated that enormous list to find our perfect eight. We've got big cakes, like the one with ground hazelnuts and a shiny glaze; small cakes with fluffy white icing and coconut flakes; and tiny cakes studded with white chocolate and honey. And don't be surprised to find a smattering of chocolate in other chapters – after all, it's too good not to share around.

People + Stories

ELZA LEVIN, an inspirational and active matriarch, recently celebrated her 90th birthday. Born in Pretoria, Elza first began cooking at her granny's, standing on a chair in the kitchen. Elza became a true friend of Monday Morning Cooking Club after appearing in *The food, the stories, the sisterhood* alongside her daughter Judy. In the last decade, we have spent countless hours with her, poring over recipes and cooking side by side. Her serious 30-year hobby of cake decorating has ensured she is the supplier of the most beautiful birthday cakes to family and friends across Sydney. And she is still cooking, inspiring us, and younger generations, to do the same.

Cooking has always been an important part of **JUDY LOWY'S** life – learning the secrets from Granny Jessie and mum, Elza, and now passing them on to her own four children. Starting out as a young just-married girl living far from home in New York City, Judy made weekly calls to her mum, who dictated recipes over the phone. Decades later, now a super-busy mother and co-founder/president of a school foundation, Judy has become the quintessential host and entertainer, enjoying traditional Jewish dishes as much as the contemporary. Her true love of cooking is fuelled by a love of eating and a love of entertaining family and friends.

JOAN McNAMARA in *Squares and Bars* (page 126)
TALIA GOLDBERG in *The Biscuit Tin* (page 16)

MARCIA FRIEDMAN'S mum taught her that the best meals involve sharing favourite foods; a golden bubbling dish of her mum's baked macaroni and cheese in the middle of the table and a spoon for each of them is really all her family needs. Italian by heritage, Jewish by choice, she celebrates this intersection of two cultures through cooking and food writing. Marcia researches recipes – particularly the older Jewish–Italian dishes – to bring the old into the new, and then updates them for busy cooks. Marcia shared her story alongside bialys for our second book. She is always mindful of the memories, traditions and heritage that have shaped her love of food through both Jewish and Italian cultures.

In a world of incomplete tasks and never-ending lists, HANNA GELLER GOLDSMITH finds complete satisfaction and a sense of accomplishment whenever a cake or a batch of cookies comes out of the oven. With a trans-Atlantic upbringing, London-born Hanna may sound English, but her heart and her baking are homegrown American. As a proud sous chef at her mother's dinner parties, Hanna learnt the power of connections made around the table and the importance of gathering around a meal for companionship, friendship, support and laughter. Now the creator of Building Feasts, Hanna builds on her background of interior design to create recipes, cooking classes and supper clubs that are as beautiful as they are delicious.

The three inseparable BENEDICT SISTERS were all wonderful bakers. CHARLOTTE CHALMERS and her husband, Hans, immigrated to Australia from Vienna in 1939 and were able to help 16 families escape the Nazis and make safe passage to Australia. Of the other sisters, ANNIE EISEMAN fled to France while EDITH HILLER and her family joined Charlotte in Sydney. Blessed with longevity, each of the sisters lived into their 90s. Edith would drive from Castlecrag to Bondi to play bridge at Charlotte's, and Annie would avoid European winters by spending six months in Sydney. They became the matriarchs of a very close family, which would often see the three sisters and three generations gathering for exquisite afternoon teas that showcased both their amazing baking and their love of family.

Drop into SUSIE CLIFFORD'S home and there will be a slice of cake on offer and a recipe to discuss; the house exudes warmth with an open–door policy. Susie affectionately remembers Omama (her grandmother) Irma Wohlstein, a prolific baker, who lived in Vienna until forced to flee from the rising tide of anti-semitism in 1938. She and her family arrived on the very first boat of refugees allowed in Sydney and appeared on the front page of the *Sydney Morning Herald* the next day. 'If you love me, you'll eat it,' she would say, coaxing her grandchildren to take just a little bit more. Omama remained an inspiring role model, living independently and baking for all the neighbours until the ripe old age of 102. Now Susie is a grandmother, and bakes with the same skill and intuition, paying forward the legacy.

White Chocolate and Honey Madeleines

We were first given a taste of these madeleines many years ago, thanks to our friend Judy. The recipe is from Stephanie Alexander, one of Australia's great food writers and educators, and Judy can now whip up a batch with her eyes closed. We added the white chocolate when we discovered Valrhona's Dulcey – an outstanding caramelised white chocolate and excellent addition to pretty much anything. Best eaten straight out of the oven, or at the very least on the day of baking.

90 g (3¼ oz) unsalted butter

2 teaspoons honey

2 eggs

75 g (⅓ cup/2⅔ oz) caster (superfine) sugar

1 tablespoon brown sugar

⅛ teaspoon vanilla extract

pinch of salt

90 g (3¼ oz) plain (all-purpose) flour, plus extra

1 teaspoon baking powder

60 g (2 oz) caramelised white chocolate, chopped

1 tablespoon unsalted butter, just melted, for greasing

icing (confectioners') sugar, for sprinkling

The batter is best made up to 1 day or at least 3 hours ahead of baking.

You will need a madeleine tin made especially for these small, shell-shaped cakes.

Melt the butter and honey together then set aside and allow to cool. In a food processor, or in a large bowl using a stick blender, combine the eggs, caster and brown sugars, vanilla and salt. Sift the flour and the baking powder together, and add to the batter, along with the butter and honey. Process briefly to combine then allow the batter to rest overnight, or for at least 3 hours.

When ready to bake, preheat the oven to 180°C (350°F/Gas 4).

Using a pastry brush, paint the tin with the melted butter then sprinkle generously with flour. Remove any excess flour by tapping the tin upside down on the bench. Gently stir the chocolate through the batter, then spoon into the prepared tin, filling each mould two-thirds full. Bake for 9 minutes or until just cooked. Cool for a minute then knock the madeleines out of the tin onto the benchtop. Repeat with the remaining batter. Serve warm, sprinkled with icing sugar.

Makes 16

Recipe credit — Based on a recipe by Stephanie Alexander in *The Cook's Companion: The complete book of ingredients and recipes*, published by Penguin Books Australia, 2007. Adapted and printed with permission of Stephanie Alexander.

Chocolate Cupcakes with Coconut Frosting

JOAN McNAMARA

These gorgeous cupcakes come from our incredibly generous friend Joan, from Joan's on Third in Los Angeles. Lisa and Natanya will never forget the first time they spotted these beauties in Joan's sumptuous cake display. Two cupcakes were quickly passed over the counter, they took a bite, turned to each other and in unison nodded and mmmmed. They had never tasted a cupcake with such an incredible texture; this is the chocolate cupcake of all chocolate cupcakes.

230 g (1 cup/8 oz) caster (superfine) sugar
125 g (1 cup less 2 tablespoons/4½ oz) plain (all-purpose) flour
60 g (½ cup/2 oz) unsweetened Dutch cocoa powder
½ teaspoon bicarb soda (baking soda)
¼ teaspoon baking powder
¼ teaspoon salt
65 g (2⅓ oz) dark chocolate, chopped
125 ml (½ cup/4¼ fl oz) boiling water
1 egg
125 ml (½ cup/4¼ fl oz) buttermilk
60 ml (¼ cup/2 fl oz) oil
¼ teaspoon vanilla extract

COCONUT FROSTING

115 g (4 oz) cream cheese, at room temperature, chopped
75 g (2⅔ oz) unsalted butter, at room temperature, chopped
¼ teaspoon vanilla extract
280 g (1¾ cups/10 oz) icing (confectioners') sugar
100 g (1 cup/3½ oz) coconut flakes

Preheat the oven to 160°C (325°F/Gas 3). You will need a 12-cup muffin pan lined with paper patty pans (cupcake liners).

In a large bowl (or the bowl of a stand mixer) combine the sugar, flour, cocoa powder, bicarb, baking powder and salt in a large bowl, and whisk by hand to combine.

Place the chocolate in a heatproof bowl and pour the boiling water over it. Set aside for 5 minutes until the chocolate melts, then whisk by hand until smooth.

In a separate bowl, combine the egg, buttermilk, oil and vanilla, and whisk to blend.

Using an electric mixer on low speed, add the melted chocolate to the dry ingredients, beating until well combined. Add the egg mixture slowly and continue beating until just smooth.

Pour the batter into the prepared pans, filling each to two-thirds full. Bake in the middle of the oven for 25 minutes or until the cakes springs back when touched. Cool completely before frosting.

To make the frosting, beat the butter and cream cheese on a low speed until combined and smooth. Add the vanilla and scrape down the sides.

Add the icing sugar all at once and mix on low speed until combined, then increase speed to medium and beat for about 3 minutes or until light and fluffy.

Place the coconut flakes on a plate. Spread or pipe a generous amount (20 g/¾ oz) of frosting onto each cupcake then gently roll in the coconut flakes to get a nice coating of flakes on top.

Makes 12

Flourless Chocolate Brownies

Marcia's mission when writing her book *Meatballs and Matzah Balls: Recipes and Reflections from a Jewish and Italian Life* was to explore her Jewish and Italian culinary roots. It was also about sharing food with family and friends. These outstanding gluten-free brownies are eminently shareable, great for Passover and loved by all. It warms our hearts that Marcia dedicates this recipe to her dear friend the late Ron Gilbert and his generous spirit, as he was the first person to try her recipe. She was overwhelmed at a dinner party at his place when he made the brownies for dessert – it was the very first time someone had served her something from her book, a very special gift indeed.

225 g (8 oz) dark chocolate (70%), chopped
225 g (8 oz) unsalted butter, chopped
100 g (1 cup/3½ oz) almond meal (see Kitchen Notes page 11)
50 g (¼ cup/1¾ oz) potato flour (potato starch)
4 eggs
165 g (¾ cup, firmly packed/5¾ oz) brown sugar
170 g (¾ cup/6 oz) caster (superfine) sugar
2 teaspoons vanilla extract
¼ teaspoon ground cinnamon
½ teaspoon salt

Preheat the oven to 180°C (350°F/Gas 4).

Grease and line a 33 x 23 cm (13 x 9 inch) rectangular baking tin, leaving an overhang of baking paper up the sides to make lifting the slab out easier.

Melt the chocolate and butter together in the microwave or a double boiler (see Kitchen Notes page 11). Set aside to cool. In a small bowl, combine the almond meal and potato flour and set aside.

In a large bowl, beat the eggs, brown sugar, caster sugar, vanilla, cinnamon and salt together. Add the chocolate mixture and beat well. Gently fold in the almond mixture until just combined.

Pour the batter into the prepared tin and smooth the top with a spatula. Bake for 25 minutes or until beginning to brown at the edges and the centre is just set and still a bit soft. It will continue to set as it cools down. Allow to cool in the tin.

To cut the brownies, run a long sharp knife under hot water before cutting. Serve at room temperature.

Makes 12 large or 24 small brownies

Chocolate Coconut Milk Cake

Hanna found a version of this recipe many years ago and was immediately drawn to the combination of coconut milk and chocolate. Over the years, it has morphed into an unusually rich dairy-free cake. It is now one of her go-to chocolate cakes, and will be one of ours as well, reminding us of the coconut rough chocolates we loved as children. This recipe uses a 400 ml (14 fl oz) tin of coconut milk – some for the cake and some for the ganache icing.

55 g (2 oz) dark chocolate, chopped

85 g (⅔ cup/3 oz) unsweetened Dutch cocoa powder, sifted

185 ml (¾ cup/6 fl oz) hot brewed coffee

150 g (1 cup/5⅓ oz) plain (all-purpose) flour

1 teaspoon baking powder

½ teaspoon bicarb soda (baking soda)

¼ teaspoon salt

230 g (1 cup/8 oz) caster (superfine) sugar

50 g (¼ cup/1¾ oz) dark muscovado or brown sugar

2 eggs

90 g (3¼ oz) coconut oil, melted, or 5 tablespoons (3½ fl oz) oil

275 ml (1 cup + 5 teaspoons/9⅓ fl oz) coconut milk

COCONUT GANACHE ICING

125 g (4¼ oz) dark chocolate, chopped

125 ml (½ cup/4¼ fl oz) coconut milk

1 teaspoon light corn syrup (optional)

ALSO NEEDED

coconut flakes, toasted

Preheat the oven to 180°C (350°F/Gas 4). Line the base and sides of a 24 cm (9½ inch) springform cake tin. Shake the tin of coconut milk well and divide it into the amounts for the cake and icing.

To make the cake, place the chocolate in a heatproof bowl with the cocoa powder. Pour over the hot coffee and allow to stand for a couple of minutes, then whisk by hand until the mixture is smooth. Set aside.

Sift together the flour, baking powder, bicarb and salt, then set aside.

Using an electric mixer, combine the caster and muscovado sugars and the eggs, and whisk until pale and thick. Add the coconut oil or oil and whisk until well combined.

Add the melted chocolate and then the coconut milk for the cake, continuing to mix on low speed and scraping down the sides as needed, until the mixture is smooth. Add the dry ingredients and whisk on low speed until just incorporated.

Pour the batter into the prepared tin and bake in the bottom third of the oven for 50 minutes or until a skewer inserted into the centre comes out clean. Place on a wire rack and allow to cool before removing from the tin.

When the cake has completely cooled, make the icing. Place the chocolate in a heatproof bowl. In a small saucepan, heat the coconut milk with the corn syrup (if using) until it just comes to the boil, and pour over the chocolate. Leave for 2 minutes and then stir until it is smooth and shiny. Allow to cool for 10 minutes before pouring over the cake. Sprinkle with the toasted coconut.

Serves about 10

Chocolate and Hazelnut Cake

SUSIE CLIFFORD

This rich, fudgy chocolate cake is a regular fixture in the Clifford house. Susie remembers her *omama* Irma Wohlstein each time she makes this Passover specialty, even decorating the cake to look exactly like her grandmother's rendition. Use gluten-free breadcrumbs if needed, but don't omit the crumbs – they add texture.

180 g (1¾ cups/6⅓ oz) ground hazelnuts
180 g (¾ cups/6⅓ oz) caster (superfine) sugar
180 g (6⅓ oz) dark chocolate, chopped
280 ml (1 cup + 2 tablespoons/ 9½ fl oz) water
2 tablespoons instant coffee granules
4 tablespoons fine matzo meal (cake meal) (see Kitchen Notes page 11) or fine breadcrumbs
80 ml (⅓ cup/2¾ fl oz) oil
7 eggs, separated

CHOCOLATE GLAZE

100 g (3½ oz) dark chocolate, chopped
1 tablespoon caster (superfine) sugar
1 teaspoon unsalted butter or oil
60 ml (¼ cup/2 fl oz) water

ALSO NEEDED

50 g (⅓ cup/1¾ oz) roasted hazelnuts (see page 75)

Preheat the oven to 180°C (350°F/Gas 4). Line the base and sides of a 26 cm (10½ inch) springform cake tin.

In a medium saucepan, combine the ground hazelnuts, sugar, chocolate, water and coffee granules. Cook over medium–low heat, stirring from time to time, until the chocolate has melted and the mixture is smooth. Continue to cook on low heat, stirring constantly, for 3 minutes. Remove from the heat and add the matzo meal or breadcrumbs and the oil, stirring well.

Pour the mixture into a large mixing bowl and allow to cool slightly, then add the egg yolks, beating well to combine. Using an electric mixer, whisk the egg whites until stiff peaks form. With a metal spoon or spatula, gently fold the egg whites into the chocolate mixture.

Pour into the prepared tin and bake for 40 minutes or until a skewer inserted into the cake comes out clean. Remove from the oven, undo the latch on the cake tin and allow it to cool completely on a wire rack.

To make the glaze, place the chocolate, sugar, butter and water in a small saucepan and heat over low heat, stirring from time to time, until it is a smooth and shiny glaze. Set aside to cool until it is a thick consistency.

To serve, place the cake on a serving plate and spread the chocolate glaze over the top, encouraging it to drip down the sides of the cake. If you wish, scatter the hazelnuts on top (we forgot!).

Serves about 12

Double Chocolate Nut Cake

For years, Lisa's husband, Danny, spoke of his late mother's chocolate cake being the best in the world. Lisa was like, 'Yeah, yeah, yeah, everyone thinks their mother's cake is the best,' but she had never seen the recipe, nor could she recall ever tasting it. One day she asked her sister-in-law Kathy about it, and finally tried making it. Lisa tasted it and said, 'Ah, yes. Now I understand!' This is an exceptional cake – flourless and rich, with the most fabulous, glossy, whipped milk-chocolate icing that you want to dive right into.

100 g (3½ oz) dark chocolate, chopped
45 g (1½ oz) unsalted butter
220 g (2 cups/7¾ oz) walnut halves
6 eggs, separated
¼ teaspoon salt
230 g (1 cup/8 oz) caster (superfine) sugar

MILK CHOCOLATE ICING

200 g (7 oz) milk chocolate, chopped
40 g (2 tablespoons/1½ oz) unsalted butter
2 eggs, separated
1 tablespoon caster (superfine) sugar
1½ tablespoons brandy

Grease a 26 cm (10½ inch) springform cake tin. Preheat the oven to 160°C (325°F/Gas 3).

To make the cake, melt the chocolate and butter together in the microwave or using the double boiler method (see Kitchen Notes page 11). Set aside. Chop the walnuts in a food processor until finely ground, taking care to not make a paste.

Using an electric mixer, whisk the egg whites with the salt until white and foamy. Continuing to whisk, gradually add the sugar and continue until soft peaks form. While still whisking, add the egg yolks one at a time. Using a spatula, fold in the ground walnuts and the melted chocolate mixture.

Pour into the prepared tin and bake for 45 minutes or until a skewer inserted in the centre comes out clean. Allow to cool completely before removing the cake from the tin and icing it.

To make the icing, melt the chocolate and butter together (as above) and set aside to cool slightly. In a small bowl, using an electric mixer or by hand, whisk the egg whites with the sugar until stiff peaks form. While continuing to whisk, add the egg yolks to the whites, one at a time. Add the brandy and the melted chocolate mixture and keep whisking until combined and smooth. Spread the icing over the top and side of the cake. Serve immediately.

As the icing contains raw egg, any leftovers must be stored in an airtight container in the fridge.

Serves about 12

Note — This dish contains raw eggs (see Kitchen Notes page 10).

Chocolate Hazelnut Bon Vivant

Early in her marriage, Merelyn tasted a bon vivant cake made by her husband's aunt Edith, and she begged and pleaded until she shared the recipe with her. Edith's secret trick of roasting the hazelnuts before grinding gave her cake such a depth of flavour, and the family savoured it at every cousins' gathering. Her children, grandchildren and cousins remember her fondly, and we are thrilled that Edith's daughter, Maya Reed, now passes on the recipe.

BASE

250 g (1⅔ cups/9 oz) roasted
   hazelnuts (see note)
8 egg whites
250 g (1 cup + 1 tablespoon/9 oz)
   caster (superfine) sugar

TOPPING

200 g (7 oz) dark chocolate (70%),
   chopped
8 egg yolks
160 g (⅔ cup/5⅔ oz) caster
   (superfine) sugar
200 g (7 oz) unsalted butter, at room
   temperature, chopped

Preheat the oven to 180°C (350°F/Gas 4). Line a 33 x 22 cm (13 x 8½ inch) baking tin, leaving enough of an overhang that you can hold on to it when lifting the cake out.

Place the hazelnuts in a food processor and process until they resemble breadcrumbs.

To make the base, use an electric mixer to whisk the egg whites until soft peaks form and then, continuing to whisk, slowly add the sugar until stiff peaks form. With a metal spoon or spatula, gently fold in the hazelnuts.

Pour the mixture into the prepared tin and bake for 40 minutes or until firm to the touch and golden on top. Cool completely before adding the topping.

To make the topping, melt the chocolate in the microwave or using the double boiler method (see Kitchen Notes page 11). Set aside to cool slightly. With an electric mixer, beat the egg yolks with the sugar until thick and pale, then add the butter a little at a time until well combined. Add the melted chocolate and mix again.

Pour the chocolate mixture on top of the base and spread evenly. Bake for 20 minutes or until set. The topping will still wobble a little but will continue to set as it cools.

Place on a wire rack to cool, then into the fridge to chill completely before slicing.

To avoid cracking when serving, using a sharp knife dipped in hot water, and slice the cake while still cold, then allow it to come to room temperature before serving. The cake can also be placed in the freezer and sliced while still frozen, then defrost to serve.

Serves about 18

Note — To roast the hazelnuts, place on a baking tray and cook for 10 minutes or until lightly golden. Allow to cool, then rub them in a tea towel to remove their loose skins.

Chocolate & Marmalade
Celebration Cake
P.78

Chocolate and Marmalade Celebration Cake

ELZA LEVIN
AND MMCC

Elza uses this cake as a base for all her magnificently decorated cakes. The recipe was published in our first book, and it may be the most frequently baked cake in our collection. It is really a make-it-with-your-eyes-closed, you've-got-everything-in-your-pantry kind of cake. We have given you the recipe for one cake, but you will need to double the ingredients and make two for this oversized celebration of double chocolate goodness. We have added our touch with a homemade marmalade and chocolate ganache.

250 g (9 oz) unsalted butter, chopped
200 g (7 oz) dark chocolate, chopped
1 tablespoon instant coffee granules
375 ml (1½ cups/12½ fl oz) hot water
460 g (2 cups/1 lb) caster (superfine) sugar
185 g (1¼ cups/6½ oz) self-raising (self-rising) flour
75 g (½ cup/2⅔ oz) plain (all-purpose) flour
30 g (¼ cup/1 oz) unsweetened Dutch cocoa powder
2 eggs
2 teaspoons vanilla extract

ALSO NEEDED

200 g (heaped ½ cup/7 oz) orange marmalade (see opposite)
candied orange peel or peel from the marmalade (see opposite)

BUTTERCREAM ICING

250 g (9 oz) unsalted butter, at room temperature, chopped
400 g (2½ cups/14 oz) icing (confectioners') sugar
60 g (½ cup/2 oz) unsweetened Dutch cocoa powder
80 ml (⅓ cup/2¾ fl oz) milk
2 teaspoons vanilla extract
½ teaspoon salt

You will need to make 2 cakes to make this double chocolate marmalade cake.

To make 1 cake, preheat the oven to 150°C (300°F/Gas 2). Grease and line the base and sides of a 24 cm (9½ inch) springform cake tin. It is a very liquid batter, so if your tin leaks, secure a piece of foil around the outside of the base and side.

Melt the butter in a medium saucepan over medium heat and add the chocolate, stirring to melt. Add the coffee, water and sugar, stirring until you have a smooth mixture. Remove from the heat and pour into a large mixing bowl. Cool for 5 minutes.

Sift the flours and the cocoa powder into the chocolate mixture and stir through. Lightly whisk the eggs with the vanilla then add them to the bowl, beating well by hand or with an electric beater until you have a smooth batter.

Pour the batter into the prepared tin and bake for 1½ hours or until a skewer inserted into the centre comes out clean. The top will be crusty and cracked. If you prefer a smoother top, cut a piece of baking paper the same size as the cake, and place it on top of the mixture during baking.

Allow the cake to cool completely before removing it from the tin. Repeat and make a second cake.

To make the buttercream icing, beat the butter in an electric mixer until pale and thick. Sift the icing sugar and cocoa powder together and add to the butter, beating at low speed until combined. Add the vanilla, milk and salt, and beat well until you have a smooth icing.

Halve each cake so you end up with 2 round layers. Lay 1 layer of cake on a serving plate, spread one-third of the marmalade all over it, then a quarter of the buttercream, then top with the next layer of cake and repeat. On the last layer of cake, top only with buttercream. Decorate with pieces of orange rind from the marmalade or fresh flowers, as you wish.

Serves about 20

ORANGE MARMALADE AND PEEL

4 oranges
1.5 litres (6 cups/1½ quarts) water
660 g (3 cups/1 lb 7 oz) white
　(granulated) sugar
1 tablespoon brandy

Halve and thinly slice the oranges, remove any seeds then place into a heavy-based medium saucepan. Add the water and bring to the boil, then reduce the heat and simmer, uncovered, for 1 hour or until the fruit is soft. Add the sugar and simmer for at least 1 hour until a rich syrup forms. The syrup should reduce to about 500 ml (2 cups).

Once it has reduced, add the brandy and stir. Strain through a colander to separate the peel from the fruity syrup as you will need the peel for decoration. You may need to remove any orange flesh still attached to the peel and put it back in with the fruity syrup.

Pour the fruity syrup into a jar and allow to cool and set into marmalade. Set the orange peel aside to cool. You will need all the peel but only half the marmalade for this recipe.

The marmalade recipe has been adapted from Kathy Miller's Mandarin Marmalade in *It's Always About the Food*, with thanks!

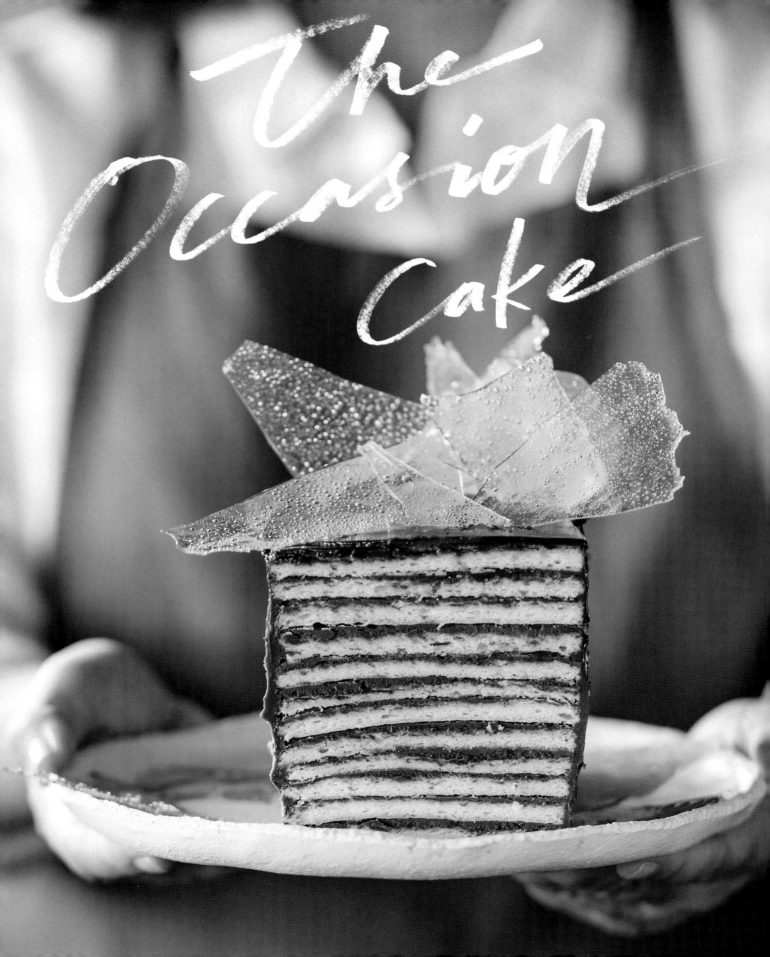

The Occasion Cake

We are often inspired by memories of our grandmothers' afternoon tea tables, fully laden, a floral teapot complete with delicate cups and tiny teaspoons and – in the centre of it all – an impressive, gorgeous, statement of a cake. Our own afternoon tea spreads are built on those memories. Of course, two generations later, there is a more contemporary touch, but the cakes are the same – just as delicious and impressive as our childhood memories would suggest. These are cakes with history, cakes to feed a crowd, to mark a special moment, to share some sweet love. Cakes you will come back to for every afternoon tea, any family gathering, many celebrations and all special occasions.

Jacqui first met **GEORGE STERNFELD** – and his gorgeous array of bow ties – while volunteering at the Sydney Jewish Museum. We were delighted to meet him when his family-favourite rack of veal was included in our third book. George's passion to educate people through the lessons of history, his authentic love of cooking and his upbeat nature make him such a pleasure to know. The poignant title of George's book, *From Chocolate to Anzac Biscuits*, best describes his life. From Warsaw to surviving the war in Siberia, to moving to Australia, George remembers his early life as one with very little food under the most trying circumstances. Now in Australia, he celebrates life and an ever-growing family, with wife Liz by his side.

As the oldest grandchild, **SHARON ALLENTUCK** spent a lot of time in the kitchen with her grandmother *Baba* Ida, who came to Saskatchewan, Canada, from Russia. Her grandmother was widowed in 1939 and had to learn to fend for herself and her seven children. She knew how to cook and bake for a crowd, all without the conveniences of a modern kitchen, and, decades later, Sharon would watch in amazement. The extended family would gather at *Baba* Ida's house every Sunday afternoon for tea – seven children, their spouses and a horde of cousins, all shmoozing, playing together and devouring her amazing baking. Now, Sharon carries on the tradition. She loves to bake with two of her young granddaughters who are already expert *hamantashen* rollers and fillers.

Born in the Ukraine, **ETHEL BARANOVSKY TARSHIS** immigrated to Canada in 1927 at age six. The village where Ethel was born, Bobrinitz, was in the Ukraine but came under the umbrella of Russia; Eastern European Jewish culture was always a big part of her life. She only spoke Yiddish when they arrived in Montreal; her father put her on the front stoop, closed the door and told her to learn English. She eventually learnt English and went on to receive a degree in teaching. Unbelievably, the Jewish girls were told they would not be hired to actually teach in the city of Montreal because of their religion. Most went on to do other things, and Ethel was grateful for the education. Her mother, Manya, was a wonderful baker and Ethel learnt from her – the master. She is greatly missed by her three daughters and loving husband, Robert, and her memory lives on.

NAOMI ALTHAUS and **NECHAMA WERDIGER** share a special recipe, and a special family history. Two different families intertwined when their journeys followed the same path – it almost seemed like destiny, *beshert* (meant to be). Soon after World War II, Naomi's grandparents and Nechama's parents escaped Russia together via Paris, and were then sent by the *Lubavitcher Rebbe* to Australia. They all lived in rural Shepparton before moving to Melbourne, and both became founding families of the *Yeshivah* (centre for Jewish learning). Nechama, the matriarch of the Werdiger family, and her late husband, Nathan, have over 80 great-grandchildren. Naomi's grandparents opened the kosher guesthouse, Chedva, in Sherbrooke Forest near Melbourne – a place that gave so many Holocaust survivors a feeling of the extended family they had lost. Naomi continues her grandparents' legacy by nurturing through food and, like her mother before her, is a renowned kosher caterer.

ELZA LEVIN in *The Chocolate Cake* (page 60)

Having settled in Perth from Liverpool, England, **CAROLYN LEVITT'S** mother, an acclaimed dessert cook, often served a classic English rice pudding to the family. Carolyn was 11 when she arrived in Australia, and to this day she'll fight with her brothers to snare the golden, caramelised skin of their favourite dessert. She learnt to bake by her mother's side, and soon earned her own excellent reputation for sweets. For a while, Carolyn baked for her local café but now she focuses on feeding family and friends at her own *Shabbat* (Friday night) dinners and Jewish festival celebrations. Everyone always leaves her table with a parcel of leftovers, and she hand-delivers and posts biscuits all over the country, to wherever her children live.

'The rule is TLC – tender loving care,' wrote **MAIDA HEATTER** about baking. Over the course of many decades, Maida influenced how Americans made desserts. Today, her many books are still a resource to anyone who wants a clear-cut path to baking success. Interestingly, Maida never attended cooking school; she credits her mother (as well as a lot of trial and error) for her baking skills. Her career changed from illustrator to jewellery maker to baking doyenne when she started making cakes for a restaurant she owned with her husband. From there, she started teaching baking classes, and the *New York Times* suggested she write a cookbook. Nine books, three James Beard awards and an induction into the Foundation Hall of Fame followed. Maida lived to the grand age of 102 and sadly passed away while we were writing this book.

Happiness for **NETA GREENBERG-TOUBOUL** is feeding her loved ones, art and dancing. She finds herself in the kitchen, feeding hungry stomachs with absolute joy. Her kitchen is the spiritual centre of her home, the place where the best and worst conversations take place. Born and raised in Israel till the age of 16, Neta lived in Los Angeles with her family, then moved to Bellevue, Washington, in search of a smaller city. She has Polish heritage on both sides; her parents met in Israel after the war. Neta's life is greatly influenced by art and she loves working with clay, specialising in functional pottery.

Cinnamon Swirl
Coffee Cake

NETA GREENBERG-TOUBOUL

We just adore a cake with a swirl. This swoon-worthy cake has become a regular part of Neta's repertoire. We have tweaked Neta's translation of the original Hebrew recipe, which came from Israeli pastry chef Carine Goren.

200 g (7 oz) unsalted butter, at room temperature, chopped, plus extra for greasing

300 g (1⅓ cups/10½ oz) caster (superfine) sugar

1 teaspoon vanilla extract

3 eggs

420 g (2¾ cups/15 oz) plain (all-purpose) flour, plus extra for dusting

1 tablespoon baking powder

1 teaspoon bicarb soda (baking soda)

½ teaspoon salt

500 ml (2 cups/17 fl oz) sour cream

FILLING

120 g (⅔ cup, lightly packed/4¼ oz) brown sugar

65 g (⅔ cup/2⅓ oz) walnuts, finely chopped

2 teaspoons ground cinnamon

1½ teaspoons unsweetened Dutch cocoa powder

ALSO NEEDED

icing (confectioners') sugar

Generously butter a large 10-cup bundt (fluted tube) tin and lightly dust with flour. Place the tin in the freezer until ready to use. Preheat the oven to 180°C (350°F/Gas 4).

Using an electric mixer beat together the butter, the sugar and the vanilla until pale and creamy. Add the eggs one at a time, beating well between each addition.

In a separate bowl, sift together the flour, baking powder, bicarb and salt. On a low speed, add the flour mixture in 3 lots, alternating with the sour cream and ending with flour.

To make the filling, combine the brown sugar, walnuts, cinnamon and cocoa powder. Spoon one-third of the batter into the prepared tin, then sprinkle over half of the filling. Spoon another third of the batter into the tin and sprinkle with the remaining filling. Top with the remaining batter. Using a knife, swirl the filling through the batter.

Bake for 50 minutes or until a skewer inserted into the cake comes out clean. Allow to cool and sprinkle with icing sugar to serve.

Serves about 12

Recipe credit — Translated, adapted and printed with permission of the author, *from Sweet Secrets 2* by Carine Goren, 2011.

Upside-down Peach Cake

ELZA LEVIN

Elza met Norma Holmes many years ago, when they were part of a group of women in the 70-plus age bracket, chatting in the change room after weekly aqua aerobics classes. They all felt such a great camaraderie that they began meeting for monthly lunches to get to know each other better. Norma had owned a café called The Gum Nut Tea Garden in one of Sydney's historic neighbourhoods, The Rocks. She'd served her upside-down peach cake at the café, and when she made it for the aqua aerobics ladies' lunch, they went crazy for it. Norma generously shared the recipe with Elza, and here it is. And they are all still doing lunch.

3 yellow peaches
115 g (1 stick/4 oz) unsalted butter, at room temperature, chopped
230 g (1 cup/8 oz) caster (superfine) sugar
2 eggs
225 g (1½ cups/8 oz) plain (all-purpose) flour
2 teaspoons baking powder
¼ teaspoon salt
¼ teaspoon ground cardamom
finely grated zest of 1 lemon
125 ml (½ cup/4¼ fl oz) milk

SYRUP

115 g (1 stick/4 oz) unsalted butter
185 g (1 cup, lightly packed/6½ oz) brown sugar
2 tablespoons lemon juice
¼ teaspoon ground cinnamon
¼ teaspoon ground cardamom

whipped cream, to serve

Preheat the oven to 175°C (345°F/Gas 3). You will need a 25 cm (10 inch) round cake tin without a removable base. Line the base only, then grease and flour the side.

To make the syrup, combine the butter, brown sugar, lemon juice, cinnamon and cardamom in a medium saucepan. Cook over medium heat, stirring until the sugar is dissolved. Remove from the heat and set aside.

Slice the peaches and arrange them around the base of the prepared tin. Pour the syrup over the peaches and set aside while making the cake batter.

To make the cake batter, use an electric mixer to beat the butter and sugar until pale and creamy. Add the eggs one at a time, beating well after each addition. In a separate bowl, sift together the flour, baking powder, salt and cardamom, then add the lemon zest. On low speed, beat in the flour mixture, alternating with the milk until just combined.

Carefully spoon the cake batter over the peaches and syrup and smooth the top. Bake for 1 hour or until a skewer inserted into the centre comes out clean. Allow to rest for a few minutes, then invert onto a serving platter. Serve at room temperature. Lovely with a dollop of whipped cream.

Serves about 12

Almond Meringue Torte

GEORGE STERNFELD

We adore George, and we're so pleased Jacqui introduced us to him. We are in awe of his work at the Jewish Museum, and we also love his curiosity and exploration in the kitchen. This is his go-to Passover dessert; George tells us it was devoured again this year, and likely to be reproduced next year by popular demand. Unlike most layer cakes, this torte can be served as soon as it is made, or kept in the fridge for up to two days before serving.

MERINGUE NUT LAYER

75 g (½ cup/2⅔ oz) roasted almonds
4 egg whites
250 g (1½ cups/9 oz) icing
    (confectioners') sugar
1 tablespoon white vinegar
30 g (¼ cup/1 oz) unsweetened
    Dutch cocoa powder

FILLING

600 ml (2½ scant cups/20 fl oz)
    thickened (whipping) cream
75 g (½ cup/2⅔ oz) roasted almonds,
    chopped
100 g (3½ oz) dark chocolate,
    finely chopped
135 g (1 cup/4¾ oz) raspberries
165 g (1 cup/5¾ oz) blueberries
165 g (1 cup/5¾ oz) strawberries,
    quartered

Preheat the oven to 150°C (300°F/Gas 2). Line 2 large baking trays. Trace 3 circles approximately 20 cm (8 inches) in diameter on the baking paper.

To make the meringue nut layer, place the roasted almonds in a food processor and pulse until they are ground, and resemble breadcrumbs. Set aside.

Using an electric mixer, whisk the egg whites until soft peaks form, then slowly add the icing sugar 1 tablespoon at a time, while continuing to whisk. Whisk for 10 minutes or until stiff and glossy. Using a spatula, fold in the vinegar, cocoa powder and the ground almonds.

Use the spatula to spread the meringue inside the outlines you've traced, smoothing out to the edges. Bake for 45 minutes or until the discs are crisp to the touch. Place on a wire rack to cool completely.

To make the filling, whip the cream in a bowl just until soft peaks form and set aside. In a separate bowl combine the almonds and the chocolate. In a third bowl combine the berries.

To assemble the torte, place the first disc of meringue on a serving platter and top with one-third of the cream, one-third of the almond/chocolate mixture and one-third of the berries. Repeat with the remaining discs.

Serves about 10

Dark Fruit Cake

ELZA LEVIN

Elza's foray into the new world of cake decorating saw her make many new friends. One such friend, and a wonderful teacher and mentor, was Ada Lyrus; she helped Elza take her creations to the next level. Ada shared this treasured cake, traditionally served at Greek weddings and at Christmas time, and it has now become a regular in Elza's kitchen. We all wish we were on her Christmas cake list!

500 g (2¼ cups/1 lb 2 oz) raisins

500 g (heaped 3 cups/1 lb 2 oz) sultanas (golden raisins)

250 g (1⅔ cups/9 oz) pitted dried dates

250 g (1¼ cups/9 oz) mixed (candied) fruit peel

100 g (½ cup/3½ oz) glacé cherries

250 ml (1 cup/8½ fl oz) sherry, plus extra

250 g (9 oz) unsalted butter, at room temperature, chopped

250 g (1⅓ cups, lightly packed/9 oz) brown sugar

5 eggs

1 heaped tablespoon orange marmalade

300 g (2 cups/10½ oz) plain (all-purpose) flour

1 teaspoon ground cinnamon

1 teaspoon ground nutmeg

¼ teaspoon salt

Start this recipe the day (or up to 1 month) before serving.

In a large bowl, soak the raisins, sultanas, dates, peel and cherries in half the sherry for 24 hours at room temperature, tossing from time to time.

Do NOT preheat the oven. Line the base and sides of two 18 cm (7 inch) square cake tins – use 3 layers of baking paper in each tin, one on top of the other, greasing each layer before the next goes on top.

Using an electric mixer, beat the butter and sugar together until pale and creamy. Add the eggs one at a time, beating well between each addition. Add the marmalade and continue to beat until completely combined.

Sift together the flour, cinnamon, nutmeg and salt, then toss with the soaked fruit and add to the butter mixture. Be sure to include any sherry from the bottom of the bowl. Stir through to combine.

Divide the cake mixture equally between the prepared tins and place into the cold oven. Turn on the oven to 180°C (350°F/Gas 4) and bake for 30 minutes. Reduce the heat to 120°C (250°F/Gas ½) and bake for a further 2½ hours. Remove from the oven, prick the top with a skewer and pour over the remaining sherry.

Wrap each tin in clean tea towels and allow to cool completely. Once cool, remove the cakes from the tins, tightly wrapping each cake in the layers of baking paper and then a tea towel. Set aside in a cool place. If you love the idea of a sherry-soaked cake, you can add another tablespoon of sherry to each cake every fortnight or so until you are ready to enjoy it.

Makes 2 cakes, each serves about 18

Russian Honey Cake

CAROLYN LEVITT

We'd heard whisperings of an interesting layered honey cake from Merelyn's home town, Perth. Luckily for all of us, she went visiting and brought back some of the famous cake from The Honeycake bakery. We were dreaming of how to re-create our own, so imagine how excited we were when Carolyn Levitt (also from Perth) sent a recipe for her own version of the same iconic Russian torte. It will really shake up your Rosh Hashanah.

PASTRY LAYERS

125 g (4½ oz) unsalted butter,
   at room temperature, chopped
170 g (¾ cup/6 oz) caster
   (superfine) sugar
2 eggs
90 g (¼ cup/3¼ oz) honey
2 teaspoons bicarb soda
   (baking soda)
600 g (4 cups/1 lb 5 oz) plain
   (all-purpose) flour, sifted

FILLING

500 g (1 lb 2 oz) cream cheese,
   at room temperature, chopped
120 g (¾ cup/4¼ oz) icing
   (confectioners') sugar, sifted
90 g (¼ cup/3¼ oz) honey
500 ml (2 cups/17 fl oz) pure (35% fat)
   cream

ALSO NEEDED

100 g (⅔ cup/3½ oz) roasted
   hazelnuts, chopped (see page 75)

Note — The pastry can be prepared and baked up to 3 days before assembling if it is kept in an airtight container.

Start this recipe at least 1 day before serving.

You will need a large heatproof bowl that will fit snugly over a medium saucepan. Add about 2.5 cm (1 inch) of water to the saucepan and bring to the boil. Put the butter, caster sugar, eggs and honey in the bowl, and whisk together to combine (the butter will remain in pieces). Place the bowl on top of the saucepan (make sure the bowl is not touching the water) and reduce the heat to medium so the water is simmering. Whisk the mixture constantly for 10 minutes or until the mixture is smooth and slightly thickened. Remove the bowl from the heat and allow to cool slightly.

Add the bicarb to the mixture and stir, and then add the flour. Mix with a wooden spoon to form a firm dough. Divide the dough into 8 equal pieces.

Preheat the oven to 200°C (400°F/Gas 6). You will need 2 baking trays and a 20 cm (8 inch) diameter plate or template. Roll out 1 piece of dough onto a piece of baking paper and, using the plate or template, cut out a circle. Remove the scraps of pastry from the outside of the circle and place the baking paper with the pastry circle onto one of the baking trays.

Repeat the rolling out and cutting with the next piece of dough and place either next to the first one on the baking tray (if there is room) or on the second tray. Bake for 5 minutes, or until just slightly puffed and deep golden. It will firm as it cools. Remove from the tray and cool on a wire rack. Repeat with the remaining dough.

To make the filling, use an electric mixer to whisk the cream cheese until light and fluffy. Add the icing sugar and honey and whisk until combined. Add the cream and continue to whisk until it is thick enough to spread.

To assemble the cake, spread 1 round with approximately 3 mm (⅛ inch) of the filling, top with another round and continue to do so until you have used all the layers.

Spread the remaining filling over the top and around the side of the cake, and sprinkle with the chopped hazelnuts.

Cover with plastic wrap and refrigerate at least overnight and for up to 3 days.

Serves about 16

Russian Sour Cream *Smetna* Torte

ETHEL BARANOVSKY
TARSHIS

The Canadian Tarshis family reached out to us with their mum's treasured recipe. Ethel had never given it to anyone, wanting to keep their special torte in the family. But daughter Judy decided it was time, and that it would be a great honour for Ethel's legacy to be shared through the Monday Morning Cooking Club project. Make this torte up to three days ahead of serving so the layers can soften and the flavours can meld.

PASTRY LAYERS

225 g (2 sticks/8 oz) unsalted butter, at room temperature, chopped
165 g (scant ¾ cup/5¾ oz) caster (superfine) sugar
1 egg
375 g (2½ cups/13¼ oz) plain (all-purpose) flour
1 teaspoon baking powder

FILLING

625 ml (2½ cups/21 fl oz) sour cream
180 ml (¾ cup/6 fl oz) pure (35% fat) cream
160 g (1 cup/5⅔ oz) icing (confectioners') sugar
70 g (⅔ cup/2½ oz) walnuts, finely chopped
1 teaspoon vanilla bean paste

ALSO NEEDED

50 g (½ cup/1¾ oz) walnut halves

Start this recipe at least 2 days before serving.

Preheat the oven to 175°C (350°F/Gas 4). Line a 23 cm (9 inch) springform cake tin. To make the pastry, use an electric mixer to beat the butter with the sugar until thick and creamy. Add the egg and beat to combine. In a separate bowl, combine the flour and baking powder and whisk by hand to combine.

On low speed, gradually add the flour mixture to the butter mixture, 1 cup at a time, until fully incorporated.

Divide the dough into 3 and, with your fingertips, press 1 part evenly into the base of the prepared tin. Bake for 30 minutes or until golden. Allow to cool for 10 minutes in the pan and then remove to a wire rack. Repeat with the remaining 2 parts. When all 3 layers of pastry are completely cooled, make the filling.

To make the filling, put the sour cream, cream, icing sugar, vanilla and finely chopped walnuts in a mixing bowl and whisk together to combine. It should have the consistency of heavy cream.

To assemble the cake, line the base and side of a 23 cm (9 inch) springform cake tin. Place 1 pastry layer into the tin and spread one-third of the cream filling on top to cover the whole surface. Repeat with the remaining pastry layers, filling and pressing down gently as you go. Cover with plastic wrap and refrigerate for at least 2 days. When ready to serve, remove the torte from the pan. Sprinkle with walnut halves and serve the torte whole, or slice it in the traditional way – into diamond wedges.

Serves about 14

Cinnamon Layer Torte

SHARON ALLENTUCK

In 2018, we addressed the world conference of the International Council of Jewish Women in Sydney. There were women from all over the world, so we asked them to please put the call out to their communities for recipes for our collection. The ladies of Canada delivered – they sent us wonderful recipes. This one, a Winnipeg wedding and Bar/Bat Mitzvah classic for generations, stole our hearts. It looks spectacular and the taste is cinnamon heaven.

PASTRY LAYERS

375 g (13¼ oz) unsalted butter, at room temperature, chopped
345 g (1½ cups/12¼ oz) caster (superfine) sugar
2 eggs
480 g (3¼ cups/1 lb 1 oz) plain (all-purpose) flour, plus extra
1½ tablespoons ground cinnamon
1 teaspoon baking powder

FILLING

1 litre (4 cups/33¾ fl oz) thickened (whipping) cream
55 g (⅓ cup/2 oz) icing (confectioners') sugar, sifted
1 teaspoon vanilla extract

ALSO NEEDED

75 g (2⅔ oz) dark chocolate shavings

Note — The pastry layers may be made several days ahead and stored in an airtight container before assembling. Once assembled, the torte can be stored in the fridge for up to three days, making it a great do-ahead cake.

Start this recipe the day before serving.

To make the pastry layers, using an electric mixer beat the butter and sugar until pale and creamy. Add the eggs one at a time, and beat well. In a separate bowl combine the flour, cinnamon and baking powder then add to the butter mixture in 3 lots, gently beating to just combine after each addition. You will have a very soft dough. Form the dough into a log, wrap it in plastic wrap and refrigerate for at least 1 hour.

Preheat the oven to 180°C (350°F/Gas 4). You will need 2 baking trays and a stencil or template that is 22 cm (8½ inches) in diameter – the base of a springform tin is ideal – as you will be rolling and cutting out 10 pastry circles, and baking each one on the paper you roll it out on.

Remove the dough from the fridge and divide it into 9 pieces. Work with 1 piece at a time, returning the remaining pieces to the fridge to keep cold. Lightly flour a 30 cm (12 inch) square of baking paper. With a floured hand, form the dough into a ball and press it into the middle of the baking paper. Using a well-floured rolling pin, roll the dough out into a circle slightly bigger than the stencil. Place the stencil onto the pastry and, using a small knife, cut around the outside. Remove the stencil, set the trimmings aside, and place the baking paper together with the dough circle onto one of the baking trays. Repeat with the next ball of dough and place either next to the first one on the baking tray (if it fits) or on the second tray.

Bake for 10 minutes or until deep golden brown. Remove from the oven, set the baking paper and pastry discs aside and repeat with the remaining dough. Use all the trimmings to make a tenth circle. Allow the discs to cool.

To make the filling, whisk the cream with the icing sugar and the vanilla until soft peaks form. Set aside 1½ cups of the whipped cream for the topping.

To assemble the torte, place one disc on a clean square of baking paper. Spread one-ninth of the cream (about 80 g/⅓ cup) all over and right to the edge of the first disc, then place the next disc on top. Repeat filling and stacking the discs until you've used them all up, finishing with a disc.

Spread the reserved cream over the top of the torte and decorate with the chocolate shavings. Cover with plastic wrap and refrigerate for at least 24 hours (and up to 3 days) before serving to allow the layers to soften.

Serves about 16

Napoleon Cake

NAOMI ALTHAUS AND
NECHAMA WERDIGER

This recipe has a heartwarming collaborative history of two families. It started before Naomi's grandmother Manya made Nechama a very special dress, and before Nechama's mother made this Russian layered custard cake for her daughter's third birthday. It has evolved over the years; the custard was originally made when a saucepan and spoon were the only utensils. Nechama's close family friend Raya Shifrin tweaked it to its current form. The pastry layer recipe comes from Manya and has now been perfected by Naomi. Russian traditionalists may tell you it should have more layers, or be decorated with crushed pastry, but we love this one just like it is.

BUTTERCREAM

5 eggs
575 g (2½ cups/1 lb 4 oz) caster (superfine) sugar, plus extra
150 g (1 cup/5⅓ oz) plain (all-purpose) flour
1.25 litres (5 cups/42 fl oz) milk
625 g (1 lb 6 oz) unsalted butter, softened, chopped
80 ml (⅓ cup/2¾ fl oz) vodka
1 tablespoon vanilla bean paste

PASTRY LAYERS

150 g (heaped ½ cup/5⅓ oz) sour cream
2 tablespoons caster (superfine) sugar
3 eggs, lightly beaten
125 g (4½ oz) unsalted butter, melted and cooled
260 g (1¾ cups/9¼ oz) plain (all-purpose) flour, plus extra
260 g (1¾ cups/9¼ oz) self-raising (self-rising) flour

ALSO NEEDED

150 g (5⅓ oz) dark chocolate, grated

Start this recipe 2 days before serving.

To start the buttercream, first make a custard (check out How to Custard on page 232). You can do this on the stove or in the microwave. If making on the stove, whisk together the eggs, caster sugar and flour in a large, wide saucepan. Add the milk, whisking to combine. Cook over medium to medium–low heat, stirring continuously to prevent the mixture from catching, for about 20 minutes or until the mixture coats the back of a spoon and is thick. If lumps form along the way, whisk until smooth.

If you prefer using a microwave, place the eggs, caster sugar and flour in an extra-large heatproof bowl, and whisk by hand until smooth. Add the milk and whisk gently till combined. Cook on high for 24 minutes, stopping every 8 minutes to whisk the mixture well. It will thicken to a custard. If lumps form along the way, whisk until smooth.

When the custard is ready (the temperature should be around 80°C/175°F on a sugar thermometer), pour it into a large heatproof bowl and while it's still hot, sprinkle a layer of caster sugar on the top of the custard to prevent a film forming. Allow to cool and then cover with plastic wrap and refrigerate overnight.

To make the pastry, combine the sour cream and caster sugar in a medium bowl and whisk by hand until smooth. Add the eggs and the melted butter and whisk until combined. Add the plain flour and self-raising flour, fold in with a wooden spoon and then mix with your hands to form a smooth pastry.

Weigh the pastry and divide it into 7 equal parts (around 140 g/5 oz each). Shape each piece into a small rectangle, wrap individually in plastic wrap, and refrigerate for 30 minutes.

→

←

Preheat the oven to 180°C (350°F/Gas 4). Grease the back of a 43 x 33 cm (17 x 13 inch) baking tray. You only need to grease it for the first piece of pastry.

On a lightly floured benchtop, roll 1 piece of pastry to the size of the prepared tray. Use the rolling pin to lift it off the benchtop and place it on the (back of the) tray. Prick the entire surface with a fork and bake for 6 minutes or until just starting to brown at the edges. Remove from the oven to a wire rack and repeat with the remaining pieces. Allow the pastry layers to cool.

When ready to assemble the Napoleon, finish the buttercream by beating the butter until pale and creamy. While beating, add the custard, one spoonful at a time (and no more!), until it is incorporated into the butter. Add the vodka and the vanilla and beat until completely smooth. Divide the buttercream into 7 parts.

Place a piece of baking paper (bigger than the size of a pastry layer) on a flat tray. Place one pastry layer on the tray and spread one part of the buttercream evenly on top from edge to edge. Place the next pastry layer on top and spread with buttercream. Repeat using all the pastry layers and all the buttercream, ending with buttercream on the top. Sprinkle with the grated chocolate.

Refrigerate for 24 hours to ensure the layers are soft enough to cut. Remove from the fridge and trim the edges so they are straight.

Store well covered in the fridge for up to 5 days.

Serves about 50

Dobos Torte

Hungarian Layered Sponge

We searched high and low for a recipe for the elusive Dobos Torte. When we tried Deb Perelman's (from *The Smitten Kitchen* blog), we were blown away. She had used Maida Heatter's recipe for the cake layers and ganache, which we now have permission to reprint here in its original, lovely and chatty format (with no changes). We loved the look of Deb Perelman's cake, and we wanted ours to look just like hers, so after Maida's recipe you will find our instructions (on page 104) for assembling a 12-layer rectangular version with toffee shards.

MAIDA HEATTER'S
DOBOSH TORTE

7 eggs, separated
3 egg yolks
450 g (2¾ cups/1 lb) icing
  (confectioners') sugar
110 g (¾ cup/3¾ oz) sifted plain
  (all-purpose) flour
3 teaspoons lemon juice
⅛ teaspoon salt

In Maida Heatter's words:

To prepare for baking seven cake layers (the usual number): cut seven pieces of baking paper (parchment), each about 28 cm (11 inches) square. Trace a 23 cm (9 inch) circle on each paper. Turn the papers upside down. Butter an area a little larger than the traced circle (which will show through). Sift flour over the buttered papers; shake and tilt the papers to shake off excess flour. Set papers aside.

Place rack in the centre of the oven and preheat to 230°C (450°F/Gas 8).

In the large bowl of an electric mixer at high speed, beat the ten egg yolks for a few minutes until they are pale lemon coloured. Reduce speed and gradually add sugar. Increase speed to high again and beat for 5 minutes until very thick. Reduce speed and gradually add the flour, then again increase it to high and beat for 5 minutes more (mixture will be almost stiff), scraping the bowl occasionally with a rubber spatula. Mix in the lemon juice and remove from mixer. (The mixture will be very thick – use your fingers to get it all off the beaters.)

In a clean bowl with clean beaters, beat the seven egg whites with the salt until they hold a point – stiff but not dry. Since the yolk mixture is very thick, actually stir a few spoonsful of the whites in to lighten it a bit. Then fold in a few large spoonsful three or four times until the mixture lightens. Gently fold in the remaining whites.

Although a Dobosh Torte is generally seven layer high, I pride myself on the number and thinness of my layers. If you only make seven layers, that's perfectly all right – trying for more is one of my own personal hang-ups.

With a large serving spoon, place one or two large spoonsful of the batter on a piece of the prepared paper. Using an offset spatula or the back of a spoon, spread the batter thin, slowly rotating the paper with your left hand as you spread the batter with your right hand. Make it thin but do not leave any holes in it. A 6 mm (¼ inch) thickness should give you seven layers. Do not make the edges too thin. Follow the lines closely, but don't worry – the edges may be trimmed later.

Slide a cookie sheet under the paper and bake for 5 to 7 minutes or until the top is golden brown with dark brown spots. If the layers are thicker than mine are, they will take longer to bake. If they are not baked long enough, they will stick to the paper. Repeat with remaining layers.

When a layer is baked and out of the oven, lift the corners of the paper and invert onto a rack. Peel off the paper and immediately invert the layer onto another rack to cool, right side up. (If you let the layer cool upside down it will stick to the rack). When you run out of racks, layers may cool on smooth towelling that has been dusted with icing (confectioners') sugar. When you run out of room, cooled layers may be stacked if you sprinkle the tops lightly with icing sugar and place wax paper between them.

Cooled layers may be trimmed to even the edges. Working on a board, place a 22–23 cm (8½–9 inch) pot cover or cake pan on the layer. Cut around with a small sharp knife or trace with the knife and then cut with scissors.

FILLING AND ICING FOR DOBOSH TORTE

225 g (½ lb/8 oz) semisweet or bittersweet (dark, at least 70%) chocolate
225 g (2 sticks/8 oz) butter
1 teaspoon vanilla extract
3 egg yolks
2 tablespoons icing (confectioners') sugar

Prepare the following:

Melt the chocolate in the top of a small double boiler over hot water on moderate heat. Remove from heat, stir until smooth, and set aside to cool completely. In small bowl of electric mixer beat the butter until soft. Add vanilla and egg yolks and beat well. Add sugar and cooled chocolate. Beat until thoroughly mixed, scraping the bowl with a rubber spatula.

Place four strips of baking parchment or wax paper around the outer edges of a cake plate. Place one cake layer on the plate and with a long, narrow metal spatula spread with a thin layer of the chocolate filling. If you have more than seven layers, the filling must be spread very thin, in order to have enough for all. Place another layer on top, adjusting it carefully so that the edges are lined up evenly. Continue icing the layers, stacking them as evenly as possible. If necessary, trim the edges again.

Spread the remaining chocolate smooth around the sides first and then over the top. Remove paper strips by pulling each one out by a narrow end and refrigerate cake for at least several hours to set the icing. Store in refrigerator and serve cold.

Serves 12

Note — This dish contains raw eggs (see Kitchen Notes page 10).

→

To assemble our version of the Dobos Torte

THE TORTE

Line the base and sides of a 33 x 23 cm (13 x 9 inch) swiss roll tin. Weigh and divide the batter into 4 equal parts. Scrape 1 part into the prepared tin and spread evenly. Bake at 230°C (450°F/Gas 8) for 8 minutes or until golden brown with dark brown spots. Follow Maida's instruction on removal from the tin, and then repeat with the remaining batter. (Once cool, the stacks can be layered with baking paper, put into an airtight container and frozen.)

THE ICING

Weigh and divide the icing into 6 parts, reserving 2 of them. Spread 1 part of the icing on the first layer of cake. Place the second layer of cake on top and spread with icing. Repeat with the third and fourth layers of cake. Trim the edges. Cut the stack of 4 cakes crossways into 3 equal parts (use a ruler!). Layer these 3 stacks of cakes on top of each other to create a cake of 12 layers. Trim again if necessary. Spread the remaining icing over the sides of the cake and over the top if necessary. If the icing hardens while spreading, warm gently in the microwave to soften.

THE DECORATION

If you are new to making toffee, check out How to Sugar on page 266.

To make the toffee shards, lay out a 40 cm (16 inch) sheet of baking paper on the benchtop. In a small saucepan, combine 170 g (¾ cup/6 oz) of white (granulated) sugar with ¼ cup of water. Over medium heat, stir continuously until dissolved then bring to the boil. Simmer on medium heat for about 5 minutes, without stirring, swirling from time to time, until deep golden and 170°C (338°F) on a sugar thermometer. Very carefully (it is hot!) pour the toffee onto the baking paper. Very carefully lift the corners (away from you), so it spreads down the paper to create a thin layer. Lift the sides of the paper all around to help spread the toffee as thinly and evenly as possible across the paper. When cool, break the shards on top of the Dobos Torte to decorate. The toffee shards can be made ahead and stored in the freezer.

Serves about 12

The Chiffon Cake

Icon of the Monday Morning Cooking Club
kitchen: the custard chiffon cake. After years
of begging and pleading, Merelyn's mother,
Yolan, finally relented and bestowed on
her a 50-year-old secret recipe. The chiffon
has become our go-to special delivery cake.
If a baby is born, a friend is in need or a
celebration is to be had, we are there, chiffon
in hand. Buy yourself a chiffon or angel cake
tin that will be yours for a lifetime, choose
one of these six unique recipes, follow our
steps in How to Chiffon on page 110 and
let the chiffon joy begin. Once mastered,
there is no turning back.

People + Stories

Growing up in Shanghai, zoology professor and food writer **GREG PATENT** was entranced watching his granny beat egg whites to soft peaks. When the family moved to San Francisco in 1950, Greg would rush home from school to watch Edith Green on TV, and he made his first batch of biscuits from the *Betty Crocker Cookbook*. Greg developed a passion for food – jotting down recipes from Julia Child and, over the course of a year and a half, baking every sweet treat found in Maida Heatter's classic *Book of Great Desserts*. Greg also relished the traditional recipes connected to his Jewish background and Siberian, Iraqi and Russian heritage. For his award-winning cookbook, *A Baker's Odyssey*, Greg visited the homes and kitchens of more than 60 immigrants to the U.S. to document their culinary history.

SANDRA GOLDBERG'S mother was a formidable cook, with a perfectionism drilled into her by going to the best school in Pretoria, which happened to be the local convent. While adoring her mother's cooking, Sandra developed a more relaxed kitchen philosophy. She believes entertaining is not only an art form but also a way of enjoying herself. Sandra trained as a home economics teacher, married a farmer and spent many years in Bethal, a small farming town in Mpumalanga, a region rich in maize, sunflower seeds, sorghum, rye and potatoes. Sandra creates recipes with new combinations to serve food that not only tastes great, but is also healthy and part of a beautifully presented table. Now living in Johannesburg and part of a very connected family, Sandra loves baking for her grandchildren, wherever in the world they have settled.

'Organised chaos' is what the late **IRENE ISRAEL** would say as friends, neighbours and family bustled into her house on a Friday afternoon. The doorbell rang, the stove was crammed with bubbling pots, the oven was full, the benchtop was covered with dishes. Someone always popped over for a cuppa, and at the same time Irene would be on the phone, inviting an extra to join the *Shabbat* (Friday night) table. Though she left Hungary at an early age, arriving in Australia with her family at the age of two, Irene's Jewish–Hungarian heritage was integral to her life in Melbourne. She was a renowned and welcoming host, described by her family simply as 'always inclusive'. A box of handwritten recipes, many scribbled on the back of envelopes, is now lovingly stored in her daughter Emily's kitchen. Emily still cooks her mother's food, but on reflection says that it never tastes quite the same, and wonders if it is Irene's love and warmth that is missing.

Merelyn's mother, **YOLAN SONNENSCHEIN FRANK**, never dreamt of a homemaker's life, yet she became one of the best home bakers you could find. The dream of running her Hungarian family's crystal and porcelain business was stolen from her, first by the war and then by communism. After immigrating to Australia and marrying Kopel, feeding their growing family became her newfound career. Always nocturnal, she could be found making strudel pastry at midnight – when the kitchen cooled down during Perth's scorching summers. She made apricot and plum jams to remind her of the old country and diligently pasted cut-out newspaper recipes in her old-fashioned binder. She used to interrupt Merelyn swatting the textbooks, insisting she touch the pastry or fold the egg whites, so that one day Merelyn would remember and then instinctively know how to do it. And her strategy worked; Merelyn often tells all of us in the Monday Morning Cooking Club kitchen, 'That's how Mum used to do it.'

How to Chiffon

A chiffon is a light, airy sponge cake, typically using oil instead of butter.

Before you begin: You will need a high-sided angel cake (chiffon) tin that is not non-stick, has a centre funnel and removable base. Do not grease it. Before starting the cake, find a bottle that will fit into the top of the funnel – you will need to use this as soon as the cake comes out of the oven.

1. Mix and sift the dry ingredients together to ensure they are fully combined.

2. Using a stand mixer with the paddle beater attachment, beat the egg yolks with the sugar until thick and pale. Beat well until the sugar has almost dissolved. (You can also use a handheld electric beater.)

3. Continuing to beat, gradually add the oil and beat until well incorporated. While continuing to beat on low speed, alternate between adding the other wet ingredients (milk, juice, etc.) with the dry ingredients (flour, cocoa powder, baking powder, etc.) in about 3 lots, and beat until just combined.

4. In a separate bowl, using the whisk attachment on medium speed, whisk the egg whites until soft peaks form. Gradually add the remaining sugar while continuing to whisk on medium speed, and whisk until they are just stiff but not dry.

5. With a metal spoon or silicone spatula, very carefully fold the egg whites into the batter (in 2 parts if that's easier) until just incorporated. (To fold means to gently mix in a circular motion, pushing the spoon down the side of the mixture to the bottom and then back over the top, turning the bowl and repeating.) It is essential to keep the air in the whites to keep the mixture, and the cake, light.

6. Pour into the cake tin, using a spatula to scrape all the mixture out of the bowl. Bake as directed until completely cooked through.

WHEN IS YOUR CAKE COOKED?

Merelyn looks for a deep golden colour, Lisa lightly touches the surface to feel if it is firm, Natanya waits for the slight fall after it has finished rising and Jacqui inserts a skewer into the cake to see if it comes out clean. Don't be tempted to take it out of the oven early; an undercooked cake may fall out of the tin when inverted (yes, it's happened to us all).

7.   After removing the cake from the oven, insert the bottle neck into the funnel and immediately invert the bottle and the tin in one movement so the tin is balancing on the neck of the bottle. The cake will be dangling upside down. It is important for the cake to be inverted and suspended upside down until it is completely cool to stop it from collapsing.

8.   When cool, turn the tin right side up and run a knife around the outside of the cake and the funnel, literally cutting the cake away from the sides of the tin.

9.   Holding the funnel, lift the base out of the tin.

10.   Use the knife to cut between the cake and the base.

11.   Invert onto a lightweight plate, remove the funnel piece.

12.   Invert once again onto your serving plate.

Custard Chiffon

It's hard for Merelyn to believe her humble but elegant Hungarian mother has become the torchbearer and gold-standard holder for chiffon cake. From a secret recipe guarded for over 50 years, to a published recipe baked all over the world, we had to share this poster-girl cake again. It still breaks our hearts just a little that Yolan passed away just months before her recipe was published in our first book; sadly, she never got to see her chiffon masterpiece in all its glory. We are so proud that she lives on through her cake, a true culinary legacy. See How to Chiffon (page 110) for our step-by-step guide.

180 g (1 cup + 2½ tablespoons/
   6⅓ oz) self-raising (self-rising) flour
1 teaspoon cream of tartar
35 g (¼ cup/1¼ oz) custard powder
6 eggs, separated
345 g (1½ cups/12¼ oz) caster
   (superfine) sugar
½ teaspoon vanilla extract
80 ml (⅓ cup/2¾ fl oz) oil
   (see Kitchen Notes page 11)
170 ml (⅔ cup/5¾ fl oz) warm water
icing (confectioners') sugar, to serve

Preheat the oven to 180°C (350°F/Gas 4). You will need a high-sided angel cake (chiffon) tin that is not non-stick, has a centre funnel and removable base. Do not grease it. Before starting the cake, find a bottle that will fit into the top of the funnel – you will need to use this as soon as the cake comes out of the oven.

Sift the flour, cream of tartar and custard powder together 3 times to ensure they are fully combined.

Using an electric mixer, beat the egg yolks with 230 g (1 cup/8 oz) of the sugar until thick and pale, then add the vanilla. Pour the oil and warm water into a jug. Continuing to beat on low speed, add the flour mixture and the oil and water at the same time, beating well until you have a smooth batter.

In a separate bowl, whisk the egg whites until soft peaks form, then gradually add the remaining sugar and continue to whisk until the egg whites are stiff but not dry. Very carefully, fold the egg whites into the batter with a metal spoon or silicone spatula until just incorporated. Pour the mixture into the cake tin. Bake for 1 hour, or until a skewer inserted into the cake comes out clean.

After removing the cake from the oven, insert the bottle neck into the funnel and immediately invert the bottle and the tin in one movement so the tin is balancing on the neck of the bottle (the cake will be dangling upside down). It is important for the cake to be inverted and suspended upside down until it is completely cool to stop it from collapsing.

When cool, turn the tin right side up and run a knife around the outside of the cake and the funnel. Holding the funnel, lift the base out of the tin and then use the knife to cut the cake off the base. Invert onto a lightweight plate, remove the funnel piece, and then invert once again onto your serving plate.

Once cooled, dust with icing sugar before serving.

Serves about 12

Glazed Honey Chiffon

A beautiful, light, high, lemon-glazed chance to steer away from the traditional, heavier Rosh Hashanah honey cakes. We've absolutely fallen in love with this divine ode to honey that Natanya has created. It's like no other. See How to Chiffon (page 110) for our step-by-step guide.

6 eggs, separated
175 g (¾ cup/6 oz) caster (superfine) sugar
180 ml (¾ cup/6 fl oz) oil
275 g (¾ cup/9¾ oz) honey
60 ml (¼ cup/2 fl oz) freshly brewed black tea
225 g (1½ cups/8 oz) self-raising (self-rising) flour
½ teaspoon bicarb soda (baking soda)

LEMON GLAZE

juice of ½ lemon
80 g (½ cup/2¾ oz) pure icing (confectioners') sugar

Preheat the oven to 180°C (350°F/Gas 4). You will need a high-sided angel cake (chiffon) tin that is not non-stick, has a centre funnel and removable base. Do not grease it. Before starting the cake, find a bottle that will fit into the top of the funnel – you will need to use this as soon as the cake comes out of the oven.

Using an electric mixer, beat the yolks with half of the caster sugar until thick and pale. Add the oil and keep beating for a couple of minutes until well combined. Mix the honey into the hot tea. Sift the flour with the bicarb. While continuing to beat on low speed, add the honey mixture and the flour mixture, alternating between wet and dry ingredients in 3 lots, beating gently until just combined.

In a separate bowl, whisk the egg whites until soft peaks form. Slowly add the remaining sugar and continue whisking until the egg whites are stiff but not dry.

Gently fold the egg whites into the batter with a metal spoon or silicone spatula, until just mixed through. Pour the mixture into the cake tin and bake for 50 minutes, and then reduce the temperature to 160°C (325°F/Gas 3) and cook for a further 10 minutes or until a skewer inserted into the cake comes out clean.

After removing the cake from the oven, insert the bottle neck into the funnel and immediately invert the bottle and the tin in one movement so the tin is balancing on the neck of the bottle (the cake will be dangling upside down). It is important for the cake to be inverted and suspended upside down until it is completely cool to stop it from collapsing.

When cool, turn the tin right side up and run a knife around the outside of the cake and the funnel. Holding the funnel, lift the base out of the tin and then use the knife to cut the cake off the base. Invert onto a lightweight plate, remove the funnel piece, and then invert once again onto your serving plate.

To make the glaze, add the lemon juice (a few drops at a time) to the icing sugar until you have a thick but runny glaze. Pour over the cooled cake.

This cake is best served on the day of baking. If you make it a day ahead, leave it inverted in the tin and glaze just before serving.

Serves about 12

Custard
Chiffon p. 112

Pumpkin
Chiffon p. 118

Glazed
Honey Chiffon p. 115

Poppy Seed
Chiffon p. 121

Passover Nut
Chiffon p. 123

Passover Citrus
Sponge p. 117

Passover Citrus Sponge

GREG PATENT

Passover sponges are a challenging genre. Often with an unappealing texture and a too-obviously-Passover taste, this one is magic. Greg created this recipe based on the type of cakes his granny used to make, so to him it will always be 'Granny's Passover Citrus Sponge'. See How to Chiffon (page 110) for our step-by-step guide.

70 g (½ cup/2½ oz) superfine matzo
    meal (cake meal) (see Kitchen
    Notes page 11)
45 g (¼ cup/1½ oz) potato flour
    (potato starch)
30 g (¼ cup/1 oz) tapioca starch
¼ teaspoon salt
finely grated zest of 1 orange
finely grated zest of 1 lemon
60 ml (¼ cup/2 fl oz) orange juice
1 teaspoon lemon juice
290 g (1¼ cups/10¼ oz) caster
    (superfine) sugar
8 eggs, separated

Note — If you aren't making this cake for Passover, substitute 150 g (1 cup/5 ⅓ oz) plain (all-purpose) flour for the matzo meal, potato flour and tapioca starch, and increase the orange juice to 90 ml (⅓ cup + 2 teaspoons/3 fl oz).

Do not preheat the oven. You will need a high-sided angel cake (chiffon) tin that is not non-stick, has a centre funnel and removable base. Do not grease it. Before starting the cake, find a bottle that will fit into the top of the funnel – you will need to use this as soon as the cake comes out of the oven.

In a medium bowl, whisk together the matzo meal, potato flour, tapioca starch and salt. Set aside 75 g (⅓ cup/2⅔ oz) of the sugar for the egg whites. In a small mortar with a pestle (or with the end of a rolling pin in a small bowl), mash the citrus zests with 3 tablespoons of the remaining sugar.

Using an electric mixer, beat the egg yolks on medium speed for a couple of minutes until they thicken slightly. Add the citrus sugar and continue to beat, gradually adding the remaining sugar in a steady stream. Increase the speed to medium–high and beat for a further 3 to 4 minutes until the yolks are very thick and pale and form a ribbon when the beater is lifted. On a low speed, add the orange juice and then the dry ingredients, beating only until just incorporated.

In a separate bowl, whisk the egg whites on medium speed until frothy. Add the lemon juice and whisk until soft peaks form. Continue to whisk, adding the reserved ⅓ cup sugar, 1 spoonful at a time. Increase the speed to medium–high and whisk until the whites are thick, shiny and form firm peaks.

Fold a quarter of the egg whites into the batter to lighten it, and then fold in the remaining egg whites in 2 parts, just until no whites show.

Rinse the cake tin under running hot water and shake out any excess water. Pour the batter into the tin and level the top with a spatula. Place the tin into the cold oven. Turn the oven on to 165°C (325°F/Gas 3) and bake for 50 minutes or until the cake is golden brown and springs back when gently pressed.

After removing the cake from the oven, insert the bottle neck into the funnel and immediately invert the bottle and the tin in one movement so the tin is balancing on the neck of the bottle (the cake will be dangling upside down). It is important for the cake to be inverted and suspended upside down until it is completely cool to stop it from collapsing.

When cool, turn the tin right side up and run a knife around the outside of the cake and the funnel. Holding the funnel, lift the base out of the tin and then use the knife to cut the cake off the base. Invert onto a lightweight plate, remove the funnel piece, and then invert once again onto your serving plate.

Serves about 12

Pumpkin Chiffon

SANDRA GOLDBERG

This is one of the best cakes we have ever eaten. Big call, we know. But who would've thought that putting puréed pumpkin into a chiffon cake would produce a cake with such incredible texture and bite. Truly remarkable. See How to Chiffon (page 110) for our step-by-step guide.

300 g (2 cups/10½ oz) plain
   (all-purpose) flour
3 teaspoons baking powder
2 teaspoons ground cinnamon
⅛ teaspoon ground cloves
½ teaspoon ground nutmeg
7 eggs, separated
345 g (1½ cups/12¼ oz) caster
   (superfine) sugar
1 teaspoon vanilla extract
125 ml (½ cup/4¼ fl oz) oil
125 ml (½ cup/4¼ fl oz) water
260 g (1 cup/9¼ oz) puréed
   or mashed pumpkin, drained
   (see note page 120)
½ teaspoon cream of tartar

MOLASSES BUTTERCREAM

375 g (13¼ oz) unsalted butter,
   at room temperature, chopped
300 g (2 scant cups/10½ oz) icing
   (confectioners') sugar
2 tablespoons molasses (treacle)
1 tablespoon maple syrup
1 teaspoon vanilla extract
¼ teaspoon salt

Preheat the oven to 170°C (340°F/Gas 3). You will need a high-sided angel cake (chiffon) tin that is not non-stick, has a centre funnel and removable base. Do not grease it. Before starting the cake, find a bottle that will fit into the top of the funnel – you will need to use this as soon as the cake comes out of the oven.

Sift together the flour, baking powder, cinnamon, cloves and nutmeg. Set aside. Using an electric mixer, beat the yolks with 230 g (1 cup/8 oz) of the caster sugar until thick and pale, then add the vanilla.

Pour the oil and water into a jug. Continuing to beat on low speed, add the oil and water and the flour mixture, alternating between wet and dry ingredients in 3 lots, beating until just incorporated. Beat in the puréed pumpkin until well combined.

In a separate bowl, whisk the egg whites with the cream of tartar until soft peaks form, then add the remaining sugar and continue to whisk until the egg whites are stiff but not dry. Very carefully fold the egg whites into the batter with a metal spoon or silicone spatula until just incorporated. Pour the mixture into the cake tin.

Bake for 55 minutes, then turn the oven up to 180°C (350°F/Gas 4) and bake for a further 15 minutes or until a skewer inserted into the cake comes out clean.

After removing the cake from the oven, insert the bottle neck into the funnel and immediately invert the bottle and the tin in one movement so the tin is balancing on the neck of the bottle (the cake will be dangling upside down). It is important for the cake to be inverted and suspended upside down until it is completely cool to stop it from collapsing.

→

←

When cool, turn the tin right side up and run a knife around the outside of the cake and the funnel. Holding the funnel, lift the base out of the tin and then use the knife to cut the cake off the base. Invert onto a lightweight plate, remove the funnel piece, and then invert once again onto your serving plate.

To make the molasses buttercream, beat together the butter and icing sugar until pale and creamy. Add in the molasses, maple syrup, vanilla and salt, and continue to beat until you have a smooth, very pale caramel-coloured buttercream. Spread over the top and side of the cake.

Serves about 12

Note — To make pumpkin purée, buy half a Kent (Japanese) pumpkin with skin and seeds. Preheat the oven to 200°C (400°F/Gas 6). Line a baking tray. Place, cut side down, on the prepared tray. Cook for 50 minutes or until you can insert a knife easily into the pumpkin. Allow to cool and then scoop out the flesh, discarding the seeds and skin. Purée the pumpkin in a food processor until smooth. A 1.7 kg (3 lb 12 oz) pumpkin will yield about 1 litre (4 cups) of purée, which freezes well in sealed containers for later use.

Poppy Seed Chiffon

Merelyn's mother, Yolan, made many different varieties of chiffon cake, but it was her poppy seed chiffon that was famous all over Perth. Merelyn even had a request from friends in France to bring it with her on the airplane. After many, many years of being a well-kept secret, this recipe can now go public. Yolan used to ice the cake simply with melted dark chocolate, but we prefer the smooth shiny finish of the chocolate glaze on page 70 (with the Chocolate and Hazelnut Cake). See How to Chiffon (page 110) for our step-by-step guide.

180 g (1 cup + 2½ tablespoons/6⅓ oz)
   self-raising (self-rising) flour
1 teaspoon cream of tartar
65 g (½ cup/2⅓ oz) ground poppy seeds
6 eggs, separated
345 g (1½ cups/12¼ oz) caster
   (superfine) sugar
½ teaspoon vanilla bean paste
80 ml (⅓ cup/2¾ fl oz) oil (see Kitchen
   Notes page 11)
170 ml (⅔ cup/5¾ fl oz) warm water

Preheat the oven to 180°C (350°F/Gas 4). You will need a high-sided angel cake (chiffon) tin that is not non-stick, has a centre funnel and removable base. Do not grease it. Before starting the cake, find a bottle that will fit into the top of the funnel – you will need to use this as soon as the cake comes out of the oven.

Sift the flour, cream of tartar and ground poppy seeds together 3 times to ensure they are fully combined. If any poppy seeds remain in the sieve, they can be added back into the flour mixture.

Using an electric mixer, beat the egg yolks with 230 g (1 cup/8 oz) of the sugar until thick and pale, then add the vanilla. Combine the oil and warm water in a jug. Continuing to beat on low speed, add the flour mixture and the oil and water at the same time, beating until just incorporated.

In a separate bowl, whisk the egg whites until soft peaks form, then add the remaining sugar and continue to whisk until the egg whites are stiff but not dry. Very carefully, fold the egg whites into the batter with a metal spoon or silicone spatula until just combined.

Pour the mixture into the cake tin. Bake for 1 hour or until a skewer inserted into the cake comes out clean.

After removing the cake from the oven, insert the bottle neck into the funnel and immediately invert the bottle and the tin in one movement so the tin is balancing on the neck of the bottle (the cake will be dangling upside down). It is important for the cake to be inverted and suspended upside down until it is completely cool to stop it from collapsing.

When cool, turn the tin right side up and run a knife around the outside of the cake and the funnel. Holding the funnel, lift the base out of the tin and then use the knife to cut the cake off the base. Invert onto a lightweight plate, remove the funnel piece, and then invert once again onto your serving plate.

If you wish, spread chocolate glaze (page 70) over the cake and allow to set before serving.

Serves about 12

Passover Nut Chiffon

IRENE ISRAEL

Passover is a time when we all try – for eight entire days – to bake delicious cakes and biscuits that taste as good as all the cakes and biscuits we bake during the rest of the year. The challenge of Passover is that we don't cook with wheat flour or yeast, but we can bake with matzo meal and potato flour. So everything often tastes like matzo meal and has the claggy mouthfeel that potato flour gives. This cake is different. It just tastes marvellous! Irene learnt much about cooking, particularly wonderful continental cakes, from her 'aunt' Leah Heimler, and this recipe was inspired by her. See How to Chiffon (page 110) for our step-by-step guide.

115 g (¾ cup/4 oz) superfine matzo
    meal (cake meal) (see Kitchen
    Notes page 11)
35 g (¼ cup/1¼ oz) potato flour
    (potato starch)
130 g (1 cup/4½ oz) coarsely ground
    walnuts
finely grated zest and juice of 1 orange
finely grated zest and juice of 1 lemon
10 eggs, separated
230 g (1 cup/8 oz) caster (superfine)
    sugar
125 ml (½ cup/4¼ fl oz) oil
¼ teaspoon salt
icing (confectioners') sugar,
    for sprinkling

Preheat the oven to 180°C (350°F/Gas 4). You will need a high-sided angel cake (chiffon) tin that is not non-stick, has a centre funnel and removable base. Do not grease it. Before starting the cake, find a bottle that will fit into the top of the funnel – you will need to use this as soon as the cake comes out of the oven.

Sift the matzo meal with the potato flour, add the walnuts and stir through. Combine the citrus zests and juices.

Using an electric mixer, beat the yolks with half of the caster sugar until thick and pale. Add the oil and keep beating for a couple of minutes until well combined. Add the flour mixture and the juice, alternating between wet and dry ingredients in 3 lots, to the egg yolk mixture, beating gently until just combined.

In a separate bowl, whisk the egg whites and salt until soft peaks form. Slowly add the remaining caster sugar and continue whisking until the egg whites are stiff but not dry.

Gently fold one-third of the egg whites into the cake mixture with a metal spoon or silicone spatula, until just mixed through. Fold through the remaining egg whites until just combined. Pour the mixture into the cake tin and bake for 1 hour or until a skewer inserted into the cake comes out clean.

After removing the cake from the oven, insert the bottle neck into the funnel and immediately invert the bottle and the tin in one movement so the tin is balancing on the neck of the bottle (the cake will be dangling upside down). It is important for the cake to be inverted and suspended upside down until it is completely cool to stop it from collapsing.

When cool, turn the tin right side up and run a knife around the outside of the cake and the funnel. Holding the funnel, lift the base out of the tin and then use the knife to cut the cake off the base. Invert onto a lightweight plate, remove the funnel piece, and then invert once again onto your serving plate.

Sprinkle with icing sugar, to serve (this also goes nicely with the chocolate glaze on page 70).

Serves about 12

Squares and Bars

Any time of the day, any time of the week, any time at all. That's what we love about this chapter. Squares, bars, slabs or slices – take your pick. Whether it's walnuts or pecans, lemon or orange, ginger or passionfruit, choose a slice you can whip up in no time. We love how easy it is to bake a slab of one of these 'irresistibles'. Carefully slide the squares into a cellophane bag, tie with a ribbon and voilà! You've got a perfect homemade birthday/hostess/anytime gift. So grab your lamington tin, these recipes will soon be on high rotation for you, as they already are for us.

We may just have a chef-crush on **NEIL GOTTHEINER**. Perhaps it's his quirky sense of humour or perhaps it's his outstanding café/restaurant, our local, Lox Stock and Barrel. Together with sister Lianne, he combines the essentials of Jewish comfort food with the essentials of modern Australian fare – all with that healthy spin that has become so Bondi Beach. Born in South Africa, Neil reminisces about the fish barbecues in his grandparents' backyard and the awe-inspiring croquembouche at his aunt's 60th. After immigrating to Brisbane, where he finished high school and started law school, Neil took a break to start an apprenticeship in Sydney. He never went back. Neil doesn't let his heritage dictate what he should eat, and enthusiastically tries almost everything, but *Shabbat* (Friday night) with chopped liver, *challah*, chicken soup and, of course, cake makes him happy.

PHYLLIS SHUB believes cooking is integral to a child's education; it teaches them maths (measuring and fractions) and science (mixing and changing matter). Now an English teacher, Los Angeles-based Phyllis started her teaching career working in early childhood centres, and has always incorporated cooking into her own curriculum for preschoolers. It took us a while to find Phyllis. When we took our third book on tour to the U.S. in 2017, we met *@TheCookbookHunter* (in real life she is the lovely Helena G.), first via Instagram and then in person. She showed us the *B'nai Tikva Nursery School Cookbook*, which she had picked up at a garage sale. The book was filled with nostalgia-inducing recipes, and we started searching for, and miraculously found, Phyllis – a contributor to that book. Now a grandmother of three, teaching and cooking are still a huge part of her life.

Growing up, **SARANNE CHAIT** could smell *Shabbat* (Sabbath) and *Yom Tov* (celebration days) in the air. The heady fragrance of chicken soup, *kneidlach* (matzo balls), *chrain* (horseradish), *tzimmes* (sweet carrot) and jam would fill the house. Memories were built sharing food, breaking bread and laughing around the table. Saranne's mother was her teacher in all things food, with a steady stream of visitors dropping by for *sukkot* (the festival celebrating the harvest) teas. After hospitality school, Saranne and her sister Jodi started their business, Radical Food Catering, in Cape Town. Now in Sydney, Saranne emulates what her parents did for her. Maintaining family traditions in her new home, she is already compiling a cookbook of family specialities for her young twin boys.

Perfectionist, entrepreneur, tastemaker, chef, founder and curator of all things, **JOAN McNAMARA** has created a Los Angeles food institution. Joan, the daughter of Czech immigrants and a mother and grandmother herself, has become our American sister. She grew up in a hardworking home where life revolved around the kitchen. Joan's On Third has become our home away from home in L.A. Her authentic warmth, support of our project, generosity in hosting our book launches, and downright sheer deliciousness make Joan magnetic. After penning the foreword to our last book, and sharing her sublime chocolate brownie recipe, she has delivered yet again.

ELZA LEVIN in *The Chocolate Cake* (page 60)

HELEN GOLDREIN was inspired by her grandmother, who lovingly made *tsimmes* for 30 people. And not just any *tsimmes*, but a grand one, complete with carrot, potato, meat and studded with *kneidlach*. Growing up in Bury, Northern England, Helen was also inspired by her mother's enthusiasm for cooking, whose golden rule was to cook one new recipe each week. Armed with an Evelyn Rose cookbook, lessons in home economics from school and her mother's recipes, Helen moved to Cambridge and married. Trying to define British–Jewish food is an ongoing project for her; she's been experimenting in the kitchen for over three decades. Now, Helen's daughter is enthusiastically cooking *Shabbat* dinners for the family, and planning which new recipe to make next.

To this day, when **MARCELLE ROM** bakes in her Sydney kitchen, she hears the voices of both her grannies giving her tips. Growing up in Benoni, South Africa, Marcelle and her girlfriends would sneak out of school for lunch at Granny Ray's, sitting around the table discussing recipes and shmoozing with her. Marcelle's other granny, Becca, in Johannesburg, was such a perfectionist baker that her husband made templates for each variety of biscuit so they were the exact size and shape. After Marcelle immigrated, weekly expensive international phone calls were spent briefly catching up on news, then exchanging recipes in great detail. Even now, Marcelle's mother watches the food channel, scribbling down recipes to pass along to her daughters.

SYLVIA STRICKER still takes great pleasure in always making dessert for her family's *Shabbat* table, and as we hear time and time again from so many in the community, it is a ritual that brings people together, week after week. Sylvia arrived in Australia in 1950 to start a new life after challenging early years. Her German-born parents were interned in the Italian Ferramonti concentration camp during World War II; Sylvia was one of a handful of babies born there. They moved to British Palestine in 1945, in the very difficult early pioneering days of Israel. She learnt to bake from her mother and, once settled in Sydney, Sylvia would madly translate the recipes for her mother's cakes – they were all in German – trying to impress her father with the traditional sweets that he adored.

Dried Apricot Jam

ELZA LEVIN

We love stories of intergenerational cooking. Elza's mother created this jam recipe by accident when a batch of *pletzlach* (dried apricot sweets) she was making didn't set as they were supposed to, and she thought it would be delicious *shmeared* on matzo instead. This discovery led to an annual tradition of four generations of Levins working side by side: the oldies taking turns to stir the thick jam, the littlies mincing apricots, and everyone filling jars so 20 kg of *Pesach* jam could be gifted to lucky family and friends. This jam needs the tartness of Australian (or Californian) dried apricots in halves, rather than the sweeter whole Turkish (or Mediterranean) apricots.

1 kg (2 lb 3 oz) Australian
(or Californian) dried apricots
1.3 kg (6 cups/3 lb) white (granulated)
sugar

You will need 4 x 500 ml (2 cups/17 fl oz) glass jars (or other containers of equivalent volume) for the jam. To sterilise the containers and their lids, wash them well in hot, soapy water, then dry and place in a cold oven. Set the oven to 120°C (235°F/Gas ½) and heat the containers and lids for 15 minutes. Alternatively, you could wash them by hand and then put them through a hot dishwasher cycle. Cool before using.

Soak the apricots by placing them in a large non-reactive (non-aluminium) bowl and cover with warm tap water. Allow to soak at room temperature for at least 3 hours. Drain well. Mince the apricots in a mincer (food grinder) or process in a food processor until almost smooth.

Place the apricot purée and the sugar in a 4 litre (1 gallon) non-stick (if possible) saucepan or stockpot and cook, stirring constantly, over medium–low heat, for 1½ hours or until glossy and sticky. You will know it's ready when a wooden spoon can almost stand in the centre without being held.

Taking care with the hot jam, use a jam funnel or a pointy-ended spoon to fill the jars with jam. Seal each jar with baking paper and a lid, and store in a cool place until opened. Once opened, store in the fridge for up to 3 months.

Makes about 8 cups

Three-layer Jam Diamonds

ELZA LEVIN

The recipe for these moreish jam diamonds comes from Elza's aunt Lily, an amazing pastry cook who would bring her precisely cut diamond-shaped slices to family get-togethers. Trying hard to make them just as Lily did by sight, Elza would use a ruler to measure and cut, but they were never quite as perfect. We love how rustic they are, and the edge trimmings are the cook's treat.

115 g (1 stick/4 oz) unsalted butter, at room temperature, chopped
55 g (¼ cup/2 oz) caster (superfine) sugar
2 eggs
¼ teaspoon vanilla extract
265 g (1¾ cups/9¼ oz) plain (all-purpose) flour, plus extra
¾ teaspoon baking powder
400 g (14 oz) Dried Apricot Jam (see recipe on page 128)
1 tablespoon milk
icing (confectioners') sugar, to serve

Using an electric mixer, beat the butter and caster sugar together until pale and creamy. Add the eggs one at a time, while still beating. Add the vanilla. The mixture will curdle, but do not worry.

Sift the flour and baking powder together and mix into the wet ingredients slowly, until just incorporated to form a very soft dough. Divide into 3, then wrap with baking paper or plastic wrap and refrigerate for at least 1 hour.

Preheat the oven to 180°C (350°F/Gas 4). Grease a baking tray.

Lay out one piece of baking paper (approximately 35 cm/14 inches in length) and sprinkle with flour. Remove the first piece of dough from the fridge and roll it out on the baking paper to form a thin rectangle of pastry, approximately 27 x 19 cm (10¾ x 7½ inches). Use your hands to help shape the rectangle. Place a second piece of baking paper on top of the pastry to trace the outline of the rectangle. This will be used as a template for the next 2 pieces of pastry.

Lift the pastry (with the baking paper it was rolled on) and place it on the prepared tray. Top with half the jam, spreading it from edge to edge. Flour the baking paper template and roll out the second piece of dough to the same size as the first. Carefully, tip the pastry rectangle upside down onto the jam layer and peel off the baking paper template. Top with the remaining jam. Repeat with the third piece of dough and place on top of the second jam layer. Brush the top with milk.

Bake for 30 minutes or until dark golden on top and cooked through. Remove from the oven and allow to cool a little before cutting into diamonds, trimming the edges if you wish (cook's treat!).

When completely cool, sprinkle with the icing sugar to serve. These are at their best on the day of baking, and get softer every day after that – but are still delicious. Store in an airtight container for up to 3 days.

Makes 35

Joan's Lemon Bars

JOAN McNAMARA

In addition to how much we adore Joan, she is truly one of the best bakers we know. So when searching for the ultimate lemon bar, we remembered hers immediately. A perfect base with sweet, citrusy goodness on top makes these the most delicious morsels.

BASE

230 g (2 sticks/8 oz) unsalted butter
280 g (2 scant cups/10 oz) plain (all-purpose) flour
55 g (⅓ cup/2 oz) icing (confectioners') sugar
pinch of salt

TOPPING

460 g (2 cups/1 lb) caster (superfine) sugar
40 g (¼ cup/1½ oz) plain (all-purpose) flour
1 teaspoon baking powder
4 eggs
125 ml (½ cup/4¼ fl oz) lemon juice

ALSO NEEDED

40 g (¼ cup/1½ oz) icing (confectioners') sugar

Preheat the oven to 175°C (345°F/Gas 3). Line a 32 x 22 cm (12½ x 8½ inch) baking tin.

To make the base, melt the butter and allow to cool. Combine the flour, icing sugar and salt in a large bowl, and whisk to combine. Add the melted butter and stir until you have a pasty dough. Tip into the prepared tin, and spread out evenly across the base using a palette knife. Bake for 20 minutes or until light golden.

In the meantime, make the topping. In a large bowl, whisk together the caster sugar, flour and baking powder. Add the eggs and the lemon juice, and whisk by hand until smooth. Pour onto the hot base and return to the oven for 25 minutes or until just set.

Remove from the oven and allow to cool completely before cutting into bars. Dredge with icing sugar and serve right away, or store in the fridge in an airtight container for up to 1 week and dredge with icing sugar before serving.

Makes 18

Crunchies

This recipe comes from across the ocean, yet masquerades as an Anzac biscuit. There was always a jar of these in Saranne's mother's kitchen in Cape Town for the family to snack on, so when we were searching for that perfect biscuit to mark Anzac Day we were just so happy to discover this one with its unusual roots. We love that Saranne and her boys, who now live in Sydney, bake and deliver packets of crunchy deliciousness, tied with ribbon and rosemary, every Anzac Day to their very lucky neighbours and friends.

275 g (1½ heaped cups/9½ oz) plain (all-purpose) flour
110 g (1 cup/3¾ oz) rolled (porridge) oats
175 g (¾ cup/6 oz) caster (superfine) sugar
85 g (1 cup/3 oz) desiccated coconut
¼ teaspoon salt
220 g (7¾ oz) unsalted butter
2 heaped tablespoons golden syrup (light treacle)
1 teaspoon bicarb soda (baking soda)

Preheat the oven to 150°C (300°F/Gas 2). Line a 32 x 22 cm (12½ inch x 8½ inch) baking tin.

Mix the flour, oats, sugar, coconut and salt together in an extra-large bowl. In a medium saucepan over medium heat, melt the butter and golden syrup together, and then stir in the bicarb. Once it froths, pour it into the dry ingredients and mix well with a wooden spoon. Use your fingertips to separate any clumps that form.

Tip the mixture into the prepared tin and just smooth the top, not compressing the mixture too much. Bake for 30 minutes or until deep golden. If it is not deep golden at this stage, cook for an additional 10 minutes or so. Allow to cool for 10 minutes before turning out and slicing into squares (as big or as small as you like). Place the cut squares onto a flat baking tray then put into the still-warm oven (it should be switched off) for 2 hours or until crunchy. They will become hard and crunchy once they cool completely.

Makes 24 medium squares

Dutch Ginger Squares

These always make an appearance at Helen's family celebrations and are ready and waiting when family arrive from overseas. It's an incredibly forgiving recipe, so if they are slightly undercooked they have a moist, chewy texture, and if slightly overdone, they become a bit more biscuity. These are delicious either way, although Natanya and Jacqui really fell for the chewier version.

190 g (6¾ oz) unsalted butter
150 g (1 cup/5⅓ oz) plain (all-purpose) flour
60 g (heaped ⅓ cup/2 oz) self-raising (self-rising) flour
220 g (1 scant cup/7¾ oz) caster (superfine) sugar
125 g (4½ oz) crystallised ginger, finely chopped
1 egg
1 egg, lightly beaten, for egg wash
50 g (½ cup/1¾ oz) flaked almonds, for sprinkling

Preheat the oven to 180°C (350°F/Gas 4). Line a 20 cm (8 inch) square cake tin.

Melt the butter in a small bowl in the microwave or in a small saucepan and allow it to cool slightly.

Combine the plain and the self-raising flours with the sugar and ginger in a large bowl and mix well. Add the egg to the melted butter and whisk to combine. Pour the butter mixture into the flour mixture and stir with a wooden spoon to combine. It will be very thick and almost dough-like.

Place the mixture in the prepared tin, patting it into the corners. Brush the top with the egg wash (you may not need it all) and sprinkle with the flaked almonds.

Bake for 40 minutes or until a skewer inserted into the centre comes out clean. Cool for a few minutes in the tin, then turn out and allow to cool on a wire rack. Cut into squares.

Makes 16

Pecan and Date Squares

Better known as Granny Becca's Date and Pecan Squares, these biscuity slices, a little soft in the middle, a little crisp on the edges, a little sugary on the outside, are just perfect with a cup of tea.

115 g (1 stick/4 oz) unsalted butter, at room temperature, chopped
115 g (½ cup/4 oz) caster (superfine) sugar
1 egg, beaten
70 g (heaped ½ cup/2½ oz) pecans, chopped
225 g (8 oz) pitted dried dates, chopped
150 g (1 cup/5⅓ oz) plain (all-purpose) flour
pinch of salt
½ teaspoon ground cinnamon
½ teaspoon bicarb soda (baking soda)
2 teaspoons boiling water
55 g (¼ cup/2 oz) caster (superfine) sugar, for dusting

Preheat the oven to 175°C (345°F/Gas 3). Line a 33 x 23 cm (13 x 9 inch) baking tin.

Beat the butter and caster sugar until pale and creamy. Add the egg and beat well. Add the pecans and dates and beat until incorporated.

Sift together the flour, salt and cinnamon, and add to the mixture, beating until just combined. Mix the bicarb with the boiling water and pour into the mixture, beating until combined.

Spread the batter into the prepared tin. It will be a thin layer. Place in the oven, turn the temperature down to 160°C (325°F/Gas 3), and bake for 20 minutes or until golden brown and just firm to the touch.

Dust with the extra caster sugar as soon as it comes out of the oven. Allow to cool in the tin then cut into 20 squares to serve.

Makes 20

Dutch Ginger
Squares

Pecan & Date
Squares

Linzer Torte

Some recipes are really hard to benchmark. A simple jam slice can be an Italian *crostata*, an Eastern European *linzer*, or a tart from the local Aussie bakery. So a lot of discussions ensued in our kitchen on which one we loved the most. The fact that this is a true heirloom recipe from Sylvia's late mother, Miriam Weiss, only adds to its pole position.

175 g (1 heaped cup/6 oz) plain (all-purpose) flour, plus extra
100 g (scant ½ cup/3½ oz) caster (superfine) sugar
50 g (½ cup/1¾ oz) ground walnuts
¼ teaspoon ground cinnamon
175 g (6 oz) unsalted butter, at room temperature, chopped
2 egg yolks, lightly beaten
finely grated zest of 1 lemon
¼ teaspoon lemon juice
375 g (13¼ oz) plum jam (jelly)

Preheat the oven to 180°C (350°F/Gas 4). Grease or line a 26 x 18 cm (10½ x 7 inch) shallow rectangular tin.

In a large bowl, combine the flour, sugar, walnuts and cinnamon. Add the chopped butter to the dry ingredients and crumble together using your fingertips or a pastry blender until the mixture resembles coarse breadcrumbs.

Add the egg yolks, lemon zest and juice to the mixture. Use your fingertips or a wooden spoon to combine the liquid with the dry mixture until a rough dough forms. Lightly knead to bring it together to form a smooth dough, being careful not to overwork it.

Cut off a quarter of the dough (approximately 140 g/5 oz) to use for the lattice top, wrap tightly and refrigerate for 15 minutes. With lightly floured hands, break off and press pieces of the remaining dough into the prepared tin until the base is evenly covered. Spread the jam evenly on top, from edge to edge.

Remove the lattice dough from the fridge. On a well-floured board, roll out the dough into a long rectangle of pastry about 3 mm (⅛ inch) thick. Place the board and pastry in the fridge for another 15 minutes. Using a ruler as a guide, cut the pastry into equal-width strips, between 5 and 10 mm (¼–½ inch) wide, and carefully arrange these in a crisscross (lattice) pattern on top of the jam.

Bake for 40 minutes or until golden brown. Allow to cool before removing from the tin. Cut into squares to serve.

Makes 18

Orange Almond Bars

PHYLLIS SHUB

These mighty delicious three-layered iced bars have always been a part of Phyllis's baking repertoire. She shared the recipe in a cookbook for the nursery school where she taught, which we came across decades later. It amazed us to discover it was originally a prize-winning recipe from Pillsbury's 9th Grand National Bake-Off in 1958, created by Mrs Alice Lacher from Los Angeles in the 'new brides' category. Thanks to J.M. Smucker (previous owner of the Pillsbury brand) for allowing us to share the recipe.

BASE

300 g (2 cups/10½ oz) plain
  (all-purpose) flour, plus extra
75 g (⅓ cup/2⅔ oz) caster (superfine)
  sugar
1½ teaspoons baking powder
½ teaspoon salt
160 g (5⅔ oz) cold unsalted butter,
  chopped
1 egg, lightly beaten
1 teaspoon vanilla extract

FILLING

200 g (2 cups/7 oz) almond meal
150 g (⅔ cup/5⅓ oz) caster
  (superfine) sugar
finely grated zest of 1 orange
125 ml (½ cup/4¼ fl oz) orange juice
1 tablespoon lemon juice

ORANGE ICING

240 g (1½ cups/8½ oz) pure icing
  (confectioners') sugar, sifted
2 tablespoons orange juice

Preheat the oven to 175°C (345°F/Gas 3). Line a 31 x 21 cm (12½ x 8¼ inch) baking tin, leaving an overhang of baking paper on the longer sides.

Put the flour, caster sugar, baking powder and salt into a large bowl, and whisk to combine. Add the chopped butter to the dry ingredients and crumble together using your fingertips or a pastry blender until the mixture resembles breadcrumbs.

Combine the egg and vanilla then add to the bowl, mixing with a wooden spoon at first, and then with your hands to form a dough. Divide the dough into 2 discs, wrap each one tightly and refrigerate while you make the filling.

Prepare the filling by combining the almond meal, caster sugar, orange zest, orange juice and lemon juice in a bowl, and mix well.

On a lightly floured piece of baking paper, roll out one piece of dough to the size of the prepared tin and place it in the tin. Don't worry if you have to patch and press the pastry to fit the tin; it will be covered with filling or icing.

Spread the filling over the pastry in the tin. Roll out the remaining piece of dough to the size of the tin and place it on top of the filling, patching and pressing as needed. Prick generously with a fork, then bake for 35 minutes or until the top is golden.

With 10 minutes cooking time remaining, make the icing. In a small bowl, combine the icing sugar and orange juice, and mix until it is a smooth, thick paste.

Remove the slice from the oven and spread the icing over the top while still warm. Allow to cool before cutting into bars.

Makes 24

Coconut and Passionfruit Slab Cake

NEIL GOTTHEINER

We first ate this cake when we were having lunch at our local, Bondi's Lox Stock and Barrel. After we'd demolished a few pastrami sandwiches, co-owner and chef Neil kindly sent out a piece of this super-delicious coconut cake with a tart passionfruit icing. He then shared the recipe with us and, given its incredible crumb and cakey texture, we could not believe it was flourless – it surprised us all.

170 g (6 oz) unsalted butter, at room temperature, chopped
270 g (scant 1¼ cups/9½ oz) caster (superfine) sugar
1 teaspoon vanilla extract
5 eggs
150 g (1¾ cups/5⅓ oz) desiccated coconut
350 g (3½ cups/12⅓ oz) almond meal
1 tablespoon baking powder

PASSIONFRUIT ICING

500 g (3 cups + 6 tsp/1 lb 2 oz) pure icing (confectioners') sugar, sifted
15 g (½ oz) unsalted butter, melted
50 ml (2½ tablespoons) lemon juice
40 g (1½ oz) passionfruit pulp (1–2 passionfruit)
pinch of salt

Preheat the oven to 170°C (340°F/Gas 3). Line a 32 x 22 cm (12½ x 8½ inch) rectangular tin (see note). Beat the butter, caster sugar and vanilla together until pale and creamy. Add the eggs one at a time, beating well after each addition.

In a separate large bowl, combine the coconut, almond meal and baking powder. Using a whisk, stir well to combine. Add the dry ingredients to the butter mixture and beat until well combined.

Pour the batter into the prepared tin and smooth the top. Bake for 28 minutes, then reduce the temperature to 160°C (325°F/Gas 3) and bake for an additional 4 minutes or until the top is golden brown and a skewer inserted into the centre comes out clean. Allow to cool completely before icing.

To make the icing, mix (by hand or using an electric mixer) the icing sugar with the melted butter in a medium bowl. Add the lemon juice and stir through – the icing will still be powdery – and then the passionfruit pulp and stir until smooth. Ice the cake and allow the icing to set.

Serves about 16

Note — This also works well in a 23 cm (9 inch) round springform tin. Cook for 30 minutes at 170°C (340°F/Gas 3) then turn the oven down to 160°C (325°F/Gas 3) and cook for 15 minutes.

Pastries and Tarts

Magic can be created with flour and butter, the building blocks of pastry. And the options are endless. The cooks of the previous generation were resourceful; if they made one batch, they made two, leaving a disc of pastry in the freezer for a rainy day. With the basics down pat, we can journey back to Eastern Europe and roll pastry with jam, chocolate and dried fruit. We can whip up a stone fruit galette for a summer get-together or amaze with a do-ahead *mille-feuille* for a decadent afternoon tea. Make a quick batch in the food processor or take the time to crumble the butter and flour with eager fingertips. From delightfully simple to slightly more challenging – and with our helpful How to Pastry on page 148 – let's get rolling.

People + Stories

Meeting **LENA GOLDSTEIN** for the first time was one of the most moving and significant moments in our Monday Morning Cooking Club journey. She welcomed us into her home and kitchen, sharing not only her exceptional recipes but also a glimpse into her life before immigrating to Australia. Lena survived the war in the unimaginable Warsaw Ghetto and later in a claustrophobic underground bunker. Lena was thankfully reunited with her sister after the war, and was able, together with husband Olec to create a life and a family in Sydney. Lena continued to share her story through the Sydney Jewish Museum and the community at large until she passed away peacefully at the age of 100. Lena was, and is, truly an inspiration to us all.

Until she celebrated her Bat Mitzvah in Buenos Aires, **SANDRA SUCHIN KOFMAN'S** only connection with Jewish culture came from her grandmothers' cooking. Her Polish *bobe* (grandmother) filled the kitchen with *knishes*, *gefilte* fish and yeasted baked goods. *Bobe's* first greeting was always, 'What do you want to eat?' and, as she farewelled the family at the end of the visit, she meticulously packaged up leftovers for each of them to take home. Sandra's Argentinian–Moroccan grandmother, Blanca, created many sweet delicacies, and Sandra enthusiastically learnt by her side, becoming her sous chef. Attorney Sandra and her husband enjoyed ten years in Texas before moving to Miami so their daughters could enjoy a more Jewish upbringing.

NADINE LEVIN has a strong connection to the Sydney Jewish Museum, building on her foundation as an educator. She wanted to give back to the community that welcomed her and husband David from Johannesburg, fulfilling their dream to plan a safe future for their family. Together they embraced other immigrants and created large *Shabbat* (Friday night) dinners and festival celebrations with friends to compensate for so much family left behind in South Africa. Their table was always full, with classic chopped liver and herring for *Shabbat*, rich chicken soup with matzo balls and succulent roast turkey for *Pesach* (Passover) or dripping golden *teiglach* (golden syrup pastries) and caramel nut tart for Rosh Hashanah (Jewish New Year).

SUSAN LEVIN, a third-generation American and a business school professor, lives in San Francisco where she has retired with her husband. She spends her time cooking, hiking in the California hills and travelling. A self-taught cook, her cooking, and particularly baking, skills grew with curiosity, drive and chutzpah – and her sweet-toothed husband was a willing tester at every stage. Now spending a lot of time in the kitchen with her two granddaughters, she loves sharing and teaching them the family's traditional recipes. Sue felt such enormous pride when her youngest granddaughter made the Thanksgiving apple pie for the first time, having passed the 'supervised' test the previous year.

As a young girl, whether mixing cake batter with a wooden spoon, or watching whisked cream transform into soft folds, **LIOR MASHIACH** was totally fascinated by cooking. Years later, when Lior started working in the tough commercial kitchen of Raphael restaurant in Tel Aviv, she realised she was hooked. Whether studying pastry and bread making in New York, working at Eataly and The Mercer Kitchen, interning at Copenhagen's Noma or teaching baking workshops back home in Israel, Lior never seems to stop baking. When Lior was young, her grandmother used to send every family member home with a *babke* for their freezer, just in case. She wishes her grandma could see her now, an established pastry chef in Israel, selling dozens of *babke* each week. And that's just for starters.

Having lived through the Depression after immigrating to Australia from Russia, **DIANA ADONIS'S** grandmother used to quip that she could make soup out of a nail. Decades later, she would catch two buses to deliver freshly cooked potato *knishes* (Eastern European pastries) to the family at their holiday beach house. Diana recalls her mother's kitchen being a hive of activity following days of enormous preparation for biscuit baking days, when Diana was only allowed to perform menial tasks, like putting cherries on the tops. She has a come a long way; now a grandmother herself, Diana bakes all the cakes and biscuits for her son's Perth café and keeps her grandmother's heritage alive through the recipes she makes.

Israeli-born **EVY ROYAL** has been with us since the start. Her magnificent *hamantashen* (three-cornered pastries) filled with halva and chocolate (that we have now revamped with two new fillings), and her exotic icing sugar-dredged date- and nut-stuffed *mamoul* biscuits, embody the inspiration from her Moroccan heritage. Her Israeli great-grandmother arrived at their doorstep every Friday night, laden with boxes overflowing with dessert after dessert. Decades later, living in Sydney with her own family, Evy still regrets not asking for those recipes at the time, as they are now long gone.

The greatest compliment to be paid to a Sephardi cook is *manus bendichas* – 'may your hands be blessed' – and **LAURA GLUCKMAN'S** hands are blessed indeed. Now living in Sydney, Laura was born in Zimbabwe (or Rhodesia, as it was then known) of Egyptian, Greek and Turkish descent. Her encyclopaedic knowledge of Sephardi baking enabled her to teach us some of her time-honoured sweet baking traditions, for which we are so grateful. For Laura, the lines blur beautifully when combining heritage and food. Her deep understanding of the food of her ancestors combined with her training as a pastry chef, and the need for specific measurements, temperatures and time, produce perfect results.

How to Pastry

Before you begin: Most pastry recipes in this book can be made by hand or using a food processor, regardless of what the recipe suggests. Both methods are outlined below; we hope this guide helps you master the utter joy of pastry-making.

The food processor method is quicker and may give you that minute for a cup of tea.

BY HAND

1. Mix the dry ingredients together in a bowl.

2. Add the chopped butter to the dry ingredients.

3. Crumble together with your fingertips or with a pastry blender until the mixture resembles coarse breadcrumbs.

4. Combine the egg (if using) and liquid in a glass and tip into the mixture.

5. Use your fingertips or a wooden spoon to combine the liquid with the dry mixture until a rough dough forms.

6. Lightly knead to bring it together to form a smooth dough, being careful not to overwork it.

7. Shape into a disc.

8. Wrap tightly in baking paper or plastic wrap.

9. Refrigerate before rolling to rest the dough, as directed in the recipe.

USING A FOOD PROCESSOR

1. Pulse the dry ingredients in a food processor with the blade attachment.

2. Add the chopped butter to the dry ingredients.

3. Pulse until the mixture resembles coarse breadcrumbs.

4. Combine the egg (if using) and liquid in a glass and then tip into the mixture.

5. Pulse until a rough dough forms

6. Continue to pulse until a ball of dough forms around the blade.

7. Carefully remove from the blade from the food processor, and tip out the dough.

8. Shape into a disc and wrap tightly in baking paper or plastic wrap.

9. Refrigerate before rolling to rest the dough, as directed in the recipe.

Hamantashen
Three-cornered Pastries

Evy's is the best *hamantashen* pastry we have tasted (it's in *The food, the stories, the sisterhood*), and we've spent more than a decade trying others. We've created two new fillings to indulge our cravings: a Middle Eastern baklava-inspired one with a nutty filling that reminds Natanya of trips to Israel and another with a thick strawberry jam that reminds Lisa of childhood jam tarts from old-fashioned Australian cake shops. It also luckily solves the problem of regular jam leaking out of the *hamantashen* all over the baking tray.

PASTRY

450 g (3 cups/1 lb) plain (all-purpose) flour, plus extra
115 g (½ cup/4 oz) caster sugar
½ teaspoon baking powder
½ teaspoon finely grated lemon zest
pinch of salt
200 g (7 oz) unsalted butter, at room temperature, chopped
150 g (heaped ½ cup/5⅓ oz) sour cream
3 egg yolks, lightly beaten
½ teaspoon vanilla extract

HONEY–NUT FILLING

80 g (½ cup/2¾ oz) shelled pistachios, finely chopped
50 g (½ cup/1¾ oz) walnuts, finely chopped
75 g (½ cup/2⅔ oz) almonds, finely chopped
90 g (¼ cup/3¼ oz) honey
60 ml (¼ cup/2 fl oz) orange juice
110 g (½ cup, firmly packed/3¾ oz) brown sugar
40 g (2 tablespoons) unsalted butter
½ teaspoon sea salt
½ teaspoon orange blossom water
finely grated zest of 1 orange

STRAWBERRY JAM FILLING

740 g (2 cups) strawberry jam
1 teaspoon vanilla extract

TO GLAZE

1 egg white, beaten
white (granulated) sugar

To make the pastry, place the flour, sugar, baking powder, zest and salt in the bowl of the food processor and pulse to combine. Add the butter and pulse until the mixture resembles breadcrumbs. Add the sour cream, egg yolks and vanilla and pulse just until a ball of dough forms around the blade. To make it by hand, check out How to Pastry on page 148.

Divide the dough into 3 discs, and wrap each disc tightly in plastic wrap and refrigerate for 1 hour. While your dough rests, make your filling(s).

To make the honey–nut filling, place those ingredients in a medium saucepan and bring to the boil over medium heat. Reduce the heat to medium–low and simmer, stirring often, until the liquid is thickened – about 10 minutes. Allow to cool, stirring from time to time. Refrigerate until needed.

To make the strawberry jam filling, place the jam and vanilla in a saucepan and cook over medium heat, stirring often, until the mixture has reduced to about 460 ml (1¾ cups/15½ fl oz) – this will take about 15 minutes. Careful, it is very hot. Allow to cool and refrigerate until needed.

Line 2 baking trays. On a piece of lightly floured baking paper, roll out 1 piece of the dough to a 3 mm (⅛ inch) thickness, then use an 8 cm (3¼ inch) diameter cookie cutter or glass to cut out circles. Place a teaspoon of your filling on each circle. With your fingertips, wet the outer rim of the circle. Creating 3 sides to the circle, bring the pastry up around the filling (leaving a small opening at the top if you wish) to form a triangular pastry. Pinch the three 'joined edges' to seal firmly. Place on the prepared baking trays and refrigerate for at least 30 minutes. Repeat with the remaining dough.

Preheat the oven to 180°C (350°F/Gas 4). Remove the trays from the fridge, brush the *hamantashen* lightly with the egg white, sprinkle with sugar and bake for 15 minutes or until light golden.

Makes 40

Note — The recipe makes 40 *hamantashen*, and there is enough of each filling for a full batch. If you want two varieties of *hamantashen*, adjust the filling amounts accordingly.

Summer Fruit Galette

JUDY LOWY AND MMCC

This incredible pastry from Marieke Brugman was the base of the Pear Tarte Tatin in *The food, the stories the sisterhood*, which came from the kitchen of Judy Lowy. We love it here as a galette; simple stone fruit encased with flaky, buttery pastry is a perfect summer dessert. The quantity makes enough dough for two galettes. You could bake one and whip up a batch of Anchovy Twists (page 290) with the remainder, or freeze any leftover dough for a rainy day. If you are new to pastry making, have a look at How to Pastry on page 148.

PASTRY
(ENOUGH FOR 2 GALETTES)

240 g (1½ heaped cups/8½ oz) plain (all-purpose) flour, plus extra
200 g (7 oz) cold unsalted butter, chopped
125 g (½ cup/4½ oz) sour cream
¼ teaspoon salt

FILLING FOR 1 GALETTE

2 slipstone peaches
2 nectarines
1 tablespoon caster (superfine) sugar
½ teaspoon vanilla bean paste
2 tablespoons apricot jam (jelly)
1 tablespoon almond meal
1 egg plus 1 tablespoon water, for egg wash
demerara sugar, for sprinkling

ice cream or whipped cream, to serve

To make the pastry, place the flour, butter, sour cream and salt into the bowl of a food processor and pulse just until it forms a ball. Divide into 2 and wrap each half tightly in plastic wrap and refrigerate for at least 30 minutes.

Preheat the oven to 200°C (400°F/Gas 6). Line a baking tray.

Roll out the pastry on a floured piece of baking paper to form a 26 cm (10½ inch) circle. Slice each peach and nectarine into 12 thin slices. Place in a bowl and toss gently with the caster sugar and vanilla.

Spread the jam over the base of the pastry leaving a 5 cm (2 inch) border around the outer edge. Sprinkle the almond meal over the jam. Place the fruit neatly or pile it (up to you!) in the centre of the pastry.

Fold the pastry border up and over the fruit, pleating the pastry a few times as you fold.

Beat together the egg and water and brush the pastry with the egg wash. Sprinkle with the demerara sugar then bake for 40 minutes or until the pastry is golden brown and cooked through. Slide the galette onto a wire rack to cool.

Serve with ice cream or a dollop of whipped cream.

Each galette serves about 8

Passionfruit Tart

SUZANNE RESS

Lisa remembers her parents often going to legendary afternoon teas at the Ress home back in the 1970s. They always returned with evocative stories of tables laden with an abundance of French cakes and pastries: chocolate eclairs, mini fruit tarts, meringue gateaux, almond tuiles, passionfruit tarts and many more. French-born Suzanne had a reputation to live up to and she always delivered. If you are new to making pastry, check out our How to Pastry guide on page 148.

PASTRY

250 g (1⅔ cups/9 oz) plain
   (all-purpose) flour, plus extra
1 tablespoon caster (superfine) sugar
pinch of salt
160 g (5⅔ oz) cold unsalted butter,
   chopped
1 egg
1 tablespoon iced water

FILLING

7 egg yolks
165 g (¾ cup/5¾ oz) caster
   (superfine) sugar
2 teaspoon finely grated lemon zest
185 g (⅔ cup/6½ oz) passionfruit pulp
   (about 8 passionfruit, see note)
250 ml (1 cup/8½ fl oz) thickened
   cream

TO SERVE

pulp of 3 passionfruit
whipped cream

You will need a 23 cm (9 inch) tart tin. There is no need to grease it.

To make the pastry, place the flour, sugar and salt in a food processor and pulse to mix. Add the butter and pulse again until it resembles coarse breadcrumbs. Add the egg and the water, and process just until a ball of dough starts to form around the blade. Carefully remove the dough and wrap tightly in plastic wrap and refrigerate for 20 minutes. To make the pastry by hand, follow the guide on page 148.

On a lightly floured benchtop, roll the dough out until it is just larger than the tin. Lift the pastry up using the rolling pin and place on top of the tin. Press the pastry gently into the corners and then carefully up the sides. Trim off any excess pastry. Press a piece of aluminium foil (or baking paper) into the tin, covering the base and sides, and freeze for 20 minutes.

Preheat the oven to 180°C (350°F/Gas 4). Remove the pastry from the freezer and add pastry weights (you can use dried beans or rice if you don't have weights) on top of the aluminium foil, pressing the weights into the corners. Bake for 20 minutes, remove the foil and the weights and then bake until golden, about 15 minutes. Remove from the oven and reduce the temperature to 150°C (300°F/Gas 2).

To make the filling, in a large bowl, combine the egg yolks, sugar, lemon zest and passionfruit pulp, and whisk until smooth. Add the cream and whisk gently till smooth, trying not to add air bubbles. Pour into a jug.

Place the tart tin and pastry back in the oven and pour the custard carefully onto the base without going above the top of the tin. Bake for 40 minutes or until the filling has just set. It should be a little wobbly as it will continue to set as it cools. Remove from the oven and allow to cool.

Serve at room temperature with whipped cream and extra passionfruit pulp.

Serves about 10

Note — You can choose to leave or remove the passionfruit seeds. To remove, blitz the pulp in a food processor and then strain through a sieve, discarding the seeds. If you leave the seeds in, they may sink to the bottom.

Caramel Nut Tart

NADINE LEVIN

This nut tart has always been a favourite on Nadine's table at Rosh Hashanah both in Johannesburg and Sydney, bringing family and friends together to celebrate. When the Levins' tradition started, it was a communal meal where everyone brought something, and it has grown over many years to a huge celebration where, on last count, Nadine hosted 200 people. For this recipe, we've taken the liberty of doubling Nadine's original caramel, as we just can't get enough of it. This one feeds a crowd.

PASTRY

175 g (6 oz) unsalted butter, at room temperature, chopped
115 g (½ cup/4 oz) caster (superfine) sugar
1 egg
3 teaspoons oil
375 g (2½ cups/13¼ oz) plain (all-purpose) flour
1 teaspoon baking powder
pinch of salt

FILLING

250 g (9 oz) unsalted butter
230 g (1 cup/8 oz) white (granulated) sugar
2 tablespoons honey
1 teaspoon vanilla extract
125 ml (½ cup/4¼ fl oz) milk
750 g (1 lb 10 oz) salted, roasted mixed nuts

Preheat the oven to 160°C (325°F/Gas 3). Line a 35 x 24 cm (14 x 9½ inch) baking tray with a small lip or edge.

To make the base, use an electric mixer to beat the butter and caster sugar until pale and creamy. Add the egg and oil and beat until well combined.

Sift together the flour, baking powder and salt and, with a spatula, fold into the butter mixture until it comes together into a ball. Press the dough into the base and sides of the prepared tray.

Prick all over with a fork and bake for 25 minutes or until golden and cooked through.

While it is in the oven, make the filling.

Combine the butter, white sugar, honey, vanilla and milk in a medium saucepan. Stir and bring to the boil over medium heat. Simmer for 5 minutes, stirring continuously. Add the nuts and continue to stir, simmering for a futher few minutes until they are well coated.

As soon as the pastry comes out of the oven, pour the hot nut mixture onto it and spread evenly. Return the tart to the oven to bake for a further 15 minutes or until deep golden.

Allow to cool and then remove from the tin and cut into squares to serve.

Serves about 20

Chocolate and Cherry *Kindlech*

Asking us to choose our favourite recipe is like asking us to choose a favourite child, but Lena's *kindlech* (small strudel-like pastries) from our first book is one we hold particularly close to our hearts. Apart from Lena's story, her inspirational resilience and wonderful outlook on life, her recipe is simply outstanding. This sour cream pastry is lightly flaky, easy to work with and freezes well. Her original filling of strawberry jam, chocolate hazelnut spread, walnuts and sultanas is just perfect, but over time we have played with different fillings, and this is our new spin on the classic.

PASTRY (FOR 8 ROLLS)

480 g (3¼ cups/1 lb 1 oz) plain (all-purpose) flour, plus extra
1 tablespoon white (granulated) sugar
250 g (9 oz) unsalted butter, at room temperature, chopped
150 g (heaped ½ cup/5⅓ oz) sour cream
2 egg yolks, lightly beaten
2 teaspoons vanilla extract

FILLING (FOR 1 ROLL)

1 heaped tablespoon cherry jam (jelly)
40 g (2 tablespoons/1½ oz) roughly chopped dark chocolate
30 g (1 small handful/1 oz) sultanas (golden raisins)

ALSO NEEDED

1 egg, beaten with 1 teaspoon water, for egg wash

Start this recipe the day before serving.

To make the pastry, combine the flour and white sugar in a large bowl. Add the butter and crumble together with your fingertips or with a pastry blender until the mixture resembles coarse breadcrumbs. Add the sour cream, egg yolks and vanilla, and, with your fingertips or a wooden spoon, mix until a soft and slightly sticky dough forms.

Divide the dough in 2, wrap tightly in plastic wrap and refrigerate overnight. If you wish to make the pastry in the food processor, follow How to Pastry on page 148.

Preheat the oven to 180°C (350°F/Gas 4). Grease or line a baking tray. Cut each piece of dough into 4 equal pieces (each piece will make 1 roll). Working with 1 piece at a time, lightly knead the dough on a benchtop sprinkled with a little flour. The dough may be wrapped and frozen at this stage to use in the future.

With a floured rolling pin, roll out 1 piece of the dough thinly until you have a rough rectangle measuring about 30 x 15 cm (12 x 6 inches). The pastry should be a little translucent.

Spread the jam over the pastry, right to the edges, then sprinkle with the chocolate and the sultanas. Roll up from the long side to form a log, and then place, seam side down, on the prepared tray. Brush with the egg wash and prick a few times with a fork to let the air escape and prevent cracking. Repeat with as many of the remaining pieces as you wish to make, or freeze the dough for another day.

Bake for 40 minutes or until golden. Allow to cool on the tray for 10 minutes and then gently move to a wire rack to cool completely. When cool, use a sharp serrated knife to slice into 2.5 cm (1 inch) diagonal slices.

Makes 10 kindlech per roll

Apricot *Rugelach*

SUSAN LEVIN

More than 50 years ago, Sue Levin's boyfriend had a special request – could she make her grandmother's exquisite apricot delights? Twenty years old at the time, she hastily arranged a sleepover at her granny's and the heirloom recipe was dutifully taught. The lesson was watched, intricate notes taken, and the boyfriend with the sweet tooth soon became a husband. Sue likes to joke it was only because of the recipe that she got a proposal. To Sue, they are apricot delights; to us, they are simply the best *rugelach*.

PASTRY

150 g (1 cup/5⅓ oz) plain (all-purpose) flour, plus extra
85 g (3 oz) cream cheese, at room temperature, chopped
115 g (1 stick/4 oz) unsalted butter, at room temperature, chopped

FILLING

170 g (6 oz) dried Australian (or Californian) apricot halves
125 ml (½ cup/4¼ fl oz) water
110 g (⅓ cup) strawberry jam (jelly)
40 g (¼ cup) sultanas (golden raisins)

TOPPING

25 g (¼ cup) pecans
40 g (2 tablespoons) white (granulated) sugar
1 teaspoon ground cinnamon
50 g (1¾ oz) unsalted butter, melted and cooled

To make the pastry, place the flour in a large bowl. Add the cream cheese and butter and, using a pastry blender or 2 forks, mix together to form a dough, without overworking. Divide the dough into 3 balls, shape each into a disc and wrap tightly in plastic wrap. Refrigerate for at least 2 hours.

Meanwhile, to make the filling, place the dried apricots in a medium saucepan with the water. Cover and cook over a low heat for about 15 minutes or until all the water is absorbed and the apricots are soft. Process in the food processor, add the strawberry jam and process until smooth. Stir through the sultanas and set aside.

To make the topping, process the pecans, sugar and cinnamon in the food processor until finely ground. Tip onto a plate and set aside.

When you are ready to assemble the pastries, line a large baking tray. Preheat the oven to 175°C (345°F/Gas 3).

Work with one piece of pastry at a time, leaving the others in the fridge. On a floured benchtop, roll out the disc to form a 25 cm (10 inch) circle. Cut the circle into quarters and each quarter in half to make 2 wedges – you will have 8 wedges in total. Place 1 teaspoon of filling on the wide end of each wedge and spread along the wedge towards the point.

Fold the wide corners in, and roll the dough towards the pointy end. Place on a large plate or tray, with the point underneath. Repeat with all wedges and place the rolled pastries in the fridge for at least 10 minutes. Repeat with the remaining pastry.

Remove the rolled pastries from the fridge and roll each one in the melted butter, then roll in the topping. If you prefer a nut-free topping, simply roll in white sugar or cinnamon sugar (see page 54). Place on the prepared tray and bake for 30 minutes or until golden brown.

Makes 24

rough pecan

fine pecan

sugar

Fishuelas

Pastry Coils in Honey Syrup

SANDRA SUCHIN KOFMAN

Breaking the *taanit* (the Yom Kippur fast), as Sandra's great-grandmother would call it in her North African Jewish dialect (Haketia), always starred the syrup-drenched *fishuelas* as a wish for a sweet new year. We just love that, years later, no matter where in the U.S. or Argentina the extended family lived, they received a care package of *fishuelas* from Sandra's grandmother Blanca, just in time to break the fast. Now, from their home in Miami, Sandra and her teenage daughters continue this legacy that has been carried on for five generations. The original – and traditional – recipe came to us with the oil measured using empty egg shells.

DOUGH

250 g (1⅔ cups/9 oz) plain
    (all-purpose) flour, plus extra
⅛ teaspoon salt
1 egg, lightly beaten
3 teaspoons oil
100 ml (⅓ cup + 1 tablespoon/
    3½ fl oz) water

SYRUP

440 g (2 cups/15½ oz) white
    (granulated) sugar
330 ml (1⅓ cups/11 fl oz) water
juice of ½ lemon
1 cinnamon stick
480 g (1⅓ cups/1 lb 1 oz) honey

ALSO NEEDED

oil, for deep-frying
ground cinnamon

In a large bowl, combine the flour and salt. Make a large well in the flour and add the egg, oil and water to the well. Using a fork, combine the ingredients in the well. With a wooden spoon, bring the flour into the liquid in the well bit by bit, until a rough dough is formed. Add a little more water if it is too dry. Knead the dough by hand (or use an electric mixer with a dough hook if you prefer) for 15 minutes or until smooth. Wrap the dough tightly in plastic wrap and allow to rest at room temperature for at least 1 hour.

To roll out the dough, divide it into 4 pieces. Start with 1 piece, leaving the remaining pieces covered. Using a pasta maker or a rolling pin, and with a sprinkling of flour from time to time, roll the piece into a long, super-thin strip, approximately 60 cm x 10 cm (24 x 4 inches). On a floured benchtop, cut the strip in half crossways and then into 2 long strips. Roll each strip again, and, on the floured bench, cut in half crossways. Dust them lightly with flour and hang them on a tea towel over the back of a chair while they are waiting to be cooked. You'll have 8 long, thin pieces.

Heat the oil to 180°C (350°F) in a large saucepan or a deep-fryer. The oil should be hot enough so that a small piece of dough starts bubbling immediately when it is put in the oil.

Hold the end of the dough up high with one hand as you introduce the other end to the oil with a fork in your other hand. Start turning the fork, rolling the dough around it, allowing the entire strip of dough to form a coil, and then pressing the end towards the coil to seal it. Carefully remove the fork and repeat with the next strip. Depending on the size of your deep-fryer, you should only fry a few at a time.

Fry each coil for 1–2 minutes on each side or until the pastry is golden brown all over and has bubbles on the surface. Remove from the oil and drain on paper towel. Repeat with the remaining dough until all the strips have been rolled and all the coils fried and drained.

When the coils are completely cool, prepare the syrup. If you are new to making sugar syrup, refer to How to Sugar (page 266). Combine the sugar, water, lemon juice and cinnamon stick in a medium saucepan and bring to the boil, stirring, over medium heat. Continue to simmer, without stirring, for 10 minutes or until the mixture reaches 115°C (239°F) – just below 'soft-ball' on a sugar thermometer. Stir in the honey. Immerse 4 coils at a time in the syrup and simmer for a few minutes. Remove the coils and place them in a colander to drain. Repeat with the remaining coils.

Allow the *fishuelas* to cool and serve at room temperature, sprinkled with cinnamon.

Makes 32

Florentine Tart

Diana was given this recipe nearly 50 years ago by a lovely next-door neighbour and it has since become a family favourite. We were enthralled by the filling for this tart; it's chewy from the nougat, jammy from the dried fruit and marmalade, and rich from the chocolate. It had us from the get-go.

FILLING

300 g (2 cups/10½ oz) Australian (or Californian) dried apricots, chopped
300 g (10½ oz) soft nougat, chopped
150 g (5⅓ oz) dark chocolate, chopped
105 g (¾ cup/3½ oz) slivered almonds
115 g (⅓ cup/4 oz) orange marmalade
1 tablespoon Grand Marnier (or other orange liqueur)

PASTRY

225 g (8 oz) unsalted butter, at room temperature, chopped
50 g (scant ¼ cup/1¾ oz) caster (superfine) sugar
1 teaspoon vanilla extract
1 egg
400 g (2⅔ cups/14 oz) plain (all-purpose) flour
100 g (1 cup/3½ oz) almond meal
pinch of salt

Start this recipe the day before serving.

To make the filling, combine the dried apricots in a bowl with the nougat, chocolate, almonds, marmalade and Grand Marnier. It is a sticky mixture that needs to be mixed well with a wooden spoon or with your hands. Cover and set aside overnight at room temperature to macerate.

To make the pastry, use an electric mixer to beat the butter, sugar and vanilla until pale and creamy. Add the egg and beat again. Add the flour, almond meal and salt and mix on low speed until combined. Divide the dough in 2, wrap tightly in plastic wrap and refrigerate overnight.

The next day, preheat the oven to 180°C (350°F/Gas 4). Lightly grease a 27 cm (10¾ inch) tart tin with a removable base.

To assemble the tart, use the coarse side of a box grater to grate the first half of the dough into the tin and then press evenly across the base. Spoon the filling evenly over the base. Grate the second half of the dough evenly over the top of the filling. Bake for 40 minutes or until golden brown.

Allow to cool for 10 minutes, then remove from the tin and cool completely on a wire rack.

Serves about 12

Travados

Honey and Nut Pastries

Sephardi cuisine reflects the food and tradition of the Spanish Jews until their expulsion in 1492. From there, the community scattered to other parts of the world, including North Africa, Greece, Turkey, Israel and Italy. While Sephardi cuisine was influenced by these new countries, many of the original dishes have remained unchanged for hundreds of years since. Sweet Sephardi delicacies will usually be linked to a festival in the Jewish calendar. *Travados* will most likely be found at the Rosh Hashanah table or shared to break the Yom Kippur fast, bringing a sweetness and goodness to infuse the new year. Laura's recipe is an updated version of one originally published in a little cookbook from the Sephardi ladies of Zimbabwe some decades ago.

DOUGH

150 g (1 scant cup/5⅓ oz) fine semolina
500 g (3⅓ cups/1 lb 2 oz) plain (all-purpose) flour
2 teaspoons baking powder
100 ml (⅓ cup + 1 tablespoon/ 3½ fl oz) orange juice
90 ml (⅓ cup + 2 teaspoons/ 3 fl oz) water
100 g (scant ½ cup/3½ oz) caster (superfine) sugar
1 teaspoon ground cinnamon
1 teaspoon vanilla extract
2 teaspoons baking soda
100 ml (⅓ cup + 1 tablespoon/ 3½ fl oz) water
115 ml (½ cup less 2 teaspoons/ 4 fl oz) oil
50 g (2 tablespoons/1¾ oz) honey

FILLING

300 g (3 cups/10½ oz) raw almonds, finely chopped
100 g (heaped ¼ cup/3½ oz) honey
½ teaspoon ground cinnamon
pinch of cloves

Preheat the oven to 180°C (350°F/Gas 4). Line 2 large baking trays.

To make the dough, put the semolina, flour and baking powder into a medium bowl and combine with a whisk. Set aside.

Put the orange juice into a large bowl with the 90 ml (3 fl oz) water, caster sugar, cinnamon and vanilla and whisk to combine. Add the baking soda and whisk immediately for 10 seconds or so, until the ingredients are combined and the baking soda dissolves and starts to foam. Add the 100 ml (3½ fl oz) of water, the oil and the honey and whisk again to combine.

Add the dry ingredients to the wet ingredients and stir with a wooden spoon until you have a smooth and soft dough. Do not overwork the dough and do not add any extra flour (as tempted as you might be). Allow the dough to rest on the benchtop for 10 minutes before shaping.

To make the filling, mix the chopped almonds, honey, cinnamon and cloves together in a small bowl.

Pinch off a portion of dough about the size of a walnut (about 25 g/1 oz) and shape by gently rolling into a round. Make an indentation with your thumb and fill with 1 teaspoon of the filling. With slightly damp hands, roll the dough over to seal the filling inside, then shape into an oval. Place on a prepared tray and repeat with the remaining dough and filling.

Lightly press down on the top of each oval with the tines of a fork and then make 3 rows of holes with the fork into the top layer of dough. Bake for 20 minutes or until lightly browned and cooked through, and in the meantime, make the syrup.

SYRUP

300 ml (1¼ cups/10¼ fl oz) water
560 g (2½ cups/ 1 lb 3¾ oz) white
    (granulated) sugar
90 g (¼ cup/3¼ oz) liquid glucose
3 cinnamon sticks
2 whole cloves
1 lemon, cut in half
200 g (heaped ½ cup/7 oz) honey

ALSO NEEDED

200 g (1⅓ cups/7 oz) raw almonds,
    chopped

Combine the water, white sugar, glucose, cinnamon sticks, cloves and lemon halves in a medium saucepan. Bring to the boil over medium heat, stirring, and boil for 3 minutes or until the sugar has dissolved. Stir in the honey, reduce the heat and keep warm.

When the travados come out of the oven, reheat the syrup until hot and remove the cinnamon sticks, cloves and lemon halves and discard. Place the travados in batches of 8 or so into the syrup, flipping them with a slotted spoon from time to time for around 5 minutes. Remove with a slotted spoon, place on a serving platter and sprinkle over the chopped almonds. Repeat with the remaining travados. Reserve the syrup and store it in the fridge in an airtight container for up to 2 weeks.

If you are not eating the travados the same day, best to reheat them in the hot syrup for a few minutes before serving. Drain and allow them to cool to room temperature before serving. Store them at room temperature in an airtight container for up to 3 days, or freeze for up to 2 weeks.

Makes 45

Travados
p. 168

Mille-feuille

p. 172

Mille-feuille

French Vanilla Slice

Jacqui had a hankering for a vanilla slice for some years, and lobbied for us to find a great recipe. We searched to no avail; some pastries were not flaky enough, some custards were too thin, some recipes were too complicated. She was excited, after meeting Lior in Israel, to return with this recipe. Prepare to be amazed by a rough puff pastry that is patisserie-standard, and a custard that has the custard-powder flavour we Aussies crave in a vanilla slice, combined with the French method of making a pastry cream.

All the elements can be made up to two days ahead of serving. The custard (or even the whole pastry cream) can be made ahead and refrigerated until needed. The pastry can be made and baked ahead and re-baked at 180°C (350°F/Gas 4) for 5 minutes to refresh on the day of serving. Allow the pastry to cool then layer with the pastry cream to serve. When making the custard, our How to Custard guide on page 232 may assist.

ROUGH PUFF PASTRY

250 g (1⅔ cups/9 oz) plain
   (all-purpose) flour
1 teaspoon salt
50 g (1¾ oz) unsalted butter, softened
100 ml (⅓ cup + 1 tablespoon/
   3½ fl oz) iced water
150 g (5⅓ oz) cold unsalted butter,
   cut into 1 cm (½ inch) cubes
1 tablespoon icing (confectioners')
   sugar

PASTRY CREAM

475 ml (2 cups less 1 tablespoon/
   16 fl oz) milk
100 g (scant ½ cup/3½ oz) caster
   (superfine) sugar
½ vanilla bean, split and scraped
4 egg yolks
60 g (2 oz) custard powder or pastry
   powder
75 g (2⅔ oz) cold unsalted butter,
   chopped
200 ml (heaped ¾ cup/7 fl oz)
   thickened (whipping) cream

ALSO NEEDED

icing (confectioners') sugar

To make the pastry, in a medium bowl, combine the flour, salt and softened butter. Add the cold water and mix with a wooden spoon until a rough ball forms. Place the dough in a food processor and add the cold butter. Pulse a few times until a rough ball is formed. It will still have small chunks of butter in it. Shape the dough into a small rectangle, wrap tightly with plastic wrap and refrigerate for 30 minutes.

Remove from the fridge and make a double fold in the dough as follows: on a lightly floured benchtop, with a lightly floured rolling pin, roll out the pastry to form a long rectangle, about 38 x 24 cm (15 x 9½ inches). Holding the short edge, fold the bottom-third of the rectangle up over the middle-third, then fold the top-third down to form a small rectangle (it will be a third of the size of the original). Brush off any excess flour as you go. Turn the rectangle 90 degrees, roll out again and repeat the folds. This is the first of 3 double folds.

Wrap and refrigerate the dough again for 30 minutes and then make the second double fold, as outlined above. Wrap and refrigerate for 30 minutes and then make the third and final double fold. Wrap and refrigerate for at least 30 minutes before rolling and baking.

When ready to bake, preheat the oven to 180°C (350°F/Gas 4). On baking paper, roll out the dough to form a rectangle about 3 mm (⅛ inch) thick – it will be around 38 x 24 cm (15 x 9½ inches).

Place the paper and the dough on a baking tray. Cover with another piece of baking paper and top with another baking tray, for weight. Bake for 25 minutes and then remove the top tray and baking paper and continue to bake for 10 minutes or until golden brown. Dust with the icing sugar and then bake for a further 5 minutes. Remove from the oven and allow to cool completely.

To make the pastry cream, first make a custard. Place the milk, half of the caster sugar and the vanilla bean in a saucepan over high heat and bring to a light boil. In a bowl, whisk together the remaining sugar, the egg yolks and the custard powder. Pour about half of the hot milk into the egg mixture, whisking to combine. Pour this mixture back into the saucepan and whisk to combine. Bring the mixture to the boil over medium heat and cook for 2 minutes, whisking continuously. Whisk in the butter and allow to cool with plastic wrap pressed directly on its surface to prevent a skin forming. Refrigerate the custard for at least 4 hours or overnight.

When ready to assemble, finish the pastry cream by whisking the cream until quite stiff. Whisk the cooled custard to loosen and then fold in the whipped cream. Refrigerate in the bowl, covered with plastic wrap, or spoon into a piping bag (or large plastic snap lock bag, which you can use as a piping bag by cutting off the corner) and refrigerate till needed.

Once the pastry has cooled, use a sharp knife to cut it into 3 even rectangles. Pipe or spoon the cream on one sheet of pastry, place the second one on top and repeat the piping or spooning. Place the third sheet of dough on top. Dust the top of the pastry with icing sugar to serve. Best served within 2 hours of assembling.

Serves about 8

Yeasted Dough

There is something intoxicating for us about baking with yeast – that unique scent wafting through the kitchen, our slow excitement as we wait and watch the dough rise, extraordinary softness under our fingertips, feeling the generations of cooks behind the recipes. We are besotted with these yeasted beauties. From an heirloom *challah*, updated and sweetened with apples and honey, to a unique Dutch citrus-studded bun, from the secrets of the Russian *kulich*, to the comfort of a hot jam doughnut for *Chanukah*. Baking with yeast takes time and patience, but let us extend a helping hand: How to Yeast on page 178.

People + Stories

JUNE EDELMUTH is a Sydney cooking legend and early contributor to *The food, the stories, the sisterhood.* Along with husband Steve, she has been at the forefront of the catering game for decades. June qualified as a teacher in South Africa, but her love of cooking grew into a cooking school and cookbooks that taught a generation of South African homemakers how to cook. In 2014, JunEdelmuth Catering was born, purely by accident. June was heading for retirement and looking forward to spending quality time with her grandchildren, until an old client asked her to cater their daughter's Bat Mitzvah (the celebration when she turned 12). The rest is history. June is renowned for creating exquisite tables generously laden with the most delicious and interesting dishes, both contemporary and traditional.

Growing up in the village of Voorschoten, in the western Netherlands, **RONALD VAN WEEZEL'S** childhood was filled with traditional Dutch–Jewish foods and Amsterdam specialities. Ronald adored his mother's soups – her clear vermicelli tomato and her hearty Dutch vegetable with mini meatballs are still etched in his memory. Ronald learnt to cook as part of his hotel business administration degree. Food is a huge part of both his personal life and his work as general manager of Sydney's Hilton Hotel. His cooking celebrates the unique and contrasting flavours of his Dutch heritage and his time in Indonesia, evoking memories of times and places gone by.

Dreaming up a menu to share with family and friends is one of Caracas-born **MYRIAM MACÍAS ABADY'S** happiest pastimes; she loves creating memories full of flavour and love. After spending her early years in Venezuela, the U.S. and then France, Myriam settled with her husband and three children on the idyllic Dutch Caribbean island of Curaçao. Life was slow paced and families were able to form deep bonds; Myriam completely immersed and involved herself in the small, yet strong, Jewish community. To her, the most fulfilling part of being Jewish is the customs and traditions, and she believes food is the best vehicle for passing these on. Now living in Florida, her Sephardi and Curaçao traditions remain with her every step of the way.

LILA COHEN knows she is the link between the old and the new. Living in Australia since the early 1960s, she finds herself deeply attached to those traditional European dishes that reconnect her to the past, and to the family she tragically lost in the Holocaust. Lila was born in Dagestan (Russia) after her parents fled Krakow from the invading Germans, and they returned to Poland after the war. She met and married her husband in Sydney; he came from a Jewish–Australian–Anglo family so their food traditions were vastly different but they both loved to explore new cuisines and started their own culinary journey. Now a grandmother, Lila (a contributor to *It's Always About the Food*) feels great joy when she cooks for her children and grandchildren.

GREG PATENT in *The Chiffon Cake* (page 108)

Since featuring in *The food, the stories, the sisterhood*, Irene's *Bulkas* (Cinnamon Buns) from the **MEYEROWITZ SISTERS** have been almost revered around the world. The story of Nicky, Cathy and Jane is a familiar one in Sydney: the three girls arrived from Johannesburg over the span of a decade, leaving their parents and extended family behind in search of a better and safer life. They took their love of family and tradition and created an enviable network of family and friends in their new home. Their delicious cinnamon bun tradition is to whip up a batch whenever a baby is born in the family. The dough is made as the mum goes into labour, and the baby is born into a cinnamon-infused world of warm, soft, sweet buns. A beautiful family tradition that we all dream of replicating (one day!).

Many people in Sydney's Jewish community are fortunate to have had **REBBETZIN CHANIE WOLFF** and husband Rabbi Levi as spiritual and religious leaders for nearly two decades. Chanie's '*Challah* from Heaven', a recipe from her mother-in-law, Sonia, made its public debut in our first book, and our video of that recipe has had tens of thousands of views. We've baked it in classes and on national television, and now people around the world make it each Friday. Committed to spreading the warmth and beauty of Judaism, the *challah* (traditional plaited yeast bread, for Sabbath and festivals) is the centrepiece of the Wolff family's remarkable *Shabbat* (Sabbath) lunches, put on each and every Saturday in their home for their congregation and community.

Family and community tradition is so important to Israeli-born **GIORA SHIMONI**. Giora is a food enthusiast, home cook and father of four who simply loves to delight his family and friends with memorable and delicious meals. While studying a Master of Arts in communications in the U.S. he began discovering the new opportunities around working and writing online. On his return to Israel, he created and grew an online community of kosher-food-loving cooks. Giora has since published and shared hundreds of recipes online, garnering a huge following across the world. He has helped people simplify the daunting prospect of setting up a kosher kitchen, giving much-needed guidance on how to more easily lead a kosher life.

How to Yeast

SMALL BOWL OR A WELL?

Some recipes call for the yeast to be activated (proofed) in the well you have made in the flour, rather than in a small bowl. We do it both ways. Back in the day when cooks used fresh yeast, it was necessary to activate (proof) the yeast before proceeding with the recipe. It is not actually necessary when using today's active dried yeast but we still think it is a good idea because if your yeast is old/expired/past its peak (and no longer active) it will not foam or froth; it is better to know before you waste time and other ingredients. The risk of activating it in the well of dry ingredients (rather than a small bowl) is that if it is no longer active, you may not be able to salvage the other ingredients.

1. In a small bowl, combine the dried yeast, lukewarm liquid and the sugar (if using). It is essential that the liquid is lukewarm, like a baby's bottle. If it is too hot, you may kill the yeast. If too cool, it will take longer to rise. Allow the yeast mixture to stand for 10 minutes or until the liquid becomes frothy or foamy. This indicates the yeast is active. If it does not react, get a new packet of yeast and start again.

2. Put the flour (and other dry ingredients) in a large bowl and mix to combine. Make a well by pressing a cup into the flour, or using a spoon, to leave a deep indentation that will hold the liquid. Add the liquid ingredients (such as eggs, milk, etc.) to the well, pour in the frothy yeast mixture and mix to combine using a fork or wooden spoon, keeping the liquid inside the well.

3. Slowly, using a wooden spoon, bring the flour surrounding the liquid into the well, one circle at a time, until all the flour is incorporated.

4. Using a stand mixer with a dough hook, start to mix (knead) at slow speed, and once all the ingredients are well combined, increase the speed to medium-low. Continue to knead until the dough is smooth and supple, usually 5–10 minutes. You can also do this with a hand-held mixer with a dough hook, or by hand on a floured benchtop, but be careful not to add too much extra flour (it is tempting) – it will toughen the dough.

5. Remove the dough from the bowl, lightly grease the bowl it came out of, and put the dough back in. A plastic dough scraper is really helpful for working with the dough.

6. Cover the bowl with a tea towel (or plastic wrap and then a tea towel) and put in a warm place to rise.

7. We try to find a warm corner of a room to ensure the dough rises nicely.

8. Punch down the dough by making a fist and gently punching the dough once or twice to remove any air bubbles that have formed. You can also do this by throwing the dough gently onto the benchtop a couple of times. Follow the recipe; it will indicate how to shape the dough, how long to allow for a second rise and whether to egg wash before baking.

Apple, Cinnamon and Honey *Challah*

REBBETZIN CHANIE WOLFF
AND MMCC

We've decided to sweeten the incredible *challah* from Rebbetzin Chanie Wolff just a little. We've added apples and honey for extra Rosh Hashanah joy. If you're new to baking with yeast, our guide on page 178 may help. You can plait the loaves however you wish, but a round loaf is traditional at this time of the year. We think this simple coil best suits a *challah* studded with fruit.

Chanie explains that baking your own *challah* is a special *mitzvah* (spiritual good deed) for a Jewish woman; it brings blessing to the home and family. To recite the blessing, she tells us to double the recipe (so as to make it with 2 kg/4 lb 6 oz flour) and, before plaiting, to remove a small piece of the dough and recite, '*Ba-ruch a-tah a-do-noi, elo-hai-nu me-lech ha-olam a-sher kid-sha-nu be'mitz-vo-tav v'tziva-nu l'haf-rish chal-lah.*'

DOUGH

1.05 kg (7 cups/2 lb 5 oz) plain (all-purpose) flour, plus extra
500 ml (2 cups/17 fl oz) warm water
18 g (2½ sachets/6 teaspoons) active dried yeast
115 g (½ cup/4 oz) caster (superfine) sugar
125 ml (½ cup/4¼ fl oz) oil
2 tablespoons honey
2 eggs, beaten
1 heaped tablespoon salt

APPLE FILLING

3 granny smith apples
110 g (½ cup/3¾ oz) white (granulated) sugar
110 g (⅔ cup/3¾ oz) sultanas (golden raisins)
1 teaspoon ground cinnamon

GLAZE

1 egg, beaten
2 tablespoons demerara sugar

Line an extra large baking tray that will fit 2 round *challahs*, or 2 smaller trays that will fit one each.

Put the flour in the bowl of a stand mixer (or a large bowl if making by hand). Make a large well in the flour and add the warm water. Add the yeast and caster sugar to the well and stir to combine, keeping the liquid in the well. To ensure the yeast is active, allow to stand for 15 minutes, or until foamy.

Combine the oil, honey, eggs and salt in a small bowl (or in your measuring jug) and add to the mixture in the well. Mix with a wooden spoon and gradually incorporate the flour into the mixture in the well. Once combined, using the dough hook attachment of the stand mixer, knead on low–medium speed for 6 minutes until you have a very soft, sticky dough. You can also knead it by hand for 10 minutes on your benchtop; you will need to add extra flour but add as little as possible to avoid toughening the dough.

Cover the bowl with plastic wrap and a tea towel. Set aside in a warm place and allow the dough to rise for 2 hours or until it has doubled in volume. Towards the end of the rising time, prepare the filling by peeling and finely dicing the apples then toss with the white sugar, sultanas and cinnamon.

When the dough has risen, remove with floured hands (or a dough scraper) and place on a floured benchtop. Divide into 2. Flatten 1 piece with your hands to form a long rectangle. Press half of the filling into the surface of the dough and roll the rectangle into a snake from the long side. On the prepared tray, coil the snake around itself to form a large circle. Tuck the end underneath and press to seal. Repeat with the other half of the dough to make a second loaf.

Cover the loaves with a light tea towel and allow them to rise for 45 minutes. In the meantime, preheat the oven to 180°C (350°F/Gas 4).

When the loaves have risen, brush them well (including all crevices) with the egg and sprinkle with the demerara sugar. Bake for 40 minutes or until deep golden. Allow to cool on a wire rack.

Makes 2 round challahs

Sufganiyot

Hot Jam Doughnuts

Lisa has a delicious and special memory of Sunday mornings with her dad eating so-hot-you-burnt-your-lips sugary jam doughnuts out of a paper bag on the water's edge in Port Melbourne. Because of this, hot jam doughnuts have always held a special place in Lisa's heart and these *sufganiyot* from Giora Shimoni take her right back to that place. Apart from enjoying them while watching ships pass by, these are traditionally eaten at *Chanukah* (the festival of lights). Try them filled with the Strawberry Jam on page 150 or the *Dulce de Leche* on page 33. See How to Yeast on page 178.

7 g (1 sachet/2¼ teaspoons) active dry yeast

450 g (3 cups/1 lb) plain (all-purpose) flour, plus extra

55 g (¼ cup/2 oz) caster (superfine) sugar

310 ml (1½ cups/11 fl oz) warm water

60 g (2 oz) unsalted butter, melted

2 egg yolks

¼ teaspoon salt

75 g (¼ cup/2⅔ oz) strawberry jam (jelly)

ALSO NEEDED

oil, for deep-frying
caster (superfine) sugar

In a small bowl, combine the yeast with 1 tablespoon of the flour, 1 tablespoon of the caster sugar and the water. Mix and allow to stand for 10 minutes or until the mixture becomes frothy, to ensure the yeast is active.

Put the remaining flour in a separate large bowl and make a well. Add the remaining sugar, melted butter, egg yolks and salt to the well, and beat to combine, keeping the mixture in the well.

Add the frothy yeast mixture to the well and mix to combine. Slowly bring in the flour mixture while stirring until all the flour is incorporated and you have a soft dough. Cover the bowl with a tea towel and set aside to rise in a warm place for 1½ hours or until doubled in volume.

Remove the dough from the bowl and punch down on a lightly floured benchtop. Roll it out to a 1.5 cm (⅝ inch) thickness. Use a 6 cm (2½ inch) round cookie cutter to cut circles out of the dough.

Place 1 teaspoon of jam in the middle of one circle of dough and then cover with another circle of dough. Press and seal the edges together to ensure that the circles form a closed fat disc with the jam in the middle. Place on a floured tray.

Cover the doughnuts with a clean, slightly damp tea towel and allow to rise until puffed up (about 45 minutes).

Line a large plate with several layers of paper towel and set aside. Pour 5 cm (2 inches) of oil into a deep, heavy-bottomed pot. Heat over medium–high heat until a sugar/deep-fry thermometer registers 180°C (350°F). If you don't have a thermometer, test the oil by dropping a small piece of dough into it; the dough should sizzle immediately and start to turn golden brown without burning too quickly.

Working in batches, carefully slip the doughnuts into the oil, taking care not to crowd the pot. Fry the doughnuts for about 2–3 minutes per side or until puffed and golden brown. Carefully remove the doughnuts with a slotted spoon and transfer to the towel-lined plate to drain.

Cool slightly, roll in caster sugar and serve immediately.

Makes 14

milk choc.   nutella   dark choc!

Monas de Chocolate

MYRIAM MACÍAS ABADY

Chocolate and Aniseed Buns

Myriam's great aunt Tita Chele gave her a handwritten cookbook as a wedding present. It had all the family's traditional dishes, including a recipe for these sweet aniseed-flavoured buns with a chocolate filling. Myriam remembers eating them as a child with her cousins every Saturday, either for breakfast or as a *merienda* (snack), in the afternoon. Nowadays, Myriam makes them each Friday to have as a treat for the weekend. We tried some other fillings and loved the buns with chocolate hazelnut spread (Nutella) or *Dulce de Leche* (page 33). The aniseed in the buns is an unusual and traditional element but can be omitted if it's not your thing. For some tips on baking with yeast, check out How to Yeast on page 178.

375 ml (1½ cups/12½ fl oz) milk
    or water
250 ml (1 cup/8½ fl oz) oil
230 g (1 cup/8 oz) caster (superfine)
    sugar
1 teaspoon whole aniseed
½ teaspoon salt
3 eggs
10 g (1⅓ sachets/3 teaspoons) active
    dried yeast
1 kg (6⅔ cups/2 lb 3 oz) plain
    (all-purpose) flour, plus extra
150 g (5⅓ oz) dark chocolate,
    chopped
1 egg, beaten with ½ teaspoon water,
    for egg wash
60 g (¼ cup/2 oz) white (granulated)
    sugar, for sprinkling

Place the milk, oil, caster sugar, ¼ teaspoon of the aniseed and salt in a medium saucepan and cook over medium heat, stirring from time to time, until the sugar has dissolved. Set aside until it is lukewarm.

Add the eggs to the milk mixture one at a time, mixing well after each addition, and then mix in the yeast. Add the flour and the remaining aniseed, and mix well to combine.

Tip the mixture onto the benchtop and knead for around 10 minutes or until you have a smooth and soft dough, lightly flouring the benchtop if necessary. You can also do this using a stand mixer with a dough hook attachment. Place the dough in a large greased bowl, cover the bowl with plastic wrap and a tea towel and set aside to rise for 1½ hours or until it doubles in volume.

Grease 2 baking trays. To shape the buns, divide the dough into 21 pieces. Take 1 piece and roll it into a ball. Flatten and shape the ball into a square about 1 cm (½ inch) thick. In the centre, place 1 tablespoon of the chocolate and press into the dough. Fold the bottom edge of the square over the chocolate and then the top edge of the square over the top. Pinch the seam and sides closed, and place on the prepared tray, seam side down. Repeat with the remaining pieces of dough, leaving room between the buns to allow them to rise. As you fill up the trays, cover with a light tea towel. After filling all the buns, allow them to rise for another hour or until puffed up.

Preheat the oven to 180°C (350°F/Gas 4). Brush the tops of the buns with the egg wash and sprinkle with the white sugar. Bake for 15 minutes or until they are light golden on the top and cooked through. Remove from the oven and place on a wire rack to cool.

Best eaten on the day of baking or reheated within 2 days. They also freeze well in snaplock (zip lock) bags and can be reheated to serve.

Makes 21

Cinnamon Streusel *Babke*

JUNE EDELMUTH

In the kitchen, June reminisces about her Russian grandmother, Minka, and honours her memory by making her deliciously dense cinnamon and sugar-swirled *babke*. June has become known all over Sydney for this legendary cake, and we totally get it. Natanya and Lisa were recently at a 50th birthday and spent far too long standing too close to the *babke*, peeling off layer after layer of doughy cinnamon deliciousness. See How to Yeast on page 178.

DOUGH

565 g (3¾ cups/1 lb 4 oz) plain (all-purpose) flour, plus extra
150 g (⅔ cup/5⅓ oz) caster (superfine) sugar
1 teaspoon salt
60 ml (¼ cup/2 fl oz) warm water
10 g (1½ sachets/3½ teaspoons) active dried yeast
1 teaspoon white (granulated) sugar
2 eggs
1 egg yolk
155 g (5½ oz) unsalted butter
80 ml (⅓ cup/2¾ fl oz) pure (35%) cream
60 ml (¼ cup/2 fl oz) milk

FILLING

100 g (3½ oz) unsalted butter, melted and lukewarm
80 g (½ cup/2¾ oz) sultanas (golden raisins)

CINNAMON SUGAR

25 g (2½ tablespoons/1 oz) ground cinnamon
375 g (1⅔ cups/13¼ oz) caster (superfine) sugar

STREUSEL TOPPING

90 g (⅔ cup/3¼ oz) plain (all-purpose) flour
45 g (1½ oz) unsalted butter, at room temperature, chopped
55 g (¼ cup/2 oz) caster (superfine) sugar

ALSO NEEDED

50 g (1¾ oz) unsalted butter, melted

Combine the flour, caster sugar and salt in the bowl of a stand mixer and make a well in the centre. In a separate bowl, combine the warm water, yeast and white sugar and allow to stand for 10 minutes or until frothy, to ensure the yeast is active. In a separate bowl, mix together the eggs and the yolk.

In a small saucepan, warm the butter, cream and milk together until the butter is just melted; do not allow the mixture to boil. Set aside until it is lukewarm. Pour the yeast mixture into the well then add the eggs and the milk mixture. Using a wooden spoon, stir to combine then gradually incorporate the flour until you have a rough dough. Using the dough hook attachment, knead on low–medium speed for 10 minutes or until you have a smooth dough that starts to come away from the sides of the bowl. Cover the bowl with baking paper and plastic wrap and allow to rise in a warm place for 3 hours or until doubled in volume.

To make the cinnamon sugar, combine the cinnamon and sugar in a bowl and set aside.

To make the streusel topping, rub together the flour, butter and sugar with your fingertips to make a fairly fine crumble. Set aside.

Line a round 30 cm (12 inch) cake tin or a deep square 25 cm (10 inch) baking dish. When the dough has risen, punch it down by throwing the dough onto a lightly floured benchtop. Do not knead or add more flour, as this will toughen the dough. Divide into 2 equal pieces. Roll out 1 piece to a large rectangle, about 65 x 40 cm (25½ x 16 inches). Brush with half the melted butter, sprinkle with half the cinnamon sugar and scatter over half the sultanas. Roll up lengthways to form a log. Repeat with the remaining dough.

Cut each log into 5 cm (2 inch) sections. Place these in a circular fashion into the prepared tin, starting from the outside, cut side up, leaving about 1 cm (½ inch) between each one. Once the pieces are all in place and evenly distributed in the tin, press down gently with your hand so they are all the same height. Brush with the extra melted butter and then sprinkle evenly with the streusel topping. Cover with a light tea towel and allow to rise for a further 2 hours or until almost doubled in volume.

Preheat the oven to 170°C (340°F/Gas 3). Bake for 1 hour or until a skewer inserted into the centre comes out clean. Remove from the oven. Serve warm or cover with a light tea towel until cool. If you wish, reheat it later, wrapped in foil.

Serves about 20

Poppy Seed Brioche

LILA COHEN

A true heirloom recipe from the old world from Lila's grandmother.
This extraordinarily soft, poppy seed swirled and yeasted loaf is a keeper.
It is one of those recipes that really connects us to generations gone by.
If you're new to baking with yeast, see How to Yeast on page 178.

DOUGH

300 g (2 cups/10½ oz) plain
   (all-purpose) flour, plus extra
pinch of salt
7 g (1 sachet/2¼ teaspoons) active
   dried yeast
150 ml (½ cup + 1 tablespoon/5 fl oz)
   warm milk
50 g (scant ¼ cup/1¾ oz) caster
   (superfine) sugar
2 egg yolks, lightly beaten
100 g (3½ oz) unsalted butter,
   softened

FILLING

180 g (2 cups, packed/6⅓ oz) ground
   poppy seeds
250 ml (1 cup/8 ½ fl oz) milk
115 g (½ cup/4 oz) caster (superfine)
   sugar
50 g (⅓ cup/1¾ oz) currants
30 g (1 oz) unsalted butter
1 tablespoon honey
50 g (½ cup/1¾ oz) walnuts, chopped
½ teaspoon ground allspice
½ teaspoon ground cinnamon
½ teaspoon vanilla extract
2 egg whites

ALSO NEEDED

1 egg, lightly beaten, for egg wash

Grease a bundt (fluted tube) or large loaf (bar) tin. This dough is best made using a stand mixer.

To make the dough, put the flour and salt in the bowl of a stand mixer. Make a well in the flour and add the yeast, half the warm milk and a spoonful of the caster sugar into the well. Stir to combine, keeping the liquid in the well. To ensure the yeast is active, allow to stand for 15 minutes, or until foamy.

Add the remaining milk, caster sugar and the egg yolks to the mixture in the well. Stir with a wooden spoon, and gradually incorporate the flour into the mixture. Once combined, using the dough hook attachment of the mixer, knead for a few minutes on low–medium speed until you have a stiff dough.

Add the butter 1 tablespoon at a time, while continuing to knead, making sure each spoonful is incorporated before the next one is added. Continue to knead for 10 minutes after the last of the butter has been added, or until you have a smooth dough that comes away from the side of bowl. Cover the bowl with plastic wrap and a tea towel and set aside in a warm place and allow the dough to rise for 2 hours or until it has doubled in volume.

While the dough is rising, prepare the filling. In a medium saucepan, combine the ground poppy seeds, caster milk, sugar and currants. Cook over medium heat for about 10 minutes, stirring, until the mixture is almost dry. Remove from the heat.

Add in the butter, honey, walnuts, allspice, cinnamon and vanilla and stir well to combine. Allow to cool completely.

Lightly whisk the egg whites until foamy and fold into the poppy seed mixture.

On a lightly floured benchtop, roll the dough to form a rectangle 40 x 30 cm (16 x 12 inches).

Spread the filling over the surface of the dough, leaving a 1 cm (½ inch) border around the edges. Roll up the dough from the long edge to form a log. Place the log lengthways on the benchtop and, with a sharp knife, starting 2.5 cm (1 inch) from the top, cut in half down the centre all the way to the bottom. Twist the two halves around each other and ease the now-twisted log into the prepared tin. You may need to gently stretch the ends to meet if using a bundt tin or compress the ends to fit in the loaf tin.

Cover with a light tea towel and allow to rise for 1 hour.

Preheat the oven to 180°C (350°F/Gas 4). When ready to bake, brush the top of the brioche with the egg wash, avoiding the poppy seeds where possible. Bake for 30 minutes or until golden brown then remove from the oven and allow to cool.

Best eaten fresh on day of baking, or reheated to serve after that.

Serves about 12

Poppy Seed Brioche

p. 192

Orgeadebolus
p. 196

Orgeadebolus

Dutch Almond Buns

Ronald grew up loving his grandmother's almond *bolus* (buns). The recipe for *bolus* is one of the oldest Sephardic Jewish recipes found, dating back to the 18th century, and it is now well entrenched in Jewish cuisine in Amsterdam. There was a famous kosher bakery, Theeboom, which produced it for over 100 years until it closed its doors in 2008. On the bottom of each bun was a wafer indicating it was kosher. The recipe was passed on to another bakery in the city, van Schaik – now the place to get *bolus*, complete with wafer. This recipe comes from Bea Polak, a Jewish–Dutch food writer and friend of Ronald's family, who gave her 1955 cookbook, *Recepten uit de Joodse Keuken*, to Ronald. See How to Yeast on page 178.

DOUGH

375 g (2½ cups/13¼ oz) plain (all-purpose) flour, plus extra
1 teaspoon salt
200 ml (¾ cup + 1 tablespoon/6¾ fl oz) lukewarm milk
7 g (1 sachet/2¼ teaspoons) active dried yeast
1 egg
50 g (scant ½ cup/1¾ oz) caster (superfine) sugar
100 g (3½ oz) unsalted butter, softened

To make the dough, put the flour and salt in the bowl of a stand mixer. Make a well in the flour and add the milk and the yeast to the well. Stir to combine, keeping the liquid in the well. To ensure the yeast is active, allow to stand for 15 minutes or until foamy. In a small bowl, mix together the caster sugar, egg and butter and add to the well. With a wooden spoon, gradually incorporate the flour into the mixture in the well. Once combined, using the dough hook attachment of the mixer, knead on low–medium speed for 10 minutes or until you have an elastic and smooth dough.

Cover the bowl with plastic wrap and a tea towel and set aside in a warm place to rise for 45 minutes or until doubled in volume. Meanwhile, make the filling by combining the almonds, candied peel, caster sugar, butter and orange zest.

To make the syrup, combine the water and sugar over medium heat and stir to dissolve. Add the butter and vanilla, stir well until melted and keep warm over low heat.

Preheat the oven to 140°C (275°F/Gas 1). Grease 8 x ¾–1 cup pudding moulds (or equivalent size muffin tins).

Divide the dough into 8. Take 1 piece and roll it out into a rectangle measuring 30 x 13 cm (12 x 5 in). Sprinkle the surface of the rectangle with roughly 1 teaspoon of brown sugar, and press it in lightly. Flip the rectangle over and sprinkle another teaspoon of brown sugar on the surface. Make sure to reserve enough brown sugar for the remaining pieces. If the rolling pin or the bench get sticky, sprinkle with a little flour.

Recipe credit — Translated, adapted and printed with permission of the publisher Amphora Books, from *Recepten uit de Joodse Keuken* by Bea Polak, 1980.

FILLING

150 g (1 cup/5⅓ oz) blanched
    almonds, roughly chopped
100 g (½ cup/3 ½ oz) candied peel,
    finely chopped
1 tablespoon caster (superfine) sugar
30 g (1 oz) unsalted butter, melted
finely grated zest of 1 orange
75 g (⅓ cup, firmly packed/2⅔ oz)
    brown sugar, for sprinkling

SYRUP

125 ml (½ cup/4¼ fl oz) water
75 g (⅓ cup/2⅔ oz) white
    (granulated) sugar
115 g (1 stick/4 oz) unsalted butter,
    chopped
1 vanilla bean, split and scraped

ALSO NEEDED

2 tablespoons ground nutmeg
    or chopped blanched almonds

Divide the filling into 8. Spread 1 part of the filling onto the surface of the rectangle and fold the long sides on top of each other (folding it in half lengthways) to create a seal. Stretch the dough and roll from the short side, creating a snail, and then tuck the end into the bottom to secure. Gently squash down to widen, and place into the prepared mould. Repeat with the remaining dough, brown sugar and filling, then cover with a light tea towel and allow to rise for 15 minutes.

Brush some of the syrup on top of the buns and bake for 1 hour or until golden and cooked through, basting with more syrup every 15 minutes or so during baking.

Remove from the oven and baste with the remaining syrup. Sprinkle over the nutmeg or almonds and then serve warm or at room temperature. These are best eaten on the day of baking, or can be reheated to serve.

Makes 8

Kulich

Russian Easter Bread

Kulich is a tall, sweet dried fruit–studded bread, traditionally served with a creamy sweet cheese (*pashka*) on the side. Greg's father would take him to visit their Russian friends during Easter, and he tasted many versions of both *kulich* and *paskha*. He got to know whose was best and saved his appetite until he got to that person's home. Greg particularly remembers this version from his Russian grandmother, *Baba*; she baked and shared this with her Shanghai Russian friends every year.

Start this recipe two or three days ahead of serving as there is a lot of rising to be done. Trust us, it will be worth it in the end. This dough is best made using a stand mixer; if you are new to baking with yeast, have a look at our How to Yeast guide on page 178.

RAISINS AND RUM

75 g (⅓ cup/2⅔ oz) raisins
55 g (⅓ cup/2 oz) sultanas
    (golden raisins)
80 ml (⅓ cup/2¾ fl oz) dark rum

YEAST SPONGE

125 ml (½ cup/4¼ fl oz) milk
375 g (2½ cups/13¼ oz) plain
    (all-purpose) flour, plus extra
1 tablespoon white (granulated) sugar
7 g (1 sachet/2¼ teaspoons) active
    dried yeast
1 egg

DOUGH

2 tablespoons of the drained rum
1 egg
95 g (⅓ cup + 1 tablespoon/3¼ oz)
    caster (superfine) sugar
2 teaspoons vanilla bean paste
½ teaspoon salt
145 g (1¼ sticks/5¼ oz) unsalted
    butter, softened, plus extra

You will need a panettone tin or mould (around 3 litres/12 cups) (see note).

In a small non-reactive (non aluminium) bowl, combine the raisins, sultanas and rum. Cover with plastic wrap and set aside overnight. The next day, drain the fruit, reserving the rum. Transfer the drained fruit to paper towels to fully dry.

To make the yeast sponge, put the milk into a small saucepan and scald over medium heat (heat until you see small bubbles around the edge, without boiling) and allow to cool for 10 minutes. In the bowl of a stand mixer, put 75 g (½ cup/2⅔ oz) of the flour with the white sugar and the yeast. Stir with a wooden spoon and then add the warm milk. Using the paddle attachment on low speed, beat for about 30 seconds or until smooth. Add the egg and beat until combined.

Sprinkle the remaining flour evenly over the batter, but do not mix it in. Cover the bowl tightly with plastic wrap and allow to stand at room temperature for 3 hours or until the yeast mixture has bubbled up and almost completely engulfed the flour. (Instead of the 3-hour rise, this can be left overnight in the fridge if you prefer.)

To make the dough, combine the drained rum, egg, caster sugar, vanilla and salt in a small bowl. Add this to the yeast sponge and, using the dough hook attachment, knead on low speed to combine. Increase the speed to medium, and knead for a couple more minutes. On low speed, add the butter, 1 spoonful at a time, and knead until each is completely incorporated before adding the next.

Once all the butter is incorporated, knead on medium speed for 2 minutes. The dough should feel smooth, supple and not too sticky. Remove the dough and set aside. Grease the bowl with the extra butter, shape the dough into a ball, put it back in the bowl and cover tightly with plastic wrap. Allow to rise at room temperature for 3 hours or until it has tripled in volume.

$\longrightarrow$

Sweet Cheese

Don't expect a standard cheesecake chapter here. We've searched high and low for the interesting, the exciting, the unusual. And of course, the very best. From a polenta-crusted just-sweet Romanian loaf to a classic New Yorker with a twist, and a revered *knafeh* to a unique apricot-studded *kolac* slice. And, by popular demand, bringing back a tweaked version of the people's favourite, the 'South African Cheesecake' from *The food, the stories, the sisterhood*. The cheesy festival of *Shavuot* will never be the same again.

People + Stories

For 60 years, from 1958, the iconic **GELATO BAR** at Bondi Beach was synonymous with comfort food and continental cooking. If you grew up in Sydney – or even if you were only visiting – walks on the beach promenade were spent dreaming about which cake you would choose afterwards; the café's lavish display, built high on a tiered grandstand in the window, was irresistibly inviting. Nilly Berger, a friend of ours since she and her uncle Jack were featured in *The Feast Goes On*, married into the family behind the Gelato Bar. Nilly has become a custodian of these nostalgic Eastern European recipes and we can't thank her enough for sharing some of Gelato Bar's precious secrets.

When we first met Israeli-born chef and restaurateur **ROY NER**, we were inspired by his passion for sharing the incredible diversity and joy of Middle Eastern food. Now settled in Sydney, his journey has taken him from growing up in Israel to learning French technique at Le Cordon Bleu and immersing himself in classic fine dining at Sydney's Aria restaurant. Today, his dedication, discipline and commitment for freshness and seasonality border on fanaticism. It seems his Sydney restaurants are just the beginning of his own empire. Working alongside chefs from many countries in the region, Roy highlights flavours of a very old Middle Eastern story – 3000 years of history, many countries, old and new cities, and cultures all coming together through food.

One of **DEBBIE LEVI'S** nostalgic memories is walking through the Arab *shuk* (market) in Haifa with her father. She recalls the smells and colours, the bounty of fresh produce and the taste of exotic rose in the Turkish delight. Moving to Sydney as a young girl from Israel, Debbie was taught by her Romanian *safta* (grandmother), a wonderful European cook, how to do everything from scratch. She supervised her peeling and chopping charred eggplants for *chatzilim* (eggplant salad) and, to this day, Debbie always has eggplant, ready charred and chopped, in the freezer. Returning to Israel in her 30s to embark upon a career in food, she then came home to set up her now well-established Sydney catering company, Delen.

Cultures came together for fourth-generation Australian **LEONIE VICKERS**, who credits her Czech mother-in-law, Marta, with providing the inspiration for her cooking. Sunday dinners were spent eating Marta's beautiful roast duck, sauerkraut, crumbed mushrooms and cauliflower with a hearty side portion of *knedliky* (bread dumplings). Leonie came to adore Eastern European comfort food – so different from the food of her Australian upbringing – and understood the power of passing down traditions to the next generation. Now retired from running her travel agency, nothing makes her happier than seeing her children and grandchildren gathered around a table enjoying heartwarming foods from times gone by.

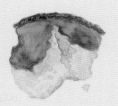

FELICIA KAHN grew up believing that the kitchen was the heart of the home, setting the foundation for her future career. It was where the family always gathered, gravitating to where her mother, Helene, spent most of her days. When Felicia got married, she followed suit and the kitchen became her haven; when visitors arrived, they would be shown in through the kitchen rather than the front door. Felicia and husband Stanley run Amaze in Taste, one of Sydney's largest kosher caterers. They have seen generations of families grow, quietly witnessing their Bat/Bar Mitzvahs (celebrations when a girl turns 12 and a boy 13) and weddings, and the births of their children from the sidelines, while ferrying delicious and abundant platters of food.

For South African-born Sydney artist **DORRYCE ROCK**, art is her meditation. Dorryce was born into a talented cooking family and, as much as she loves making desserts, her passion lies in art. A multi-disciplinary artist and former events designer, Dorryce transitioned into painting in 2005 and has exhibited her gorgeous works around Australia and New York. As a mother and grandmother, Dorryce relishes the custom in her family where four generations, headed by her mum 'the chief', Elza, gather twice a year to make herring for Rosh Hashanah (Jewish New Year) and Apricot Jam for Passover (the festival celebrating freedom). For Dorryce, these traditions around food bring comfort and ensure cultural continuity.

For psychologist **NAOMI HERSH**, baking is a passion that has taken her from London's Le Cordon Bleu to her own Roel Bakery in Sydney – a baking school and supplier of homemade custard scrolls. She learnt to cook sitting on the kitchen bench on a Friday afternoon watching her mother and remembers the excitement of being allowed to stir, measure ingredients or crack an egg. Later, when Naomi moved out of home to a different city, she had the foresight (that so many of us wish we had) to sit her mother down and type out all the recipes that only existed in her mother's head. Today, with a family of her own, the meditative process of baking is the perfect antidote to the mental rigour of work and life.

Baking cakes was **STEVEN GLASS'S** antidote to a jam-packed life of litigation and defending the rights of those in need. As the child of refugees, Steven never forgot the opportunities Australia gave his family and he most definitely paid it forward. Steven studied engineering, and worked in the earliest days of IT before making a complete switch to study law, eventually becoming a commercial litigator with a mission to help the underprivileged at the same time. He spoilt his family and friends with his famous decadent cheesecake on birthdays and other special occasions, always loving that he baked the dish that stole the show. Steven will always be remembered through his work, the person that he was and his cheesecake.

Romanian *Malai*

DEBBIE LEVI

Polenta Cheesecake

Growing up, Debbie didn't know many people with Romanian heritage. It was only as an adult travelling in Israel and Romania that she realised this crisp, golden cheesecake with polenta (her mother's regular Friday night dessert) was actually a traditional dish. Also called *alivanca*, it can be made in many different ways; some are flat, some are high, some are flavoured with honey rather than sugar. Debbie told us it is so delicious eaten straight out of the oven with a dollop of sour cream, and we agree entirely.

3 eggs
230 g (1 cup/8 oz) caster (superfine) sugar
60 ml (¼ cup/2 fl oz) oil
500 g (1 lb 2 oz) farm (pressed cottage) cheese, chopped
125 g (scant ¾ cup/4½ oz) polenta (cornmeal)
finely grated zest of ½ an orange or lemon
¼ teaspoon salt
sour cream, to serve

Preheat the oven to 180°C (350°F/Gas 4). Grease a 23 x 13 cm (9 x 5 inch) loaf (bar) tin generously with butter or oil and leave unlined as this will give the *malai* a lovely crisp edge.

Using an electric mixer, beat the eggs with the sugar until thick and pale. With the mixer on low, pour in the oil and beat until combined. Add the cheese and beat well, then add the polenta, zest and salt. Continue to beat until well combined. Don't be concerned if you can still see lumps of cheese.

Pour into the prepared tin and bake for 45 minutes or until a skewer inserted into the centre comes out clean. Allow to cool in the tin for 10 minutes before turning out onto a wire rack.

Serve warm or at room temperature with a dollop of sour cream. Store any leftovers in an airtight container in the fridge.

Serves about 10

South African Cheesecake

DORRYCE ROCK

This story charts the evolution of a cheesecake. Not just any cheesecake, but the South African cheesecake from *The food, the stories, the sisterhood*, which Monday Morning Cooking Club founding member Lauren Fink shared with us, and which we consider to be one of the best that has crossed our kitchen threshold. It was originally given to her by Dorryce, whose recipe evolved from a '2 egg/1 *"bakkie"* (tub) cream cheese' recipe in a handwritten scrawl on a scrap of paper that she first got in South Africa, circa 1975. Over the years, Dorryce has tweaked that original, and we are thrilled that we now have two fantastic South African cheesecakes to choose from.

375 g (13¼ oz) plain sweet biscuits, such as Marie or Digestives
pinch of salt
250 g (9 oz) unsalted butter, melted
8 eggs, separated
230 g (1 cup/8 oz) caster (superfine) sugar
750 g (1 lb 10 oz) cream cheese, at room temperature, chopped
150 ml (½ cup + 1 tablespoon/5 fl oz) pure (35%) cream

Preheat the oven to 180°C (350°F/Gas 4). You will need a deep 3 litre (12 cup) baking dish. To make the cheesecake base, put the biscuits and salt in a food processor and process until they resemble breadcrumbs. Add the butter and pulse to combine. Tip the mixture into the base of the baking dish and press it evenly into the base and up the sides.

Using an electric mixer, beat the egg yolks until light and fluffy, adding the sugar gradually. Add the cream cheese one-third at a time, and beat on high speed to ensure there are no lumps. On medium speed, slowly add the cream and beat until smooth.

In a separate bowl, whisk the egg whites just until stiff peaks form. Using a spatula or metal spoon, gently fold the egg whites into the cream cheese mixture, one-third at a time, then pour the mixture into the prepared crust. Bake for 45 minutes or until golden brown on top (probably with cracks) but still quite wobbly.

Turn the oven off and leave it to set in the oven for 10 minutes. Serve at room temperature. To serve, scoop with a large spoon straight from the baking dish to a plate. Refrigerate any leftovers.

Serves about 12

Note — This cake can also be made in a lined 26 cm (10½ inch) springform tin. When completely cool, remove from the tin and slice to serve.

Traditional Cheese *Blintzes*

FELICIA KAHN

A *blintz* is a filled and rolled crêpe; Felicia's cheese *blintzes* are the ultimate traditional version. In *The food, the stories, the sisterhood*, we shared Melanie Knep's unique version, bathed and baked in cream to render a soft parcel with a slightly puffy crisp top.

Felicia's hands have rolled thousands and thousands of blintzes and not only does she get joy from the making but from watching so many people devour them over the decades. Felicia's *blintzes* are baked in the oven to serve but if you (like Natanya) prefer a golden outside, gently fry them on both sides in a knob of butter. Lisa likes them with our tart blueberry compote and a dollop of sour cream, just like her parents enjoyed back in the day.

CRÊPE BATTER

500 ml (2 cups/17 fl oz) milk
2 eggs
75 g (2⅔ oz) unsalted butter, melted
2 teaspoons caster (superfine) sugar
1 teaspoon vanilla extract
½ teaspoon salt
150 g (1 cup/5⅓ oz) plain
    (all-purpose) flour
1 tablespoon unsalted butter, for frying

CHEESE FILLING

500 g (1 lb 2 oz) cream cheese,
    at room temperature, chopped
125 g (heaped ½ cup/4½ oz) caster
    (superfine) sugar
50 g (2½ tablespoons) sour cream
3 teaspoons finely grated lemon zest
1 teaspoon vanilla extract

ALSO NEEDED

MMCC's Blueberry Compote
    (see recipe opposite)
sour cream

Preheat the oven to 160°C (325°F/Gas 3). Butter a 28 x 22 cm (11 x 8½ inch) baking dish.

To make the crêpe batter, combine the milk, eggs, butter, sugar, vanilla and salt in a medium bowl. Using a stick blender or whisking by hand, combine the ingredients. Add the flour and beat or whisk until you have a smooth batter with no lumps. Transfer the batter into a jug for easy pouring and cover and refrigerate for at least 1 hour and up to 24 hours.

To fry the crêpes, heat a crêpe pan or small, non-stick frying pan over medium heat. Add a pea-sized knob of butter to the pan and swirl to coat the base. When it just starts sizzling, pour in a little batter. Swirl the pan so the batter covers the base and tip any excess back into the jug. You don't want the crêpe to be too thin or too thick. Cook gently over medium–low heat for a couple of minutes until you can gently lift an edge and peek underneath. When the underside is lightly browned all over and the top is set, flip the crêpe onto a board or large plate. You will only be cooking the underside of the crêpe. Continue with the rest of the batter, piling the crepes on top of each other. Allow to cool before filling.

To make the filling, using an electric mixer beat the cream cheese and sugar until the sugar is dissolved and the mixture is light and smooth. Add the sour cream, lemon zest and vanilla, and beat well to combine.

To fill the *blintz*, lay one crêpe flat on your benchtop, cooked side down. Place 2 tablespoons of the filling in the centre of the crêpe (on the uncooked side), and shape into a log around 7 x 2.5 cm (2¾ x 1 inch). Fold the left and right sides of the crêpe over to meet in the middle, and then roll up from the side closest to you until you have a small rectangular parcel. Continue until all the crêpes are filled. Place the *blintzes* in the prepared baking dish, seam side down. Cover the baking dish with foil and cook for 20 minutes or until the filling is hot.

The filled *blintzes* may be made ahead and refrigerated for up to 3 days, or frozen for up to 1 month before heating and serving.

If you wish, serve with blueberry compote and sour cream.

Makes 16

MMCC'S BLUEBERRY COMPOTE

1 tablespoon water
finely grated zest of 1 lemon
1 tablespoon lemon juice
pinch of salt
750 g (1 lb 10 oz) fresh blueberries
2 teaspoons unsalted butter

In a medium saucepan, combine the water, lemon zest and juice, and salt and stir until smooth. Cook over medium heat for a few minutes until the sugar is dissolved. Add two-thirds of the blueberries and mash coarsely with a potato masher. Add the butter and cook over medium heat, stirring occasionally, for about 10 minutes or until the mixture boils, thickens and becomes slightly jammy.

Remove from the heat and stir in the remaining blueberries. Set aside.

Cheese and Raisin Pastries

NAOMI HERSH

Naomi's cousin, a pastry chef in Israel, introduced her to Carine Goren's 2006 cookbook, *Sweet Secrets*. Naomi immediately fell in love with these plump, yeasted, sweet cheese pastries. Carine is an Israeli pastry chef, cookbook author and television personality. We have tweaked Carine's recipe slightly to reflect the methods we use for working with yeast. For some yeasty guidance, see How to Yeast on page 178.

DOUGH

500 g (1 lb 2 oz) plain (all-purpose) flour, plus extra
115 g (½ cup/4 oz) caster (superfine) sugar
1 teaspoon salt
7 g (1 sachet/2¼ teaspoons) active dried yeast
250 ml (1 cup/8½ fl oz) warm milk
115 g (1 stick/4 oz) unsalted butter, melted
2 egg yolks, lightly beaten
finely grated zest of ½ lemon

FILLING

500 g (1 lb 2 oz) ricotta cheese
100 g (scant ½ cup/3½ oz) caster (superfine) sugar
2 egg yolks
6 teaspoons cornflour (corn starch)
1 teaspoon vanilla extract
finely grated zest of ½ lemon
30 g (1 oz) unsalted butter, melted
80 g (½ cup/2¾ oz) raisins or sultanas (golden raisins)

ALSO NEEDED

1 egg beaten with 1 tablespoon water, for egg wash
icing (confectioners') sugar

Combine the flour, sugar and salt in the bowl of a stand mixer and make a well in the centre. In a small bowl, combine the yeast with half the milk, and add in 1 spoonful of the flour mixture. Stir and allow to stand for 10 minutes or until the mixture is frothy, to ensure the yeast is active.

Place the remaining milk and the melted butter, egg yolks and lemon zest into the well, along with the yeast mixture. Using a wooden spoon, combine the mixture in the well and gradually incorporate the flour until you have a rough dough. Using the dough hook attachment of the mixer, knead on low–medium speed for 5 minutes or until the dough is smooth and shiny. Cover the bowl with plastic wrap and a tea towel and allow to rise until doubled in volume, about 1½ hours.

Meanwhile, make the filling. In a medium bowl, combine the ricotta cheese with the sugar and set aside for a few minutes until the sugar dissolves. Add the egg yolks, cornflour, vanilla and lemon zest, and stir well. Fold in the melted butter and the sultanas then cover and refrigerate until needed.

Line 2 large baking trays. Turn the risen dough out onto a floured benchtop, punch down and divide into 2 equal pieces. Roll out 1 piece to form a rectangle, about 33 x 26 cm (13 x 10½ inches). Straighten the edges, then cut into 12 equal squares. Place 1 tablespoon of the cheese filling in the centre of each square then fold by bringing one corner over the filling and folding the opposite corner over to cover the first one. Fold the third corner over and finally the fourth corner, and then pinch together to seal. It should look like an almost-sealed envelope (see picture) but it's fine for the filling to show.

Place the pastries on the prepared trays, leaving a little space in between. Cover with a light tea towel. Allow to rise for 1 hour or until just about doubled in volume.

Preheat the oven to 180°C (350°F/Gas 4). Gently brush with the egg wash and bake for 15 minutes or until golden on the top and bottom. Allow to cool a little and sprinkle with icing sugar.

Makes 24

Recipe credit — Adapted and printed with permission of the author, from *Sweet Secrets* by Carine Goren, published by Cookie Media Ltd, 2006.

New York-style Cheesecake

Steven's family adore this cake and it was the one most regularly requested by friends. This cake is a classic New York cheesecake with a sponge layer in place of a biscuit or pastry crust. The recipe is adapted from Junior's Original NY Plain Cheesecake, with permission.

BASE

50 g (⅓ cup/1¾ oz) plain (all-purpose) flour
¾ teaspoon baking powder
pinch of salt
2 eggs, separated
75 g (⅓ cup/2⅔ oz) caster (superfine) sugar
1 teaspoon vanilla extract
finely grated zest of 1 lemon
30 g (2 tablespoons/1 oz) unsalted butter, melted
¼ teaspoon cream of tartar

CHEESE FILLING

1 kg (2 lb 3 oz) cream cheese, at room temperature, chopped
230 g (1 cup/8 oz) caster (superfine) sugar
35 g (¼ cup/1¼ oz) cornflour (corn starch)
2 eggs
180 ml (¾ cup/6 fl oz) pure (35% fat) cream
1 tablespoon vanilla extract

Preheat the oven to 180°C (350°F/Gas 4). Line a 23 cm (9 inch) springform cake tin, then tightly wrap the outside in foil so that water can't get in. You will also need a deep baking dish that can fit the cake tin inside so that the cake can cook in a water bath (bain marie).

To make the base, sift the flour, baking powder and salt into a bowl. Using an electric mixer, beat the egg yolks with half the caster sugar until pale and creamy. Add the vanilla and lemon zest, then fold in the flour mixture until just combined, followed by the melted butter.

In a separate bowl, whisk the egg whites and cream of tartar until soft peaks form, then slowly add the remaining sugar, whisking in 1 spoonful at a time until stiff peaks form. Fold the egg whites into the egg yolk mixture.

Spoon the mixture into the prepared tin, tap a few times on the benchtop to remove any large air bubbles, then bake in the centre of the oven for 10 minutes or until light golden.

Meanwhile, make the cheese filling. Using an electric mixer, beat the cheese, sugar and cornflour until well combined. Add the eggs, one at a time, then the cream and vanilla, and beat until smooth.

Remove the cake tin from the oven, spoon in the cheese filling and place the tin into the baking dish. Pour enough tap water into the baking dish to come 3 cm (1¼ inches) up the side of the cake tin and place the cake and its water bath in the oven. (Double-check that the water is below the foil and can't seep into the cake.) Bake for 1 hour or until the top of the cheesecake is light golden. Remove from the oven and carefully lift the cake tin out of the water bath. Allow to cool at room temperature for 2 hours, then refrigerate for at least 4 hours before serving.

Serves about 10

Recipe credit — Adapted and printed with permission of the publisher, from *Junior's Cheesecake Cookbook: 50 To-die-for recipes for New York-style cheesecake* by Alan Rosen and Beth Allen, published by Taunton Press Inc., 2007.

Cherry and Cheese Strudel

We could probably start a Sydney-wide argument if we asked the public to choose the best cake from the Gelato Bar, so we asked our husbands instead; they unanimously agreed on the cherry strudel. We're so thrilled to document this recipe from Nilly's memory (we've been dreaming about it since our first book), and to share it with those of you who've been craving it since the Gelato Bar closed. Huge thanks to Nilly Berger, from the Gelato Bar family, who came to our kitchen, and also to 'the strudologist' on the end of the phone, providing much-needed guidance.

PASTRY

5 sheets filo pastry
60 g (2 oz) ghee (clarified butter), melted
1 tablespoon caster (superfine) sugar, for sprinkling

HAZELNUT MIX

30 g (¼ cup/1 oz) ground hazelnuts
55 g (¼ cup/2 oz) caster (superfine) sugar
1½ tablespoons fine breadcrumbs

CHERRY FILLING (FOR CHERRY ONLY)

1 x 680 g (1 lb 8 oz) jar morello cherries in syrup (330 g/11⅔ oz drained weight)
75 g (⅔ cup/2⅔ oz) ground walnuts, plus extra if needed

CHERRY FILLING (FOR CHEESE AND CHERRY)

⅔ x 680 g jar morello cherries in syrup (220 g/7¾ oz drained weight)
50 g (heaped ⅓ cup/1¾ oz) ground walnuts, plus extra if needed

CHEESE FILLING

125 g (4½ oz) farm (pressed cottage) cheese, crumbled
125 g (4½ oz) ricotta cheese
60 g (¼ cup/2 oz) caster (superfine) sugar
1 egg yolk
2 teaspoons semolina
finely grated zest of ½ lemon

This recipe gives you the option of making 1 cherry strudel or 1 cheese and cherry strudel.

To make a cherry strudel, you'll need the cherry filling (for cherry only). To make a cheese and cherry strudel, you'll need the cherry filling (for cheese and cherry) as well as the cheese filling.

Remove the filo pastry from the fridge and allow to sit at room temperature for at least 2 hours.

To make the cherry filling, drain the cherries, discarding their juice. Allow them to drain overnight or, if time doesn't allow, wrap them in paper towel to remove as much juice as possible. Toss the drained cherries with the ground walnuts and mix well – you should have a mixture with the texture of wet sand with chunks of cherries. You may need to add a little more of the ground walnuts if the mixture is too wet.

To make the cheese filling, combine the farm cheese, ricotta, caster sugar, egg yolk, semolina and lemon zest in a bowl. If the ricotta is very dry, reduce the semolina to 1 teaspoon. Using a whisk, mix well to combine until most of the lumps have disappeared. Refrigerate until needed.

When ready to make the strudel, preheat the oven to 220°C (430°F/Gas 8). Line a large baking tray. Remove 5 sheets of filo from the pack and place on the benchtop. Cover with a damp cloth (otherwise the pastry will dry out and crack when rolled).

On a piece of muslin (or a light tea towel), lay out 2 sheets of filo pastry, one on top of the other, with nothing in between them. Paint the top layer lightly from edge to edge with the melted ghee. Sprinkle 2 tablespoons of the hazelnut mixture evenly on top.

Top with a third sheet of filo, paint with the ghee and sprinkle with another 2 tablespoons of the hazelnut mixture. Top with a fourth sheet of filo, ghee and hazelnut mixture. Then top with a fifth and final sheet of filo, ghee and hazelnut mixture.

$\rightarrow$

Make a line of filling along the front edge, about 5 cm (2 inches) from the edge, leaving a small space at both ends. If using the cherry filling, make small logs of the filling in the palm of your hand and line them up end to end, along the length of the filo. If using both cherry and cheese fillings, place a log of cherry filling along the length of the filo and then a log of the cheese filling next to the cherry filling.

Using the muslin or tea towel, guide the filo edge closest to you over the filling and roll up as tightly as possible, gently squeezing as you go. Squeeze a little less tightly if using the cheese filling as it expands while cooking.

Place the strudel, seam side down, on the prepared tray and press the ends together to seal.

Paint the top of the roll with the remaining melted ghee and sprinkle with the caster sugar.

Bake for 20 minutes then reduce the heat to 200°C (400°F/Gas 6) for a further 10 minutes or until the strudel is a deep golden brown and nicely caramelised on top. Remove from the oven and allow to cool before slicing and serving. This is best eaten on the day of baking.

Makes 1 strudel; serves about 8

Knafeh

Middle Eastern Cheese Dessert

After we ogled Roy's mouthwatering photo of *knafeh* on Instagram, he kindly arranged for young Iraqi-born chef Riyad Seewan to come to our kitchen and take us through the steps for the perfect rendition. This recipe comes from Riyad's aunt, his family's *knafeh* specialist, and she kindly agreed to share the recipe with us. Assemble ahead, keep in the fridge until cooking time, then pull out of the oven to oohs and aahs at the first crunch of the golden syrupy *kataifi* (a type of shredded filo) and a mouthful of stretchy luscious cheese. It is much easier to make than we imagined, and is now Jacqui's favourite new dessert. You can find *kataifi* pastry at Middle Eastern and specialty food stores.

CHEESE FILLING

1 litre (4 cups/1 quart) water
60 g (¼ cup/2 oz) white (granulated) sugar
200 g (7 oz) haloumi cheese, sliced
400 g (14 oz) grated Italian mozzarella
3 teaspoons fine semolina

PASTRY

215 g (7½ oz) *kataifi* pastry
100 g (3½ oz) unsalted butter
50 g (scant ¼ cup/1¾ oz) caster (superfine) sugar
1 tablespoon butter, softened, for greasing

SYRUP

200 ml (generous ¾ cup/7 fl oz) water
50 g (scant ¼ cup/1¾ oz) caster (superfine) sugar
1 tablespoon orange blossom water
2 cardamom pods (optional)

ALSO NEEDED

60 g (⅓ cup/2 oz) shelled pistachios, chopped
vanilla ice cream, to serve

You will need a 20 cm (8 inch) cast-iron deep frying pan or an ovenproof dish the same size.

To start the cheese filling, combine the water and white sugar in a large bowl and soak the haloumi for 2 hours to extract the salt.

Half an hour or so before the 2 hours is up, prepare the pastry and the syrup. Preheat the oven to 160°C (325°F/Gas 3). With scissors, cut the *kataifi* pastry into 1 cm (½ inch) lengths and use your fingers to gently separate each strand. Spread the pastry out on a baking tray. In a small saucepan over medium heat, melt the butter and caster sugar together then pour it over the pastry. Work the butter mixture through the pasty with your fingers, taking the time to separate the strands again. Spread the pastry evenly across the tray and bake for 5 minutes until a little dry.

To make the syrup, combine the water, caster sugar, orange blossom water and cardamom pods (if using) in a medium saucepan. Bring to the boil over medium heat, stirring, until the sugar dissolves. Continue to simmer without stirring for 3–4 minutes or until just starting to thicken. Set aside.

Drain the haloumi well, squeezing out any excess water. Place the haloumi in the food processor and pulse until it is the size of coarse breadcrumbs. Set aside and then process the mozzarella the same way. You could also grate the haloumi by hand and mix with the mozzarella. Combine the cheeses.

Grease the pan with the softened butter. Place half the pastry into the bottom of the pan, spread it around and press lightly to ensure a firm, even coverage. Sprinkle over half the semolina and top with the cheese mixture. Sprinkle with the remaining semolina and top with the remaining pastry, pressing lightly to create an even layer.

Sprinkle 60 ml (¼ cup) of the syrup over the top and bake for 40 minutes or until light golden brown on top. While it's in the oven, bring the remaining syrup to the boil over medium heat. Simmer for about 15 minutes or until you have around 60ml (¼ cup) of thick syrup remaining.

Remove the *knafeh* from the oven and pour the syrup over the top. Sprinkle with the pistachios and serve immediately, on its own or with ice cream.

Serves about 10

Kolac

Czech Apricot Crumble Slice

We met Leonie at a Monday Morning Cooking Club Passover cooking demonstration, and she was excited to tell us about her family's *kolac*. We had never heard of this Czech cake but when she described it as layered, buttery pastry with tart apricots and sweet cheese, all topped with a toasty crumble, we were just as excited. It was originally made with continental flour, which is now difficult to source. A good substitute is a low-protein (biscuit, pastry and cake) flour if you can find it.

PASTRY

300 g (2 cups/10½ oz) plain
   (all-purpose) flour, plus extra
75 g (⅓ cup/2⅔ oz) caster (superfine)
   sugar
¼ teaspoon salt
150 g (5⅓ oz) cold unsalted butter,
   chopped
1 egg, lightly beaten
finely grated zest and juice of ½ lemon

CRUMBLE TOPPING

250 g (1⅔ cups/9 oz) plain
   (all-purpose) flour
250 g (9 oz) cold unsalted butter,
   chopped
230 g (1 cup/8 oz) caster (superfine)
   sugar
1 teaspoon vanilla extract
finely grated zest of ½ lemon

CHEESE FILLING

500 g (1 lb 2 oz) farm (pressed
   cottage) cheese
2 eggs
115 g (½ cup/4 oz) caster (superfine)
   sugar
10 fresh apricots, halved (see note)

Preheat the oven to 180°C (350°F/Gas 4) with an oven tray inside. Line a rectangular tin 32 x 22 cm (12½ x 8½ inches), leaving an overhang of baking paper.

To make the pastry, place the flour, sugar and salt in the food processor and process to combine. Add the butter and pulse until it resembles coarse breadcrumbs. Add the egg, and the lemon zest and juice, and pulse until a dough forms around the blade. Remove the dough and shape it into a disc. Wrap tightly in plastic wrap and refrigerate for 10 minutes.

On a lightly floured benchtop, roll out the dough until it is the size of the tin. Place the pastry into the tin, ensuring the base is evenly covered. Bake for 15 minutes.

To make the crumble topping, place the flour, butter, sugar, vanilla and lemon zest in the food processor and pulse until it is a crumbly mixture. Remove from the processor and set aside.

To make the cheese filling, place the cheese, eggs and sugar in the food processor and process until it is smooth.

Spread the cheese filling on the pastry and place the apricots on top. Sprinkle the crumble topping evenly over the top.

Bake for 1 hour or until light golden. Allow to cool before serving

Serves about 18

Note — If fresh apricots are out of season, substitute 40 Australian (or Californian) dried apricot halves. Before starting the recipe, soak the apricots in boiling water for at least 30 minutes and then drain well.

At our place (yes, all of our places), before dinner has barely started, someone always asks, 'What's for dessert?' Choosing the sweet course is serious business: we evaluate carefully the meal that's been, the room that's left, the taste that's needed and the available time we have. We plot our cravings in advance – maybe a hint of meringue-y tahini caramel, a bite of steaming butterscotch, a lick of cool whisky or a dollop of smooth Marsala. The hardest part is choosing. We've narrowed it down and these are our picks – desserts that will be with you for decades, and hopefully generations.

RUTH MINK'S gorgeous spiral-bound cookbook opens with, 'For Joe, the love of my life, who loved my food.' What started as a project for her family helped her through the healing process after her dear husband of 60 years passed away. Growing up in South Africa, Ruth watched her mother preparing traditional dishes on the back *stoep* (verandah), mincing meat for *perogen* (meat pastries) and drying her handmade *lokshen* (noodles). After Ruth married and moved to Durban, she couldn't believe that her mother was not by her side to teach her these heritage recipes. With Joe's encouragement, she became a self-taught cook, devouring recipe books and requesting recipes at their favourite restaurants. Ruth is now an 'unbelievably happy' 88-year-old, loving life in Cape Town and enjoying her greatest treasures – her children.

It started in Israel with cake. **SHARON HENDLER'S** parents married and moved to Sydney soon after her father wooed her mother, not with flowers, but with boxes of freshly baked cakes. Good food was always at the centre of her Sydney childhood. Sharon has been a great Monday Morning Cooking Club supporter since she shared some extraordinary recipes in *The food, the stories, the sisterhood*. She has cooked many things we've yearned for over the years, and we sometimes seek her thoughts on the recipes we test; she is a good external barometer and we appreciate her honest feedback. Sharon is known by her friends as a prolific birthday cake baker, by her husband and adult children as a wonderful cook, and by all who know her as a relaxed and fabulous host.

CAROLE SINGER, who featured in *The food, the stories, the sisterhood* alongside daughter Debbi, is someone who really loves life and her family. When the family was young and living on Sydney's North Shore, the Singer home was *Shabbat* (Sabbath) lunch central, with a table laden with food, the dining room packed with family friends. It was a day of legendary Scrabble games and much singing. Despite living on the other side of the world in Israel, Carole's sister Judy Marks is, and always has been, her mentor in all things domestic; now, each of Carole's four children continues to host and entertain with love and generosity mentored by their *balaboosta* (excellent homemaker) mother.

Our neighbour from across the Tasman, second-generation New Zealander **SHEREE STONE** has loved entertaining since her teens. She has vivid memories of preparing food with her grandmother Esther, a traditional Jewish cook. Sheree's approach to cooking includes similar processes to her approach to her fine art practice of collage: extracting parts of recipes, transforming them with her own ingredient pairings to construct new tastes and textures, and creating something new and more than the sum of its parts. Sheree's Lavosh and Smoked Fish Pâté recipes featured in *It's Always About the Food*, and have now reached cult status around Australia.

FELICIA KAHN in *Sweet Cheese* (page 205)
RONNIE FEIN in *An Extra Something* (page 264)

YVETTE STUDNIBERG'S mother, Lydia Steidler, was always immaculate and sophisticated in her best cocktail dresses, ready to entertain Sydney society. Thanks to Yvette's grandmother, Lydia was equally adept at cooking the most memorable European delicacies such as cream cheese pancakes, *kuglof* and strudel. Yvette learnt to cook immersed in the stories and flavours of her parents' Czechoslovakian heritage. Her mother's Sophia Loren-like beauty and charm, together with her dad's business acumen, made them Sydney's go-to florists from the 1960s. John and Lydia's Kings Cross flower shop was just the start of what would become an iconic Australia-wide business. Yvette is a proud first-generation Australian, and her Jewish heritage has taught her a close sense of community.

ETTY DENTE has an exciting and diverse culinary heritage – a mix of Dutch, Yemeni and Italian. We came across Etty in a cookbook put together to support Keren Hayesod in Israel. We can imagine sitting in her Milan kitchen as she patiently stirs her favourite risotto *alla Milanese*, listening to the story of how lucky her family was to leave Tripoli in 1954, when things became difficult for the Jewish community after Libya's independence. Unlike her mother, who loved Middle Eastern/North African cooking and never used a recipe, Etty's passion is for Italian cooking. She taught herself from the classic cookbooks when she was a young, newly married woman, choosing the recipes her family loved her to make over and over.

JANETTE KORNHAUSER'S *haimish* (comfortable and homey) way of living is essential to the small but strong Jewish community in Queensland – her *Shabbat* table welcomes friends who then become like family. The continental supplies brought up from Melbourne and the hearty dose of warmth ensures community and continuity. We've loved Melbourne-born Janette from the start. She organised our first book launch on the Gold Coast, packing a local café, singing our praises and cheering us on with boundless energy. Janette's mum, Shirley, is a renowned cook who learnt from her own mother-in-law and has, in turn, taught Janette's three daughters the traditions of their European heritage.

When **KATHY GOLDBERG** married Jerome, Talia's best cooking advice to her new daughter-in-law was to find recipes that were both delicious and easy to make ahead. Kathy (who is Lisa's sister-in-law) shared their late mother-in-law, Talia's, Buche de Chocolat in *The food, the stories, the sisterhood*. Decades later, and now a grandmother of four, Kathy occasionally cooks the traditional food of her Hungarian heritage from her late mother, Elisabeth (who was also in our first book), and the family favourites that Talia made often, as they evoke heartwarming memories and comfort. But most of her cooking now stems from her desire to cook healthy food to nourish and feed her growing family, something we can all relate to.

How to Custard

We are always happy to eat a bowl of custard on its own, but it is also an important component of some recipes such as ice cream and pastry cream.

1. Place the sugar and cornflour (or flour) in a large heatproof bowl and whisk to combine. It helps to have a damp cloth underneath the bowl to keep it from moving (in step 5 particularly). Add the egg yolks and whisk together to form a paste. It is best not to leave egg yolks and sugar in the same bowl without being mixed, as the yolks will go grainy.

2. Using a small sharp knife, split the vanilla bean (if using), scrape out the seeds (using the back of a knife) and add the pod and seeds to the milk.

3. Pour the milk into a medium heavy-based saucepan. Scald the milk by heating until it is near to the boil (i.e. just about to boil but not boiling) and small bubbles form around the sides. Remove the vanilla bean, if using. While continuing to whisk the egg mixture, slowly pour about one-third of the milk into the mixture.

4. Once well combined (the eggs are now tempered), add the remaining milk.

5. Whisk to combine.

6. Give the saucepan a quick clean and pour the mixture back in.

7. Cook over medium–low heat, without allowing it to boil, stirring constantly with a flat-sided wooden spoon or heatproof spatula until it thickens to form a custard. Take care to ensure the custard does not catch (and cook) on the bottom of the pan – be vigilant in scraping your spoon across the bottom as you stir. (The time it takes to cook can be anywhere from a few to 20 minutes, depending on the recipe.)

8. The custard is ready when it 'coats the back of a spoon', i.e. when you run your finger along the back of the custard-coated spoon, a line is drawn in the custard and does not disappear when you turn the spoon. You can also use a sugar thermometer to guide you – the custard temperature should not exceed 80°C (176°F).

9. Strain the custard through a sieve into a clean bowl (sometimes there are small strands of egg that need to be removed). If not using immediately, place a piece of plastic wrap directly on the surface to prevent a skin from forming.

Vanilla Pouring Custard

A simple custard that goes with so many 'dessertables' – crumbles, pies, cakes, poached winter fruit – and is also delicious on its own. See our How to Custard guide on page 232 for some extra tips.

6 egg yolks
55 g (¼ cup/2 oz) caster
    (superfine) sugar
3 teaspoons cornflour (corn starch)
    or plain (all-purpose) flour
625 ml (2½ cups/21 fl oz) milk
1 vanilla bean, split and scraped or
    1 teaspoon vanilla bean paste

Place the egg yolks, sugar and cornflour in a large bowl and immediately whisk together to form a paste.

Heat the milk in a medium heavy-based saucepan over medium heat with the vanilla pod and seeds. Scald by bringing to a near boil then remove from the heat. Remove the vanilla bean, if using. While continuing to whisk the egg mixture, slowly pour about one-third of the hot milk into the mixture. Once well combined, add the remaining milk and whisk to combine.

Give the saucepan a quick clean and pour the mixture back in. Cook over medium–low heat without allowing it to boil; stir constantly with a flat-sided wooden spoon or heatproof spatula until it thickens to form a custard, about 5–10 minutes. Take care to ensure the custard does not catch – be vigilant in scraping your spoon or spatula across the bottom as you stir.

Strain if needed and pour into a heatproof jug to serve warm or cold.

Makes about 625 ml (2½ cups)

Espresso Prunes

Long before the Monday Morning Cooking Club days, back in the nineties, Merelyn used to travel for her PR work to cooking and wine-tasting masterclasses around the country. A definite perk of the job was looking in on the Jill Dupleix sessions as her recipes were modern yet comforting, easy yet impressive. Jill demonstrated how to make these espresso-flavoured stewed prunes and Merelyn has been serving them as a *Pesach* breakfast or dessert accompaniment ever since.

300 g (1⅓ cups/10½ oz) white
   (granulated) sugar
80 ml (⅓ cup/2¾ fl oz) freshly brewed
   espresso coffee
80 ml (⅓ cup/2¾ fl oz) brandy
   or other liqueur
500 g (1 lb 2 oz) pitted, dried prunes
250 ml (1 cup/8½ fl oz) water
thickened (whipping) cream
   or Greek yoghurt, to serve

In a medium saucepan, combine the white sugar, coffee and liqueur. Over medium heat, bring the mixture to the boil, stirring to dissolve the sugar. Boil for 1 minute and then add the prunes and the water, and boil for 25 minutes or until the prunes soften and plump up and the liquid reduces to a syrup consistency.

Remove from the heat and leave in the syrup to cool. Serve at room temperature with thickened cream or Greek yoghurt, or alongside a slice of Chocolate and Hazelnut Cake (page 70).

Store in an airtight container in the fridge.

Serves 8–10

Recipe credit — Adapted and printed with permission of Jilll Dupleix. The original recipe was later published in *Simple Food*, Hardie Grant Books, 2003.

Hungarian Fruit Soup

YVETTE STUDNIBERG

It may be a universal truth that only Hungarians and their descendants understand the concept of serving fruit soup as an entrée. Hugely popular in the days of the Austro–Hungarian empire, we have tweaked Yvette's recipe from her mother into a thicker compote style to serve as a light, refreshing dessert.

6 plums, stoned and roughly
    chopped
4 peaches, stoned and roughly
    chopped
4 nectarines, stoned and roughly
    chopped
500 g (1 lb 2 oz) cherries, pitted
2 strips lemon peel
125 ml (½ cup/4¼ fl oz) water
8 apricots, stoned and halved
60 g (¼ cup/2 oz) sour cream
1 teaspoon cornflour (corn starch)
Greek yoghurt or sour cream,
    to serve

Place the plums, peaches, nectarines, cherries and lemon peel in a large saucepan with the water. Bring to the boil, then lower the heat, cover with a lid and simmer for 10 minutes or until the fruit is just soft. Add the apricots and simmer for a further 5 minutes or until just cooked.

In a small bowl, mix the sour cream and cornflour, then add to the soup and mix well until slightly thickened. Set aside to cool, then place in the fridge until ready to serve. Serve chilled with a dollop of Greek yoghurt or sour cream.

Serves about 10

Whisky and Lime
Ice Cream

The diverse flavour spectrum of whisky was Sheree's inspiration for this recipe; its distinct flavour produces varying layers of taste and sweetness. A go-to, all-season dessert to complement a variety of dishes, as soon as we saw this recipe from Sheree we immediately knew it was a winner. No cooking or churning, flavoured beautifully with whisky and lime, and so very adaptable. It's perfect served as an *affogato* with a shot of espresso and a nip of whisky, and a 23-Minute Meringue (page 274) on the side.

4 egg yolks
250 g (1 cup + 1 tablespoon/9 oz)
    caster (superfine) sugar
125 ml (½ cup/4¼ fl oz) whisky
30 ml (1½ tablespoons/1 fl oz)
    lime juice
600 ml (2½ scant cups/20¼ fl oz)
    pure (35% fat) cream
finely grated zest of 1 lime

Start this recipe the day before serving.

You will need a 2 litre (8 cup) freezerproof container, preferably with a lid.

Whisk the egg yolks together and slowly add half of the sugar, continuing to whisk until the mixture is smooth, thick and pale. Combine the whisky and lime juice, and add to the egg mixture, briefly whisking to combine.

In a separate bowl, whisk the cream with the remaining sugar until soft peaks form. Gently fold the 2 mixtures together with the lime zest.

Pour the mixture into the container, cover and freeze overnight.

Serves about 10

Charoset Ice Cream

Dried Fruit and Cinnamon Ice Cream

RONNIE FEIN

Ronnie read about Ben & Jerry's *charoset*-flavoured ice cream with the sweet, nutty flavours of the essential Passover *shmear*. It sounded delicious, but sadly was only available in Israel. It wasn't exactly convenient to go and pick up a tub, so Ronnie came up with her own version. And we're thanking her for it – it's now going to be on all of our menus every year, and not just at *Pesach* time. If you are new to making custard (one of the elements of this recipe), have a look at How to Custard on page 232.

1 tablespoon unsalted butter

45 g (¼ cup, lightly packed/2 oz) brown sugar

1 granny smith apple, peeled and chopped

3 medjool dates, pitted and finely chopped

2 dried figs, finely chopped

2 tablespoons sultanas (golden raisins)

½ teaspoon ground cinnamon

60 ml (¼ cup/2 fl oz) sweet Passover wine or port

750 ml (3 cups/25 fl oz) thickened (whipping) cream

115 g (½ cup/4 oz) caster (superfine) sugar

3 egg yolks

⅛ teaspoon salt

50 g (⅓ cup/1¾ oz) roasted almonds, chopped

Heat the butter in a small saucepan over medium heat. When the butter has melted and looks foamy, add the brown sugar and mix it in. Add the apple and toss for a minute. Add the dates, figs and sultanas and cook, stirring, for about 1 minute, until the fruit is well coated.

Add the cinnamon and wine. Bring to the boil, then turn the heat to low, cover and cook for 10 minutes, stirring from time to time. Remove from the heat and mash the fruit slightly. Set aside.

While the fruit is cooking, place 500 ml (2 cups) of the cream in a medium heavy-based saucepan over medium heat and cook until bubbles appear around the edges. Using an electric mixer, beat the caster sugar in a bowl with the egg yolks and the salt for a few minutes until pale and thick. Gradually pour in the heated cream and beat together thoroughly. Return the mixture to the saucepan and cook over medium heat, stirring constantly, for 8 minutes or until it forms a thin custard. You should be able to lift the spoon from the saucepan and run your finger along the back, leaving a clear trail (so the custard 'coats the back of a spoon').

Pour in the remaining cream and stir to combine, followed by the fruit mixture. Refrigerate the mixture for at least 2 hours or until cold. Churn the mixture in an ice-cream maker, according to the manufacturer's directions. When the mixture is the consistency of soft ice cream, add the almonds and continue to churn until it is ready. Place in the freezer until ready to serve.

If you don't have an ice-cream maker, place the mixture in the freezer and cover with plastic wrap. Stir from time to time during the first few hours of freezing starting from when it first starts to freeze around the edges. It will still be good, just not as creamy.

Serves about 8

White Chocolate and Passionfruit Mousse

JANETTE KORNHAUSER

An easy and great dessert that we've all been making for quite a few years since Janette first shared this recipe with us. It's a perfect dessert choice when we're having trouble deciding what to make as it just ticks all our dessert boxes: make-ahead, fruity and oh-so-light.

150 g (5⅓ oz) best-quality white chocolate, chopped

3 eggs, separated

60 g (¼ cup/2 oz) caster (superfine) sugar

130 g (½ cup) fresh passionfruit pulp (about 8 large passionfruit)

300 ml (1¼ cups/10 fl oz) thickened (whipping) cream

fresh raspberries and passionfruit, to serve

You will need 6 individual serving glasses or a large (2 litre/8 cup) glass bowl.

The finished mousse needs to chill in the fridge for at least 4 hours before serving, or overnight, so make it in advance.

Melt the white chocolate in a microwave or using the double boiler method (see Kitchen Notes page 11) and allow to cool to almost room temperature – if the white chocolate is too hot, the mixture may seize. Using an electric mixer, whisk the egg yolks with half the sugar until thick and pale.

Fold half of the passionfruit pulp into the egg yolk mixture and then add half of the melted white chocolate. Repeat with the remaining passionfruit pulp and white chocolate.

Whip the cream until soft peaks form and gently fold into the passionfruit mixture in 2 batches.

In a separate bowl whisk the egg whites with the remaining sugar until stiff peaks form, and gently fold into the passionfruit cream mixture.

Spoon into a large glass bowl or divide between smaller individual glasses and refrigerate for at least 4 hours or overnight.

To serve, layer the extra passionfruit pulp over the top and then scatter over some fresh raspberries.

Serves about 6

Note — This dish contains raw eggs (see Kitchen Notes page 10).

Zabaione Freddo

Marsala Cream

A much-loved recipe passed down decades ago from Etty's dear aunt, this super-smooth, divinely-moussey Marsala dessert had us all in raptures from the first time we made it.

8 egg yolks
230 g (1 cup/8 oz) caster (superfine)
  sugar
80 ml (⅓ cup/2¾ fl oz) dry Marsala
500 ml (2 cups/17 fl oz) thickened
  (whipping) cream
3 egg whites
fresh raspberries or dark chocolate
  shards and caramelised nuts,
  to serve

The finished *zabaione* needs to sit in the fridge for at least 4 hours before serving. It is fine to make it one day ahead, but a little Marsala syrup may sink to the bottom of the dish the longer it sits.

You will need 8 individual serving glasses or a large (2 litre/8 cup) serving dish. You'll also need a large heatproof bowl and a saucepan filled with 2.5 cm (1 inch) of water. The bowl should sit snugly on top, without touching the water below.

To make the Marsala custard, using an electric mixer, whisk the egg yolks in the large heatproof bowl with 180 g (¾ cup) of the sugar until thick and pale. Add the Marsala and whisk until well combined. Bring the saucepan of water to the boil and place the bowl with the egg mixture on top. Reduce the heat to medium (the water should be simmering) and stir the mixture with a spatula until it thickens and forms a smooth custard, about 10 minutes. (If you need guidance, see How to Custard on page 232). Remove the bowl from the heat and stir continuously until the mixture is cool. You can also do this with the electric mixer on low speed.

In a separate clean bowl, whisk together the cream, the egg whites and the remaining sugar until soft peaks form. Using a spatula, gently fold into the cooled Marsala custard. Pour the mixture into the serving glasses or dish. Refrigerate for at least 4 hours then serve cold.

In the warmer months, decorate the top with fresh raspberries, and in the cooler months decorate with chocolate shards and caramelised nuts.

Serves about 8

Note — This dish contains raw egg whites (see Kitchen Notes page 10).

Apple Pie Cake

CAROLE SINGER

Carole's sister, Judy, gave her this recipe over 50 years ago, and she's been making it ever since. This recipe uses egg yolks only, so when you're making meringues and have yolks to spare, whip up a batch of this pastry and keep it in the freezer for a rainy day.

DOUGH

3 egg yolks
115 g (½ cup/4 oz) caster (superfine)
   sugar
1 teaspoon vanilla extract
115 g (1 stick/4 oz) unsalted butter,
   melted and cooled
170 g (1 cup + 1½ tablespoons/6 oz)
   self-raising (self-rising) flour,
   plus extra
pinch of salt

FILLING

5 large granny smith apples
80 g (½ cup/2¾ oz) sultanas
   (golden raisins)
3 tablespoons plum jam (jelly)
2 tablespoons desiccated
   or shredded coconut
1 teaspoon ground cinnamon
finely grated zest of 1 lemon

ALSO NEEDED

2 teaspoons cinnamon sugar (page 54)
freshly whipped cream, to serve

To make the dough, beat together the egg yolks, caster sugar and vanilla until thick and pale. Add the butter and beat to combine. Add the flour and salt and mix until just combined and you have a sticky dough. Tip it onto a well-floured bench. With floured hands, bring the dough together to form a ball. Divide in 2 discs, wrap and freeze for at least 2 hours.

To make the filling, peel and grate the apples into a colander. Allow to sit in the colander for 15 minutes, then squeeze the juice out (and either drink or discard it). In a bowl, combine the apple with the sultanas, jam, coconut, cinnamon and lemon zest.

Preheat the oven to 180°C (350°F/Gas 4). Line a 20 cm (8 inch) springform cake tin.

To assemble the cake, use a box grater to coarsely grate 1 of the frozen dough discs evenly over the base of the prepared tin, then gently press down.

Spread the apple filling evenly over the base. Grate the remaining frozen dough disc evenly over the top. Sprinkle with the cinnamon sugar.

Bake for 45 minutes or until a skewer inserted in the centre comes out clean. Allow to cool before removing from the tin.

Lovely with a dollop of freshly whipped cream.

Serves about 8

Hazelnut and Chocolate Trifle

The simple but oh-so-amazing flourless chocolate cake in this recipe is one we have shared thousands and thousands of times in its previous incarnation: the base of the *Buche de Chocolate* from Kathy Goldberg in *The food, the stories, the sisterhood*. Here, we have transformed it into something even more 'dessertable' – perfect for a crowd. Think layers and layers of chocolate cake, sweet strawberries soaked in Frangelico, whipped vanilla-specked cream and golden hazelnut praline. Grab your spoon and dig in.

CAKE

225 g (8 oz) dark chocolate, roughly chopped
1 teaspoon instant coffee dissolved in 80 ml (⅓ cup/2¾ fl oz) boiling water
7 eggs, separated
230 g (1 cup/8 oz) caster (superfine) sugar

TRIFLE

500 g (1 lb 2 oz) strawberries, hulled and quartered
2 tablespoons caster (superfine) sugar (for strawberries)
80 ml (⅓ cup/2¾ fl oz) Frangelico (or other hazelnut liqueur)
750 ml (3 cups/25 fl oz) thickened (whipping) cream
1 tablespoon caster (superfine) sugar (for cream)
2 teaspoons vanilla bean paste
1 tablespoon unsweetened Dutch cocoa powder

HAZELNUT BRITTLE

200 g (1⅓ cups/7 oz) roasted hazelnuts, skins removed (see page 75)
200 g (7 oz) liquid glucose
250 g (1 heaped cup/9 oz) white (granulated) sugar

You will need a wide glass dish or vase, approximately 3 litres (12 cups) in volume.

Preheat the oven to 170°C (340°F/Gas 3). Line the base and sides of a 38 x 26 cm (15 x 10½ inch) shallow rectangular tin.

Toss the strawberries with the caster sugar and Frangelico in a bowl then set aside to macerate.

To make the cake, using the double boiler method (see Kitchen Notes page 11) melt the chocolate with the coffee and water in a heatproof bowl over a saucepan of simmering water, stirring to combine until melted and smooth. Allow to cool slightly.

Using an electric mixer, whisk the egg whites until stiff peaks form. In a separate bowl, beat the egg yolks with the caster sugar until thick and pale, then beat in the melted chocolate mixture. Gently fold the egg whites into this mixture and pour into the prepared tin. Bake for 20 minutes or until a skewer inserted into the cake comes out clean. Leave the cake in the tin to cool.

While the cake is in the oven, make the hazelnut brittle. If you are new to caramelising sugar, check out the first few steps of our How to Sugar on page 266.

Place a 60 cm (24 inch) sheet of baking paper on your benchtop. You will need a second sheet the same size and a rolling pin. Chop the hazelnuts roughly. Melt the glucose in a medium saucepan over medium heat and gradually add the white sugar, stirring patiently until dissolved. Once dissolved, still over medium heat, bring to the boil and simmer for a few minutes until it is a deep toffee colour (and reaches 175°C/345°F on a sugar thermometer), then quickly stir in the nuts. Carefully (it is super hot), pour onto the baking paper, cover with the second sheet of baking paper and press down with a rolling pin to spread and flatten. Take care, as the molten brittle is extremely hot.

After a minute or so, peel off the top layer of baking paper and allow the brittle to cool completely. Crush the brittle with a rolling pin, saving some larger pieces for garnish. Store in the freezer if making ahead.

Whisk the cream with the tablespoon of caster sugar and the vanilla just until soft peaks form. Refrigerate until ready to use.

To remove the cake from the tin, use a knife to cut away any stuck edges. Place a piece of baking paper over the entire surface of the cake and flip it over onto the bench. Remove the tin and the baking paper.

To assemble the trifle, work out how many layers you will need to fill your dish. Cut the cake into the shape and number of pieces needed, and place the first layer in the dish. It is okay if you have to make a patchwork of cake. You will need to roughly divide all the trifle ingredients into the number of layers you have.

Sprinkle 1 part of the cocoa powder over the first layer of cake, top with 1 part of the strawberries (and their juices), then 1 part of the hazelnut brittle and then 1 part of the cream. Repeat layering until all the ingredients are used, finishing with the cream and the larger pieces of brittle. Serve immediately or refrigerate for up to 24 hours before serving.

Serves about 12

Thanks to Sydney pastry chef Lorraine Godsmark for the brittle recipe, adapted from her almond brittle in our first book.

Fig and Caramel Sour Cream Pavlova

Merelyn has always found pavlova so alluring but the meringue just too sweet. Sour cream (even more glorious whipped) is now her go-to topping, and a salted tahini caramel adds an irresistible layer of umami. The caramel recipe is tweaked from one of Katrina Meynink's in *goodfood.com.au*; she discovered it in Yotam Ottolenghi and Helen Goh's beautiful cookbook, *Sweet*. When figs are at their seasonal juicy peak, you don't need to bother grilling them. For some tips on making caramel, see How to Sugar on page 266.

PAVLOVA MERINGUE

6 egg whites, at room temperature
pinch of salt
400 g (1¾ cups/14 oz) caster (superfine) sugar
2 teaspoons cornflour (corn starch)
1½ teaspoons vanilla bean paste
1½ teaspoons white vinegar

SALTED TAHINI CARAMEL SAUCE

80 g (⅓ cup/2¾ oz) caster (superfine) sugar
2 tablespoons water
40 g (1½ oz) unsalted butter, chopped
2 tablespoons pure (35% fat) cream
50 g (¼ cup/1¾ oz) tahini (raw sesame seed paste)
¼ teaspoon sea salt

TOPPING

500 g (1 lb 2 oz) figs, quartered,
1 tablespoon honey
2 tablespoon shelled pistachios, roasted
375 g (1½ cups/13¼ oz) sour cream, whisked to soft peaks

This meringue base is best started 1 day ahead.

Preheat the oven to 150°C (300°F/Gas 2). Grease an ovenproof cake platter.

To make the meringue base, whisk the egg whites with the salt until soft peaks form, then slowly add the sugar, 1 tablespoon at a time, mixing continuously until all the sugar is incorporated. Whisk until glossy, about 5 minutes, then add the cornflour and whisk again for a few more minutes.

Test to see if all the sugar has broken down by rubbing a bit of meringue between your fingers. There should be virtually no grains of sugar remaining. Using a metal spoon or a spatula, gently fold in the vanilla and vinegar.

Pile the meringue on top of the platter and flatten a little with a spatula to form a circle of about 25 cm (10 inches). Reduce the temperature to 110°C (225°F/Gas ½) and bake for 2 hours, then turn the oven off and leave the pavlova in the closed oven until completely cool (or overnight).

To make the caramel, place the sugar and water in a small heavy-based saucepan over medium heat, and cook, stirring, until the sugar has melted. Bring to the boil, then continue to simmer over low heat for about 8 minutes or until the mixture is a rich, dark brown caramel (and just reaches 175°C/345°F on a sugar thermometer).

Remove from the heat and add the butter and cream, stirring constantly and taking care as the mixture may spit. Add the tahini and salt and whisk thoroughly until combined. The sauce can be stored in the fridge and warmed very gently in the microwave for drizzling. If it splits when warming, add 1 tablespoon of hot water and stir.

For the fig topping, preheat the oven grill to high and line a baking tray with aluminium foil. Place the figs on the tray, drizzle with the honey and grill for 5 minutes or until warmed through and slightly collapsed. Set aside to cool. Roughly chop the pistachios and set aside.

To serve, top the meringue with the sour cream, then the figs. Drizzle the tahini sauce on top and scatter over the pistachios (even though we forgot them in the photo).

Serves about 12

Spiced Apple Crumble

FELICIA KAHN

It's hard to believe how many years it took us to find the perfect crumble. And here it is. Also works well with pears, rhubarb and strawberry or summer stone fruit in place of the apples.

CRUMBLE TOPPING

300 g (2 cups/10½ oz) plain
    (all-purpose) flour
200 g (1 cup/7 oz) brown sugar
100 g (1 heaped cup/3½ oz) rolled
    (porridge) oats
50 g (⅓ cup/1¾ oz) blanched
    almonds, chopped
50 g (½ cup/1¾ oz) coconut flakes
1 tablespoon ground ginger
250 g (9 oz) unsalted butter, at room
    temperature, chopped

FILLING

50 g (1¾ oz) unsalted butter
7 granny smith apples
75 g (⅓ cup/2⅔ oz) caster (superfine)
    sugar
finely grated orange zest of 1 orange
1 teaspoon ground cinnamon
1 teaspoon ground ginger
75 g (2⅔ oz) sultanas (golden raisins)

cream, Vanilla Pouring Custard
    (recipe page 234) or ice cream,
    to serve

You will need a large (3 litre/12 cup) baking dish. Preheat the oven to 180°C (350°F/Gas 4).

Make the crumble mixture by combining the flour, brown sugar, oats, almonds, coconut and ginger in a large bowl. Add the butter to the mixture. Using your fingertips, rub the butter into the mixture, until fairly well combined. Set aside.

To make the filling, place the butter into the baking dish and put in the oven for 5 minutes or until the butter is melted. In the meantime, peel and quarter the apples, and slice each quarter into 4. Put the slices into a large bowl with the caster sugar, orange zest, cinnamon and ginger. Remove the baking dish from the oven, pour the butter over the apples and toss well to coat. Tip the apples into the baking dish and sprinkle the sultanas on top. Using your fingertips, place the crumble on top of the apples, squeezing some of the mixture to form small clumps and allowing some to fall freely.

Bake for 1 hour or until bubbly and golden brown. Allow to cool for at least 15 minutes before serving.

Serve warm with cream, vanilla custard or ice cream (or all three!).

Serves about 12

Butterscotch Pudding
with Caramel Sauce

SHARON HENDLER

Sharon picked up this recipe years ago in South Africa at the Singita Castleton Lodge, and we've been making it ever since. The first time you make a sauce like this (one that takes sugar to the edge) may be a bit nerve-racking, so How to Sugar on page 266 will help. And know that you can always take your time and make the sauce in advance, then reheat later to pour on the pudding.

PUDDING

125 g (4½ oz) unsalted butter, at room temperature, chopped
125 g (⅔ cup, lightly packed/4½ oz) dark brown sugar
2 eggs, lightly beaten
1 teaspoon vanilla extract
150 g (1 cup/5⅓ oz) self-raising (self-rising) flour
1 teaspoon baking powder
pinch of salt
125 ml (½ cup/4¼ fl oz) buttermilk

CARAMEL SAUCE

100 g (scant ½ cup/3½ oz) caster (superfine) sugar
100 g (½ cup, firmly packed/3½ oz) dark brown sugar
pinch of salt
125 ml (½ cup/4¼ fl oz) water
50 g (1¾ oz) unsalted butter
250 ml (1 cup/8½ fl oz) pure (35% fat) cream

ice cream or cream, to serve

Preheat the oven to 180°C (350°F/Gas 4). Grease a 1.5 litre (6 cup) pie dish or ovenproof dish. You will need a sugar thermometer.

Using an electric mixer, beat together the butter and brown sugar in a large bowl until light and fluffy. Gradually add the eggs and vanilla and continue to beat until the ingredients are well combined. In a separate bowl, sift the flour with the baking powder and salt.

Add the dry ingredients to the batter in batches, alternating with the buttermilk, and mix well.

Spoon into the prepared dish and bake for 40 minutes or until a skewer inserted into the centre comes out clean. Pour the sauce over the pudding as soon as it comes out of the oven.

Make the caramel sauce while the pudding is in the oven. In a saucepan over medium heat, combine the caster sugar, brown sugar, salt and water. Stir until dissolved. Use a pastry brush dipped in water to brush the sugar crystals from the side of the pan if needed. Bring to the boil, and continue cooking, without stirring, over medium heat for around 10 minutes until it reaches 'hard ball' stage (122°C/252°F on a sugar thermometer) or is frothy on the top with large bubbles around the edge.

Add the butter and stir to combine, then continue to simmer for about 5 minutes, swirling the pan from time to time, until it reaches 'hard crack' stage (154°C/309°F) or is very dark and frothy and smells of almost-burnt caramel. Carefully (it may spit), add the cream a little at a time, stirring, until well combined and smooth. Remove from the heat and pour over the hot pudding as soon as it is removed from the oven.

Serve the pudding hot, with ice cream or cream.

Serves 6–8

Note — To make ahead of time, pour one-quarter of the sauce over the pudding when it comes out of the oven and allow to cool. Reheat for 20 minutes at 180°C (350°F/Gas 4) and heat the remaining sauce using the microwave or in a small saucepan. Pour the hot sauce over the pudding just before serving.

Malva Pudding

RUTH MINK

This a classic South African baked pudding made with apricot jam. The recipe comes from a Franschhoek winery that Ruth and her husband, Joe, visited in the 1970s. In those days, no-one had heard of malva pudding and it quickly became a Mink family favourite.

PUDDING

230 g (1 cup/8 oz) caster (superfine)
    sugar
1 egg
1 tablespoon smooth apricot jam (jelly)
150 g (1 cup/5⅓ oz) plain
    (all-purpose) flour
1 teaspoon bicarb soda (baking soda)
1 teaspoon baking powder
pinch of salt
1 tablespoon unsalted butter, melted
1 teaspoon white wine vinegar
250 ml (1 cup/8½ fl oz) milk

SAUCE

220 g (1 cup/7¾ oz) white (granulated)
    sugar
250 ml (1 cup/8½ fl oz) pure (35% fat)
    cream
95 g (3¼ oz) unsalted butter
115 ml (½ cup less 2 teaspoons/4 fl oz)
    hot water

ice cream or whipped sour cream,
    to serve

Preheat the oven to 180°C (350°F/Gas 4). Grease a 1.5 litre (6 cup) baking dish.

Using an electric mixer, beat the caster sugar and the egg together in a large mixing bowl until thick and pale. Add the jam and beat to combine.

Sift together the flour, bicarb, baking powder and salt. In a small jug, combine the melted butter, vinegar and milk.

Alternate between adding the dry mixture and the wet mixture to the mixing bowl, beating well after each addition to form a smooth batter. Pour the batter into the baking dish. Bake for 45 minutes or until golden on top and just firm to the touch.

While the pudding is baking, make the sauce. In a medium saucepan combine the white sugar, cream, butter and hot water. Stir to combine over medium heat until the ingredients are melted and well combined.

As soon as the pudding comes out of the oven, gradually pour the sauce over the entire surface – it will soak in as you go – and then allow it to stand for 15 minutes or so before serving warm. Delicious with ice cream or whipped sour cream (a perfect antidote to the sweet pudding).

Serves about 10

Note — To make ahead of time, pour half the sauce over the pudding when it comes out of the oven and allow to cool. Reheat for 20 minutes at 180°C (350°F/Gas 4) and heat the remaining sauce in a small saucepan. Pour the hot sauce over the pudding and allow to stand for 15 minutes before serving.

An Extra Something

You know when you just have a hankering for an extra something. A little sweet something. We have it often; we don't quite feel like a piece of cake and it's not dessert time. When we don't want to bother with rolling pastry or rising dough, but we need to satisfy an afternoon slump or we're just craving something sweet, here are our favourites. From Jacqui's much-loved simple hedgehog-style balls, which are always in her fridge, to the layered chocolate toffee buttercrunch that requires slightly more concentration, from crisp meringues to the classic but updated (and much easier to make than you think) nougat. This is a chapter of all the extra somethings that make us very happy.

As a young man, **JOHN MULLIGAN** apprenticed with some of Sydney's best chefs, before changing tack to study computer engineering. But when he found himself in the library reading cookbooks rather than maths books, he realised it was time for another change. John decided to embark on a career in catering, preferring the ever-changing landscape of events to the routine of a restaurant; he soon became a sought-after Sydney caterer. In 2009, a school friend asked him to cater a kosher wedding, and so began John's immersion in Sydney's Jewish community with L'Amour Catering. The first lesson learnt was that he needed twice as much food and a quarter as much wine! John explains, 'Food is such an important part of a Jewish event – it's really at the centre, and this is what I love'. We agree totally. It is always about the food.

Food writer **JANNA GUR** recalls the taste of her grandma Vera's apple cake, and her grandma Rosa's eggplant salad. They were two great cooks who agreed on almost nothing except their love for their granddaughter. Evacuated to Latvia during World War II, Vera and Rosa escaped the terrible fate that befell many. The family, along with 16-year-old Janna, immigrated to Israel in the 1970s; Janna wanted nothing more than to be a real Israeli and so she embraced Hebrew and honed her language skills. She later married Ilan Gur, a journalist and publisher, and together they launched *Al Hashulchan*, which is now considered the premier Hebrew culinary magazine. Janna has spent an illustrious career writing about food, talking about food and publishing her own cookbooks of Israeli and Jewish cuisine.

Food has defined New York–raised American food writer **RONNIE FEIN'S** life. She baked a chocolate cake complete with frosting for her own Bat Mitzvah (the celebration when she turned 12). Nowadays, she continues her mother's tradition of making a dozen apple pies every October, and can still hear her saying, 'Don't kill the dough!' Ronnie's mother lived by the philosophy that cooking should be enjoyed and never a chore – she had just finished making a delicious batch of salmon croquettes on the day she died. The most important lesson her mother taught her was to have confidence in her own cooking, something she is proudly teaching her five grandchildren today. Ronnie is following her passion to bring the world of kosher food into the 21st century.

For **FREDERIQUE HALIMI-FRANK**, cooking is meditation. Time in her Jerusalem kitchen is both time out and a form of art. Descended from a dynasty of three strong, independent sisters who still all love to cook, the family's old original recipes and techniques from Morocco, Algeria and France are slowly trickling down the line. On trips back to France, photos of ingredients are taken, and videos of lined hands blanching almonds, rolling *brik* pastry, and couscous grains are shot. The cooking legacy continues; Frederique's husband and three children all love to cook, pitching in while catching up and discussing life along the way.

HANNA GELLER GOLDSMITH in *The Chocolate Cake* (page 61)

Life in Australia couldn't be more different for **MARLEN CARP** than her early years. Born in Pinsk, Poland, she lived in a Siberian prisoner-of-war camp between the ages of two to seven. The family immigrated to Melbourne when she was ten years old, starting a new life. Marlen's mother taught her to cook but it was her aunt next door who was the inspirational baker. Marlen studied law before marrying Leon, a doctor, and became a stay-at-home mum. Baking was never really her thing, but she indulged Leon's love of anything meringue (as well as his health-fuelled desire to avoid egg yolks in the 1970s and 1980s). Now in her 80s, Marlen loves to cook *Shabbat* (Friday night) dinner for her children, grandchildren and great-grandchildren, and is still making meringues.

For **JO-ANNE MERVIS**, family reunions – togetherness, shared love and spoiling each other – have always been accompanied by the aroma of freshly baked homemade delights and cups of strong Five Roses tea served in English fine bone china. Gagga, Jo's grandmother Mona Green-Abelson, lived an overnight train trip away in Bloemfontein, South Africa. When Jo and her family travelled from Johannesburg to visit, their grandparents would be waiting on the balcony of their apartment, excitement and anticipation shining on their faces. Since those early years, Gagga's recipes have moved with Jo from Johannesburg to Swaziland, Moscow, Hong Kong, Sydney and now Melbourne, so Gagga is always by her side.

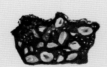

As well as raising her three boys, **ANNE ENGELMAN** volunteers as a matchmaker for a Sydney community organisation where young people meet over coffee and cake, and the occasional *Shabbat* dinner; food, once again, plays an important part in bringing people together. Perhaps thanks to her British heritage, Anne loves high tea. Scones, jam and cream are laid out on fine bone china and strong cups of tea are stirred with antique silver spoons passed down from her grandmother. Anne's father's love of chocolate has flowed down through the generations, so a batch of her chocolate biscotti, a slice of her mother's chocolate cake or her mother-in-law's chocolate nut cake are regular additions to the family table.

How to Sugar

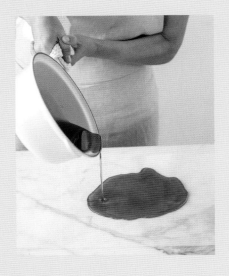

Before you begin: Some recipes require sugar to be dissolved in water to form a syrup that is then simmered until it reaches a desired stage (or sugar concentration). You can use a sugar thermometer (easy!) – a stage is reached when the syrup reaches the corresponding range of temperatures. Each stage may be marked on the thermometer as one specific or as a range of temperature/s.

You can also drop ½ teaspoon of the syrup into a glass of cold water to see how it behaves (more difficult!) – the name of each stage describes the texture of the cooled syrup. The amounts of sugar and water, the heat of your cooktop and the size and material of your saucepan will all affect the cooking time. Best to stay put (no distractions!) and watch the temperature carefully (reducing the heat if you need), paying attention to the viscosity, colour and smell of the syrup along the way. To avoid the melted sugar recrystallising (which would make the syrup grainy and opaque), ensure your utensils are clean and don't stir once it comes to the boil. Do take care – the syrup and caramel are dangerously hot.

1. Put the sugar and water into a clean heavy-based saucepan. Cook over medium heat, stirring from time to time with a wooden spoon until the sugar looks and feels completely dissolved. Stir gently (to avoid sugar crystals splashing) and don't boil the mixture before the sugar is dissolved.

2. Once the sugar is dissolved, stop stirring and let the syrup come to the boil. If sugar crystals form on the inside of the saucepan, use a clean pastry brush dipped into a glass of water to brush water over the crystals so they disappear into the liquid. You can continue to do this throughout the process if needed.

3. Place the sugar thermometer in the saucepan, and continue to simmer over medium heat. After several minutes, the clear syrup will reach the soft ball stage (112–116°C/234–241°F)(having passed through the thread stage). The bubbles will be clear, small and will pop quickly.

4. The syrup will then reach the hard ball stage (121–130°C/250–266°F), (having passed through the firm ball stage). It will still be clear but with bigger bubbles.

5. The syrup will then reach the soft crack stage (132–143°C/270–289°F). It will just start to turn the very palest shade of yellow. The bubbles will be larger and pop more slowly.

6. The syrup will then reach the hard crack stage (146–154°C/295–309°F). The bubbles will be large and slow moving and the syrup the palest golden. You might start to smell the sugar cooking.

7. The syrup will then turn golden at around 160°C (320°F), the first stage of caramel. You will be able to smell gentle caramel flavours. Some recipes head straight to caramel, melting the sugar without any water.

8. The syrup will then turn deep golden caramel at 170°C (338°F); if you are looking for the shiny patty-pan toffees of our childhood, this is it. It will turn dark amber caramel at 175°C (347°F). This happens quickly and you may need to carefully swirl the pan if one side is cooking faster than the other; the caramel is dangerously hot. The smell will border on burnt caramel, which will result in the perfect balance of bitter and sweet. Be brave!

Above 177°C (350°F), the caramel will be burnt.

Date, Coconut and Ginger Balls

This lovely and simple recipe was passed down from Gagga, Jo's grandmother, to Jo's mother; it was the first recipe Jo asked for as a new bride for her handwritten recipe binder and she has been making it ever since. Jo generously hosted a Monday Morning Cooking Club WIZO event in Melbourne some years ago where, after taking one bite of these morsels, we looked at each other and nodded.

500 g (1 lb 2 oz) medjool dates, pitted and chopped
185 g (6½ oz) unsalted butter, chopped
90 g (½ cup, loosely packed/3¼ oz) brown sugar
2 heaped teaspoons ground ginger
1 egg, lightly beaten
250 g (9 oz) Marie or plain sweet biscuits
80 g (1 cup/2¾ oz) desiccated coconut

Place the dates in a large saucepan with the butter. Cook over medium–low heat for about 10 minutes, stirring, until the dates have softened. Add the brown sugar and the ginger and continue to cook for a few minutes until the sugar has melted and the mixture is smooth. Remove from the heat and allow to cool for 5 minutes.

Add the egg and mix through quickly until you have a fairly smooth mixture. Break the biscuits into small pieces (you can put the biscuits into a large bowl and use the end of a rolling pin to break them up) and stir into the mixture.

Roll the mixture into walnut-sized balls and then roll the balls in the coconut to evenly coat. Refrigerate for at least 2 hours before serving.

Store in an airtight container in the fridge (as they contain raw egg).

Makes 50

Note — This dish contains raw egg (see Kitchen Notes page 10).

Nut and Date Coins

So simple to make and an excellent nutty treat for times when you just want a little something. We first spotted this recipe in Janna Gur's *Jewish Soul Food: From Minsk to Marrakesh*, with credit to chef Micky Shemo, who created the recipe. We have slightly tweaked the method.

50 g (½ cup/1¾ oz) walnuts
85 g (½ cup/3 oz) shelled pistachios
75 g (½ cup/2⅔ oz) almonds
60 g (½ cup/2 oz) pecans
60 g (2 tablespoons/2 oz) honey
55 g (¼ cup, firmly packed/2 oz) brown sugar
100 g (⅔ cup/3½ oz) pitted medjool dates, chopped
¼ teaspoon ground cinnamon
⅛ teaspoon ground cardamom
pinch of sea salt
100 g (¾ cup/3½ oz) white sesame seeds

Preheat the oven to 180°C (350°F/Gas 4). Line a baking tray. Put the walnuts, pistachios, almonds and pecans on the baking tray and roast for 10 minutes or until golden. Cool slightly.

Meanwhile, in a medium saucepan bring the honey and brown sugar to a boil, stirring. Add the dates and mix until broken down and combined. Remove from the heat. Add the roasted nuts, cinnamon, cardamom and salt to the mixture, and mix until well combined. Set aside for a few minutes, until just cool enough to touch, but still warm enough to be workable, then divide into 2 equal parts.

Place half of the mixture onto a piece of baking paper and, using the paper to help shape the log, roll the mixture into a log about 4 cm (1½ inches) in diameter. It does not need to be perfectly smooth. Repeat with the second half of the mixture.

Roll the logs in the sesame seeds to coat, then wrap in plastic wrap or baking paper and refrigerate. When ready to serve, slice the logs into thin coins, about 5 mm (¼ inch) thick. If it is too hard to slice straight from the fridge, leave at room temperature until soft enough to slice. Store in an airtight container in the fridge.

Makes 40

Date, Coconut & Ginger Balls

Nut & Date Coins

Cranberry, Almond and Pistachio Nougat

John has been making his (most outstanding) version of nougat for decades and Lynn Niselow (former MMCC author) shared it with us after attending his cooking class. This recipe is adapted from 'Almond Nougat' in *The Australian Women's Weekly Italian Cooking Class Cookbook*. We are amazed at how simple it is to make, and how absolutely delicious it is to eat. A sugar thermometer is essential for this recipe – if you're new to working with one, have a look at How to Sugar on page 266.

2 x A4 sheets edible (confectioners') rice paper
150 g (1 cup/5⅓ oz) toasted almonds
140 g (1 cup/5 oz) shelled pistachios
65 g (½ cup/2⅔ oz) dried cranberries
65 g (⅔ cup/2⅓ oz) dried apple, chopped
440 g (2 cups/15½ oz) white (granulated) sugar
350 g (1 cup/12⅓ oz) liquid glucose
180 g (½ cup/6⅓ oz) honey
60 ml (¼ cup/2 fl oz) water
2 egg whites
pinch of salt
½ teaspoon vanilla extract
60 g (2 oz) unsalted butter, at room temperature, chopped

This recipe is best made using a stand mixer and a sugar thermometer.

Line the base and sides of a lamington tin (30 x 20 cm/12 x 8 inches) with baking paper. You will need enough rice paper to cover the base and the top of the nougat.

Cover the base of the lined tin with 1 layer of rice paper.

Toss together the almonds, pistachios, cranberries and dried apple and set aside. Place the sugar, glucose, honey and water in a medium heavy-based saucepan. Stir over low heat until the glucose melts and the sugar dissolves. Increase the heat to medium and bring to the boil. Reduce the heat to medium–low and simmer, without stirring, for about 5 minutes or until the syrup reaches the high end of 'hard ball' stage (130°C/266°F on a sugar thermometer).

Meanwhile, using a stand mixer on medium speed, whisk the egg whites with the salt until stiff (but not dry) peaks form. While continuing to whisk, add half of the hot syrup in a slow, steady stream. Return the remaining syrup to the heat while continuing to whisk the egg white mixture. Simmer the remaining syrup for a futher couple of minutes until it reaches 'hard crack' stage (154°C/309°F on a sugar thermometer). While continuing to whisk, gradually and carefully pour the remaining syrup into the egg white mixture. Once it is all incorporated, continue to whisk until very thick, about 5 minutes. Take care not to overheat the motor.

Add in the vanilla and butter, whisking thoroughly. Then add in the fruit and nut mixture and quickly mix to combine. Working as fast as possible, pour into the prepared tin and use an oiled palette knife to smooth the top. Cover with a layer of rice paper and press down gently. Cool completely until set. Turn out onto a board and cut into 3 cm (1¼ inch) strips. Store in an airtight container in the fridge for up to 2 weeks.

Makes about 1.2 kg (2 lb 10 oz) nougat

Almond Buttercrunch

RONNIE FEIN

Abstaining from sweets when pregnant with each of her children, Ronnie's personal celebration right after they were born was to eat an entire batch of this candy. The obsession started with a version from a store called Lofts, and when it closed, Ronnie was compelled to re-create the sweet, salty, brittle. If you prefer a nuttier texture to the toffee, carefully stir in a handful of chopped almonds to the toffee (as we have done) as soon as it reaches 'soft crack' stage before continuing with the recipe.

230 g (2 sticks/8 oz) unsalted butter, chopped
165 g (¾ cup/5¾ oz) white (granulated) sugar
½ teaspoon sea salt
1½ tablespoons light corn syrup
2 tablespoons warm water
250 g (9 oz) dark chocolate (70%), roughly chopped
150 g (1 cup/5⅓ oz) roasted almonds, chopped, plus extra if you wish

Line a 33 x 23 cm (13 x 9 inch) baking tin. You will need a sugar thermometer. (Check out How to Sugar on page 266 if you are new to working with sugar.)

Place the butter into a medium saucepan and melt over low heat. Add the sugar, salt, corn syrup and water, and stir constantly with a wooden spoon, until the sugar dissolves. Continue to cook until the mixture starts to boil and then for a further 10 minutes or so, until the mixture is golden brown and reaches the high end of 'soft crack' stage (140°C/284°F) on the sugar thermometer.

Carefully (it is dangerously hot!) pour the mixture into the prepared pan and allow it to spread evenly. Immediately sprinkle the chocolate evenly across the top and allow it to stand until melted (it will take about 5 minutes) and then use an offset spatula or the back of a large spoon to spread the chocolate smoothly and evenly. Immediately sprinkle the chopped almonds on top and carefully press them in lightly using the back of a spoon.

Allow to cool for 2 hours or until the chocolate is firm and set. Break into pieces to serve.

Makes about 25 pieces

Panforte

Anne has become known among her friends for her own outstanding *panforte*, which she adapted from a recipe she found in *Australian Gourmet Traveller*, then adapted again later – taking inspiration from Yotam Ottolenghi and Helen Goh's book, *Sweet*. It is traditional but not absolutely necessary to wrap the *panforte* in edible (confectioners') rice paper, as baking paper will also work well. A sugar thermometer really helps with this recipe – if you're new to working with one, have a look at How to Sugar on page 266.

BASE

1 x A4 sheet edible (confectioners') rice paper (optional)
50 g (⅓ cup/1¾ oz) plain (all-purpose) flour
30 g (¼ cup/1 oz) unsweetened Dutch cocoa powder
3 teaspoons ground mixed spice
1 teaspoon ground ginger
100 g (3½ oz) dark chocolate (70%)
230 g (1 cup/8 oz) dried Iranian or Turkish figs
200 g (7 oz) mixed glacé (candied) fruit
110 g (¾ cup/3¾ oz) toasted almonds
80 g (¾ cup/2¾ oz) toasted walnuts
110 g (¾ cup/3¾ oz) roasted hazelnuts, skins removed (see page 75)
finely grated zest of 1 orange

SYRUP

150 g (⅔ cup/5⅓ oz) white (granulated) sugar
120 g (⅓ cup/4¼ oz) honey
60 ml (¼ cup/2 fl oz) water

ALSO NEEDED

icing (confectioners') sugar

Preheat the oven to 150°C (300°F/Gas 2). Line the base and sides of a square 20 cm (8 inch) baking tin with baking paper. Lightly grease the baking paper, and cover the lined base with the rice paper, if using, trimming to fit.

Combine and sift the flour, cocoa powder, mixed spice and ginger. Roughly chop the chocolate, figs (removing any tough stems) and glacé fruit. Place in a large bowl with the almonds, walnuts, hazelnuts and orange zest. Toss to combine then add the flour mixture and toss to coat well.

Heat the sugar, honey and water in a small saucepan over medium heat, stirring until the sugar dissolves. Bring to the boil and simmer for about 5 minutes until a golden syrup forms and reaches 'soft ball' stage: 116°C (241°F) on a sugar thermometer.

Working quickly with a lightly oiled spoon, pour the syrup over the nut mixture and mix well to combine. Tip the mixture into the prepared tin and smooth the top with an oiled spatula. Bake for 15 minutes and then remove from the oven.

When completely cool, remove from the tin, peel away the baking paper and dust both sides liberally with icing sugar. Slice to serve. It will keep, wrapped in baking paper and then plastic wrap in an airtight container in a cool place, for up to 1 month.

Serves about 20

Moroccan Almond Cigars

FREDERIQUE HALIMI-FRANK

Merelyn watched three generations of Halimi women fill and roll an enormous batch of sweet cigars for her nephew's Bar Mitzvah, and just knew she had to join the circle and learn how to make this exotic, sticky delicacy. Store-bought blanched almonds are too dry to make the filling for these, so follow the instructions below to blanch and skin your own. Add a few drops of extra water if the filling is really too dry to come together.

FILLING

250 g (1⅔ cup/9 oz) raw almonds
170 g (¾ cup/6 oz) white
    (granulated) sugar
finely grated zest of ½ lemon

PASTRY

1 packet Tunisian brick (*brik*)
    pastry (30 cm/12 inch diameter)

SYRUP

270 g (¾ cup/9½ oz) honey
3 teaspoons water

ALSO NEEDED

oil, for frying

To blanch the almonds, bring a small saucepan of water to the boil, add the almonds, and simmer for 1 minute. Drain and rinse with cold water. Pat dry on paper towels then slip the almond kernels from the skins.

To make the almond marzipan filling, process the blanched almonds in a food processor with the sugar until the nuts are finely ground. Add the lemon zest and continue to process until well combined.

With slightly wet hands, take a heaped teaspoon (around 20 g/¾ oz) of the filling and work it into a paste, then shape into a small sausage, approximately 3 x 1 cm (1¼ x ½ inch). If your nuts are very dry, you will need to work the mixture together with a little water on your hands until it comes together. Set aside on a plate until ready to fill the pastries. Repeat with the remaining filling.

Using kitchen scissors, cut 6 pastry sheets into quarters so you have 24 pieces of pastry. Take a piece of the filling and place along a straight edge of 1 piece of the pastry. Fold in the sides, then roll into a cigar. Set aside on a plate, seam side down, and repeat with the remaining filling and pastry until ready to fry. (The cigars can be stored in an airtight container in the fridge at this stage for up to 3 days, until ready to fry.)

Pour enough oil into a large frying pan to fill to 2 cm (¾ inch) deep, and heat over medium–high. Line a sieve with several pieces of paper towel, ready for the cooked cigars. Place several cigars, seam side down, in the hot oil, taking care not to overfill. Fry for 1–2 minutes on each side until evenly golden all over. Remove and drain in the lined sieve. Repeat with the remaining cigars and allow to cool completely.

To make the syrup, heat the honey and water until just boiling. Pour into a shallow baking tray. Add the cigars and coat them evenly with the syrup, then place in a serving bowl. Pour any remaining syrup on top.

Makes 24

'Come over for a drink and a nut.'
This is what Lisa's mum, Paula, always said.
Friends, family and colleagues alike were
invited home for a whisky and a bowl
of 'Dad's roasted almonds'. Pouring a hefty
4 kg (9 lb!) of raw nuts into a large, battered
old pan, Jack, Lisa's dad, would fill the house
with the smell of roasting nuts. Stirred with
a wooden spoon and tipped into a giant glass
jar, the almonds lived at the back of the pantry,
away from hungry hands, but within reach of
those in the know. We think drinks deserve a
little more than a humble nut. Here are a few
of our most revered savoury snackables to sit
alongside your most beloved G&T.

People + Stories

Young Sydney chef **ADAM WOLFERS** has become known for his contemporary takes on classic Jewish and Hungarian cuisine. Adam's career has taken him through some of the most celebrated kitchens in the world – from New York City's WD-50 to Spain's Quique Dacosta via Sydney's Yellow to Brisbane's Gerard's Bistro. Adam's grandmother met her husband in Sydney after he arrived from Hungary, having lost most of his family in the Holocaust. They both loved cooking and eating the foods from the places they had left behind as they forged a new life together. Adam created the outstanding Etelek pop-up restaurant, serving dishes inspired by this heritage. His plump, doughy, fried *langos* (we are all still dreaming about them) and unique matzo ball soup are the stuff legends are made of, honouring and remembering his grandparents in the process.

ADIRA WERDIGER'S family understands that the pot of *gribenes* (chicken skin and onions frying in chicken fat) serves a purpose, so they will always know the smell, and feel the soul, of their great-grandmother's kitchen. Coming from a large American family of rabbis and communal leaders, Adira grew up in a home where the kitchen was the central hub of daily life, always bustling and noisy. Whether cooking for a *Yom Tov* (a Jewish festival) or *Shabbat* (Friday night) dinner, celebrating the birth of a baby, or delivering a meal to someone in need, there was food to be made and recipes to be exchanged. Now in Melbourne, Adira loves when her kitchen conjures up past generations and when her five children gather around the kitchen island to share their goings on while eating the ends of her handmade *lokshen* (noodles).

As a young girl, **ELIZA LEVI**, with sisters Kate and Shana, would be dropped at her grandmother Gaga Maxine's house for Saturday lunch while her parents went to watch Aussie Rules football (as many Melbournians religiously do each week). Gaga, originally from the small town of Bunbury, Western Australia, preferred the housekeeper's food to her own, but her roast chicken, peas, potato gems and lemon cordial became a Saturday family tradition. Eliza's mum, Jan, has always loved cooking and encouraged the girls to experiment, letting them take control of meals during school holidays. A sixth-generation Australian, Eliza now loves cooking for her own family, often nostalgically making a tray of potato gems in Gaga's memory.

We also feel lucky to have known **DOV SOKONI** for some decades. Growing up with an abundance of fresh food always made from scratch, Dov (part of our project since *It's Always About the Food*) was destined to live a life immersed in food. His mum, Felicia, an amazing baker, would fill the house with the aromas of fresh baking: rising yeast, buttery pastry and melting chocolate. Way before modern Israeli cuisine was a concept, or Ottolenghi was a one-word style of cooking, Dov introduced Sydney café society to the pleasures of modern Middle Eastern food at his groundbreaking café, Dov. It was the food from his upbringing – a combination of his Israeli childhood and European heritage. Lucky for us, his food, now packaged as Yalla, is available around the country.

CHARMAINE and **REUBEN SOLOMON** have been part of our project since *The Feast Goes On*. The inimitable doyenne of Asian cooking and her late husband both craved the exotic food they left behind in Sri Lanka and Burma respectively. Sydney in the late 1950s offered no other options, so they learnt to cook for themselves. A hobby turned into a career as Charmaine went on to write 31 cookbooks, and Reuben was a showman and musician who loved nothing more than making Sri Lankan hoppers for his granddaughters. Daughter Debbie has been wonderful in connecting us to Charmaine over the years, something we have enjoyed enormously.

How wonderful that Mumbai-born **RACHEL DINGOOR** arrived in Australia with her young family, and carried close to her heart the tastes and smells of her Iraqi heritage and Indian youth. She would draw on these memories of cooking with her grandmother and mother to re-create the food of her childhood. She started with simple preparations and would add spices and seasonings – a pinch of this and a sprinkle of that until the taste of the dish was just right. We've known Rachel, now a great-grandmother herself, since her traditional Sephardi *kakas* and *babas* (traditional biscuits) were in *The Feast Goes On*, and we've had the privilege and joy of cooking with her in the MMCC kitchen with her granddaughter Orit.

Old-fashioned
Lemon Cordial

Both Eliza's mother and grandmother made this recipe whenever their neighbours' lemon trees were heavy with ripe fruit. We've had so much fun sampling this cordial – hint, it is particularly good as a mixer with gin or vodka. The recipe originally included epsom salts, but we've found it works perfectly without this medicinal ingredient.

9 or 10 lemons, washed well
1.125 kg (5 cups/2 lb 8 oz) white
   (granulated) sugar
1 tablespoon citric acid
1 tablespoon tartaric acid
1 litre (4 cups/1 quart) water

The recipe is best made the day before serving, and will keep up to 4 months in sterilised bottles. You will need enough glass bottles (or jars) to store 2 litres (8 cups) of cordial.

To sterilise the containers and their lids, wash them well in hot, soapy water, then dry and place in a cold oven. Set the oven to 120°C (235°F/Gas ½) and heat the containers and lids for 15 minutes. Alternatively, you could wash them by hand and then put them through a hot dishwasher cycle. Cool before using.

Peel the lemons. Put the peel, sugar, citric acid, tartaric acid and water into a large saucepan. Juice the lemons to yield 450 ml (just over 1¾ cups/16 fl oz) of juice, and add the juice to the saucepan.

Cook over medium heat, stirring constantly until the sugar dissolves, then increase the heat to high, bring to the boil and simmer for 5 minutes. Remove from the heat, pour into a large glass jug or bowl, and allow to cool. Cover and set aside overnight so the peel can macerate in the syrup.

The next day, strain the liquid into the sterilised containers and seal. Store any open bottles of cordial in the fridge.

Makes about 2 litres (8 cups) of concentrated lemon cordial

Note — To serve as a vodka spritzer, try a nip of vodka with 30 ml (or a nip) lemon cordial, 185 ml (¾ cup/6 fl oz) sparkling mineral water and a large slice of lemon rind, over ice.

Aperol Spritz Granita

Our Australian summers are pretty hot and Sydney can get mighty humid. The best Aussie antidote to heat is an ice cold slushy. So if you love an Aperol spritz (as we all do), then this combo is essential for those hot days. Make this gorgeous do-ahead granita as a refreshing dessert after a good Aussie barbecue lunch or for late-afternoon summer drinks.

180 ml (¾ cup/6 fl oz) Aperol
(or Campari)
250 ml (1 cup/8½ fl oz) Prosecco
(or other dry Italian sparkling wine)
220 g (1 cup/7¾ oz) white (granulated)
sugar
250 ml (1 cup/8½ fl oz) freshly
squeezed orange juice
125 ml (½ cup/4¼ fl oz) sparkling
mineral water
leaves from ½ bunch mint, to serve

Start this recipe the day before serving.

In a small saucepan, gently heat the Aperol, Prosecco and sugar over medium–low heat until the sugar is dissolved. Do not let it boil.

Add the orange juice and mineral water and stir, then remove from the heat and allow to cool.

Pour into a large freezerproof container, cover and place in the freezer overnight. The next day, use a fork to break up the ice crystals and place back in the freezer for an additional 6 hours. Use a fork to break up the crystals once again. Serve in individual glasses, garnished with torn mint leaves if you wish.

Store in an airtight container in the freezer for up to 1 month.

Serves about 6

Anchovy Twists

JUDY LOWY

Anyone who has been to Judy's over the past 20 years will have enjoyed an anchovy twist or three – perfect as a dinner party starter, an accompaniment to a cocktail or a late night snack. This incredible and versatile pastry (used in the Summer Fruit Galette on page 153 and the Pear Tarte Tatin in *The food, the stories, the sisterhood*) comes from Marieke Brugman, who taught the pastry to Judy and Lisa at the HowquaDale Gourmet Retreat in 1991 in the Victorian high country. These can be refrigerated after rolling for up to 24 hours, and can be frozen for up to three months. Bake them straight from the fridge or the freezer – if frozen, add an additional five minutes cooking time. If you are new to making pastry, see How to Pastry on page 148.

120 g (heaped ¾ cup/4¼ oz) plain (all-purpose) flour, plus extra
100 g (3½ oz) cold, unsalted butter, chopped
60 g (¼ cup/2 oz) sour cream
30 (about 160 g/5⅔ oz) best-quality anchovies in oil, drained

To make the pastry, place the flour, butter and sour cream into the bowl of a food processor and process until it just forms a ball. Wrap tightly in plastic wrap and refrigerate for 30 minutes.

Preheat the oven to 200°C (400°F/Gas 6). Line a baking tray.

Divide the dough in 2. On a well-floured bench, roll out half of the pastry into a 40 x 25 cm (16 x 10 inch) rectangle. Lay it horizontally on the bench and cut in half crossways. Line up 15 of the anchovies, vertically, on one half side by side and equally spaced (about 1 cm/½ inch apart). Place the other half of the pastry on top of the anchovies and, with your fingers, press the pastry to seal between each one. Cut the pastry right through where you have sealed, between each anchovy, making 15 anchovy-enclosed rectangles.

Pick up 1 rectangle and twist each end in the opposite direction then press to seal at the ends. Place on the prepared tray and continue with the remaining anchovies. Repeat with the second half of the dough. Bake for 20 minutes or until golden then allow to cool for 5 minutes before serving.

Makes 30

Pastry recipe credit — reprinted with permission of Marieke Brugman, former proprietor chef of HowquaDale Gourmet Retreat and director of travel concierge, Marieke's Art of Living (mariekesartofliving.com).

A DRINK AND A NUT

Spiced Cheese
Biscuits p 293

Salty Sticks
p 294

Knäckebröd
p 294

Spiced Cheese Biscuits

CHARMAINE AND
REUBEN SOLOMON

One of the great moments in our Monday Morning Cooking Club journey was meeting Charmaine and daughter Debbie back in 2012. Charmaine invited us to her home and taught us how to make Chicken Everest (a recipe from her husband, Reuben, that we shared in *The Feast Goes On*) and the most delicious daisy-shaped cheese biscuits. The story behind these biscuits is telling: the Solomons arrived in 1959 to a Sydney that was so different to the Colombo they left. With Reuben working as a musician, Charmaine spent long evenings alone cooking. She became quite good at her favourite hobby and, with Reuben's encouragement, entered a cookery competition run by a national magazine. These cheese biscuits were awarded second prize and brought the former journalist to the attention of competition judge and Aussie icon Margaret Fulton, who offered her a job as a food writer on that same magazine. It was the start of Charmaine's career.

225 g (1½ cups/8 oz) plain
    (all-purpose) flour
2 tablespoons white sesame seeds,
    toasted
1 teaspoon salt
1 teaspoon sweet paprika
½ teaspoon cayenne pepper
150 g (1½ cups/5⅓ oz) finely grated
    sharp cheddar cheese
25 g (¼ cup/1 oz) finely grated
    Parmigiano-Reggiano cheese
185 g (6½ oz) cold unsalted butter,
    chopped
40 g (⅓ cup/1½ oz) poppy seeds
    (optional), for rolling

Place the flour, sesame seeds, salt, paprika and cayenne pepper into the bowl of the food processor and process to combine. Add the cheeses and pulse to combine. Add the butter and pulse to combine, then process briefly until a rough dough is formed.

Divide the dough in 4 and roll each piece to form a log about 3.5 cm (1⅓ inches) in diameter. Roll 2 of the logs in the poppy seeds, if using. Wrap each log in plastic wrap and refrigerate for at least 1 hour.

When ready to bake, preheat the oven to 180°C (350°F/Gas 4). Line 2 large baking trays. Slice the dough into 5 mm (¼ inch) rounds and place on the prepared tray.

Bake, in batches, for 12 minutes or until light golden. Store in an airtight container. The logs of dough can also be stored in the freezer so that you can whip one out to slice and bake at a moment's notice.

Makes 4 logs, about 25 per log

Salty Sticks

Homemade bread sticks with a history. On her mother's cookbook shelf, Lisa found *Lox Stocks and Bagels*, an iconic collection of recipes from Melbourne's Jewish community published by the Women Caring for Women Committee in 1994. We have tweaked this recipe from Chana Zeiman, the house mother at a women's refuge in Haifa, Israel. Thanks to project manager Lorraine Gold, who we found through our fantastic community network, we are really excited not only to share this recipe, but also to ensure their extraordinary cookbook lives on through our book, almost 30 years after it was published. These salty sticks are great with a drink and a wedge of cheese.

250 g (1⅔ cups/9 oz) plain (all-purpose) flour
2 teaspoons baking powder
¼ teaspoon salt
50 g (1¾ oz) unsalted butter, at room temperature, chopped
80 ml (⅓ cup/2¾ fl oz) beer
60 ml (¼ cup/2 fl oz) oil
60 g (½ cup/2 oz) white sesame seeds
3 teaspoons sea salt flakes

Preheat the oven to 200°C (400°F/Gas 6). Line a large baking tray.

In a medium bowl, combine the flour, baking powder and salt. Add the butter and crumble together with your fingertips or with a pastry blender until the mixture resembles coarse breadcrumbs.

Add the beer and oil and mix well with a wooden spoon until a dough is formed.

Divide the dough in 3, then divide each of those pieces into 8, so you have 24 pieces. Cover the pieces of dough with a light tea towel while you roll the sticks.

Using your hands, roll each piece of dough into a very thin stick, approximately 20 cm (8 inches) in length.

Combine the sesame seeds and sea salt on a plate. Roll each stick in the mixture and place on the prepared tray.

Bake for 12 minutes or until golden brown.

Makes 24

Knäckebröd

Swedish Crispbread

In 2018, we were thrilled to bits to be the 'celebrity' cooks at the Glen Innes Royal Agricultural Show, and discovered such a warm friendly community of like-minded souls in rural New South Wales. When Merelyn went back to visit, local girl Belinda Norton introduced her to these very moreish Swedish crackers. Belinda was given the recipe by her friend in Sweden, Sam Seljak. Merelyn brought a batch to a working lunch, and the rest, as they say, is history.

100 g (⅔ cup/3½ oz) white sesame seeds
100 g (½ cup/3½ oz) pepitas (pumpkin seeds)
100 g (¾ cup/3½ oz) sunflower seeds
50 g (¼ cup/1¾ oz) linseeds (flaxseeds)
100 g (⅔ cup/3½ oz) besan (chickpea flour)
1 teaspoon salt
2½ tablespoons extra virgin olive oil
200 ml (¾ cup + 1 tablespoon/6¾ fl oz) warm water

Preheat the oven to 150°C (300°F/Gas 2) and line 2 baking trays.

In a medium-sized bowl, mix together the sesame seeds, pepitas, sunflower seeds, linseeds, besan and salt until well combined. In a small bowl, mix together the extra virgin olive oil and warm water, then add this to the dry mixture and stir until well combined. Set aside to rest for 15 minutes.

Using a spatula or small, angled palette knife, spread the mixture thinly on the trays to around 3 mm (⅛ inch) thick, then sprinkle with a little extra salt. Bake for 1 hour or until deep golden brown.

Allow to cool then roughly break into pieces and either serve right away or store in an airtight container.

Serves about 14

Savoury Walnut Biscuits

ADAM WOLFERS

These biscuits are inspired by the sweet nut *kipferl* Adam's Viennese grandmother used to make. They are really all about the walnuts, so use the best quality you can find. Walnuts have a short shelf life and turn rancid easily – taste and check before you start cooking.

WALNUT BISCUITS

100 g (1 cup/3½ oz) walnuts
125 g (1 scant cup/4½ oz) plain (all-purpose) flour, plus extra
¾ teaspoon salt
125 g (4½ oz) cold unsalted butter, chopped
1 egg
1 tablespoon molasses (treacle)

TO SERVE
(PER 1 LOG/45 BISCUITS)

250 g (9 oz) cream cheese, at room temperature, chopped
150 g (5⅓ oz) Atlantic salmon roe
1 bunch chives, snipped

Preheat the oven to 150°C (300°F/Gas 2). Put the walnuts on a baking tray and cook for 6 minutes or until light golden. Remove from the oven and allow to cool on the tray.

Using a food processor, finely chop the walnuts, taking care not to over process or purée. Tip the walnuts into a large mixing bowl. Add the flour, salt and butter to the food processor and pulse until it resembles coarse breadcrumbs. Add this to the walnuts and use your fingertips to combine. In a small bowl, whisk the egg and the molasses together, then add to the walnut mixture. With your hands, combine until you have a soft dough.

Divide the dough in 2. With lightly floured hands and using a piece of baking paper, roll each piece into a log approximately 20 cm (8 inches) in length, using the baking paper to help with rolling. If the dough is too soft, place it in the fridge for a little while to firm up, then roll again.

Seal each log in the baking paper, twist the ends to close, then place in the freezer for at least 2 hours or overnight. You need a log that is firm enough to slice.

When ready to bake, preheat the oven to 150°C (300°F/Gas 2). Line a baking tray (these are best baked in batches).

Remove the first log from the freezer and allow to soften for a couple of minutes so it is just soft enough to slice. Slice as thinly as possible (2–3 mm/ ⅛ inch) and place on the prepared tray. Once you have sliced enough biscuits to fill up the tray, return the remaining dough to the freezer. Bake immediately for 13 minutes or until golden brown and smelling of toasted walnuts. Cool on the oven tray. Repeat with the remaining dough and the other log, or store in the freezer for another time.

To serve, beat the cream cheese with an electric mixer for 5 minutes or until light and fluffy. Serve the biscuits with the cream cheese, salmon roe and snipped chives.

Makes 2 logs, about 45 per log

Frojalda

Turkish Cheese Bread

Frojalda is the traditional *Shavuot* (the festival where much dairy is consumed) bread baked by Jewish Turkish families. This thick, cheesy focaccia-style loaf, studded with feta and topped with melted cheese, has a super-crisp buttery edge, and a chewy, almost crumpety, inside. It is extraordinary. We found this recipe when scouring the local library for Jewish cooks from around the world – wanting to ensure we had seen every recipe that had been published from the global Jewish community. We fell in love with Janna's book *Jewish Soul Food: From Minsk to Marrakesh,* and this was just one of the many recipes that got a Post-it note on the page.

500 g (3⅓ cups/1 lb 2 oz) plain (all-purpose) flour
5 g (¾ sachet/1½ teaspoons) active dried yeast
500 ml (2 cups/17 fl oz) warm water
300 g (10½ oz) feta cheese, crumbled
150 g (5⅓ oz) unsalted butter, melted
120 g (4¼ oz) cheddar cheese, grated

You will need an extra-large rectangular (preferably non-stick) roasting pan or deep tray, 40 x 30 cm (16 x 12 inches).

Combine the flour, yeast and water in a large bowl and knead with your hands or using the dough hook in an electric mixer until a very soft (almost runny) dough is formed, about 5 minutes. Add the feta cheese and mix through the dough.

Pour half the melted butter into the roasting pan, pour the dough into the pan, flatten with a spatula and your fingertips, then top with the remaining butter, making sure the dough is covered with butter on all sides.

Cover with another roasting pan or deep tray, facing down (so the dough has room to rise), then cover with a towel and leave for 2 hours or until doubled in volume.

Preheat the oven to 200°C (400°F/Gas 6). Sprinkle the grated cheese over the dough and bake for 35 minutes or until golden and crisp on the top and bottom. Allow to cool slightly then remove from the pan onto a board and cut into large squares to serve.

Best eaten warm. Store leftovers in the fridge for up to 3 days and reheat for 15 minutes at 200°C (400°F/Gas 6), or until sizzling.

Serves about 12

Recipe credit for *Frojalda* and Nut and Date Coins —
Adapted and printed with permission of the author,
from *Jewish Soul Food: From Minsk to Marrakesh* by
Janna Gur, published by Schocken Books, 2014.

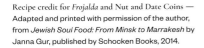

Onion *Pletzels*

LEAH KOENIG

We'd never heard of a *pletzel* before. We had eaten onion rolls growing up in Sydney and Melbourne, and a *pletzel* is pretty much a cross between an onion roll or *bialy* (like we have in *The Feast Goes On*) and a focaccia. When Jewish immigrants landed in the U.S. from Eastern Europe, these flatbreads, known as 'onion boards', were sold in Jewish bakeries. They are great served warm with butter, or with a cream cheese *shmear*.

DOUGH

7 g (1 sachet/2¼ teaspoons) active
    dried yeast
1 teaspoon white (granulated) sugar
250 ml (1 cup/8½ fl oz) lukewarm
    water
340 g (2¼ cups/12 oz) plain
    (all-purpose) flour, plus extra
1 teaspoon salt
60 ml (¼ cup/2 fl oz) oil

TOPPING

2 tablespoons oil
2 onions, finely chopped
¾ teaspoon salt
1 teaspoon dried onion flakes

ALSO NEEDED

1 teaspoon oil, for greasing
1 egg, lightly beaten, for egg wash
2 teaspoons poppy seeds

butter or cream cheese, to serve

Combine the yeast, sugar and water in a small bowl. To ensure the yeast is active, allow to stand for 10 minutes or until frothy.

Meanwhile, whisk together the flour and salt in a large bowl. Add the oil to the yeast mixture and stir to combine. Make a well in the centre of the flour and pour in the yeast mixture. Using an electric mixer with a dough hook, knead for 10 minutes, adding extra flour only if necessary, 1 tablespoon at a time, or until a supple dough forms. Cover the bowl with plastic wrap and a tea towel and stand in a warm place for 1 hour or until almost doubled in volume.

Meanwhile, make the topping. Heat the oil in a large frying pan over medium heat. Add the onions, and once they start to sizzle, cover the pan and cook (stirring occasionally) for 15 minutes or until softened and translucent.

Add the salt and the onion flakes and continue to cook, uncovered, for about 10 minutes, stirring from time to time, until just golden. Remove from the heat and allow to cool.

Preheat the oven to 220°C (430°F/Gas 8). Brush a 38 x 28 cm (15 x 11 inch) rimmed baking tray with the 1 teaspoon of oil.

Gently punch down the dough by kneading briefly to remove any air. Using your hands, press it into the prepared tray until it touches the edges on all sides. Using your fingertips, gently press indentations all over the dough. Cover with lightly greased plastic wrap or a light tea towel for about 30 minutes or until puffed up all over.

Uncover the dough and prick the top all over with a fork. Brush the top of the dough with the egg wash. You will not need it all. Spread the onions evenly over the top and sprinkle with the poppy seeds. Bake for 15 minutes or until golden and cooked through.

Transfer to a wire rack to cool slightly, then cut into squares to serve. Serve warm with butter or cream cheese. Any leftovers can be stored in an airtight container for up to 5 days and reheated in the oven or in a sandwich press.

Serves about 10

Recipe credit — Adapted and printed with permission of the publisher, from *Modern Jewish Cooking: Recipes and customs for today's kitchen* by Leah Koenig, published by Chronicle Books, 2015.

Potato *Bhaji Latkes*

RACHEL DINGOOR AND MMCC

Indian Spiced Potato Cakes

We have taken the spices and flavours of Rachel Dingoor's Indian-inspired potato *bhaji* to create a new Monday Morning Cooking Club *Chanukah* tradition: golden, spiced potato pancakes garnished with fresh coriander and red chilli. Guaranteed to shake up any *Chanukah* party.

600 g (1 lb 5 oz) desiree (or frying) potatoes
2 tablespoons oil, plus extra to fry the *latkes*
1 teaspoon yellow mustard seeds
1 teaspoon cumin seeds
1 onion, halved and finely sliced
2 teaspoons ground cumin
2 tablespoons ground coriander
½ teaspoon ground turmeric
1 teaspoon salt
1 egg, lightly beaten
1 heaped tablespoon plain (all-purpose) flour

TO SERVE

1 long red chilli, chopped
½ bunch coriander, chopped
lemon wedges

Peel and coarsely grate the potatoes. Place in a colander for 15 minutes to drain.

Meanwhile, in a large frying pan, heat the oil over medium heat. Add the mustard and cumin seeds and stir for 3 minutes. Take care, as the mustard seeds will pop. Add the onion and sauté gently for around 10 minutes, stirring occasionally, until softened. Add the cumin, coriander, turmeric and salt, and sauté for a further 3 minutes, stirring. Remove from the pan and set aside.

Squeeze the grated potato with your hands to remove any liquid and tip into a large bowl. Add the egg, flour and fried onion mixture and taste for seasoning. If necessary, add salt and pepper. Mix well.

Add enough extra oil to the frying pan to reach a depth of about 1 cm (½ inch). When the oil is hot, carefully add a tablespoon of the potato mixture to make round potato cakes. Flatten slightly and fry over medium heat for a few minutes on each side until golden brown. Drain on paper towel.

Serve hot, sprinkled with chopped chilli, fresh coriander leaves and a wedge of lemon.

Serves about 4

Plechinta

Romanian Feta Pie

We've known Dov for many years, and whenever we talk food with him, his mother is always part of the conversation. Born in Romania in 1927, Felicia studied cookery as a teenager. She told Dov rich stories about his grandmother – 'the master chef' – whom he never met. We are honoured that Dov has shared Felicia's very special *plechinta* for this book – it is truly a masterpiece of a pie. Dov's beautiful mum passed away recently, aged 91, and we hope that her memory will live on through our kitchens.

PASTRY

600 g (4 cups/1 lb 5 oz) plain
    (all-purpose) flour, plus extra
1 teaspoon salt
450 g (1 lb) cold unsalted butter,
    chopped
75 ml (2⅔ fl oz) cold water, plus extra

FILLING

2 tablespoons olive oil
2 leeks, finely sliced
1 clove garlic
2 bunches silverbeet, stalks removed
    (about 600 g/1 lb 5 oz leaves)
600 g (1 lb 5 oz) Bulgarian feta
    cheese, chopped
300 g (10½ oz) ricotta cheese
300 g (10½ oz) Parmesan cheese,
    grated
2 bunches dill
1 teaspoon salt, plus extra
½ teaspoon white pepper, plus extra
8 eggs, beaten

ALSO NEEDED

1 egg yolk
1 tablespoon milk
30 g (¼ cup/1 oz) white sesame seeds

Start this recipe the day before serving. You will need a square 23 cm (9 inch) high-sided tin; there is no need to line or grease it.

To make the pastry, place the flour and salt in a food processor and pulse to combine. Add the butter and pulse until the mixture resembles coarse breadcrumbs. Add the water and pulse again until a rough dough forms around the blade. You may need to add a little extra water so that it comes together.

Sprinkle a little flour on the benchtop and lightly knead the dough just until a ball is formed.

Divide the dough into two-thirds and one-third, and shape each piece into a flat disc. Wrap each tightly in plastic wrap and refrigerate overnight.

To make the filling, heat the olive oil in a large frying pan over medium heat. Sauté the leek and the garlic until soft. Finely chop the silverbeet and add to the pan. Cover with a lid and continue to cook until the silverbeet is wilted, then uncover and continue to cook for a further 5 minutes or until the leek is soft. Remove the pan from the heat, allow to cool and then squeeze out any excess liquid.

In a large bowl, combine the cheeses. Remove the dill fronds from the stalks and finely chop. Add the cooled silverbeet, dill, salt and pepper to the cheeses and mix well to combine. Add the eggs, combine well and season to taste.

Preheat the oven to 200°C (400°F/Gas 6). On a well-floured benchtop, roll the larger disc of dough out into a large rectangle to fit the base and sides of the tin. Carefully lay the pastry in the tin, easing it into the corners. Leave an overhang of 2 cm (¾ inch) for crimping and trimming.

Place the filling in the tin and spread it out evenly. Roll the smaller piece of dough out so it is slightly larger than the tin. Place it on top of the filling. Trim and then join or crimp the edges.

Combine the egg yolk and milk to make an egg wash. Brush the pastry with the egg wash and sprinkle with the sesame seeds.

Bake for 40 minutes and then reduce the heat to 180°C (350°F/Gas 4). Cook for another 15 minutes or until golden brown on top. Allow to cool then remove the pie from the tin by inverting it onto a board and then inverting (right way up) onto a serving plate.

Serve warm or at room temperature. This keeps well in the fridge for up to 4 days.

Serves about 16

Jerusalem *Kugel*

ADIRA WERDIGER

This is a crisp-edged, peppery, oily, salty, just-sweet baked noodle dish that is a Jerusalem tradition, known as *Yerushalmi kugel*. It stirs up nostalgic memories for Adira, whose family used to eat it every *Shabbat* lunch when they lived in Israel. Adira now makes it for her family and friends in Melbourne some 40 years later. She follows what her mother used to do and puts it in the oven on Friday night and serves it for lunch on Saturday, allowing it to cook slowly overnight (see note).

400 g (14 oz) thin egg noodles
5 eggs
2 teaspoons maple syrup
2 teaspoons brown sugar
220 g (1 cup/7¾ oz) white (granulated) sugar
125 ml (½ cup/4¼ fl oz) oil, plus extra
2 teaspoons salt
3 teaspoons ground white or black pepper, or to taste
pickled cucumbers, to serve

Generously grease a square 20 cm (8 inch) tin or 1.5 litres (6 cup) baking dish.

Preheat the oven to 180°C (350°F/Gas 4). Cook the noodles according to the instructions on the packet until they are firm to the bite, or al dente, and then drain. Drizzle a little of the extra oil through the noodles and toss well.

In a medium bowl, whisk the eggs. Add the maple syrup and brown sugar, whisking to combine. Set aside.

In a wide and deep frying pan, combine the white sugar and the oil and cook over medium heat for around 10 minutes, stirring from time to time, until the sugar is melted and dark golden brown. The oil and the sugar will stay separated. Turn off the heat and carefully (it will spit) add the noodles and toss very well so that all the noodles are coated in the caramel. Some of the caramel may harden but it will melt if you toss the noodles in the warm pan (or put it back on medium heat for a minute or so). Add the egg mixture and the salt and pepper, tossing thoroughly to combine.

Tip into the prepared tin or dish and bake for 1 hour 15 minutes or until the top is golden and crisp.

Traditionally served with pickled cucumbers.

Serves about 12

Note — For a deep caramel-coloured *kugel*, cook it overnight as follows: Cook at 180°C (350°F/Gas 4) for 30 minutes and allow to cool. At around 6 pm, double wrap in aluminium foil and bake at 100°C (200°F) for 16 hours or so.

Thanks

So here we are, 115ish recipes later, at the end of our fourth book. We are so grateful to the wonderful and still most supportive publisher Catherine Milne, for her ongoing commitment to us. We don't know where we would be without her passion and belief. It has been such an incredible pleasure to work with the head of design Mark Campbell. Mark's emails, brimming with positivity and encouragement, got us through many a day. Thanks to editorial team Barbara McClenahan, Katie Bosher and Susan McCreery for perfecting all our imperfections in the kindest way.

We are thrilled to bits to have such a super-talented creative team once again. Four books later, we still adore photographer Alan Benson for his brilliant work, big-heartedness, humour and all-day coffee service. We love David Morgan, our super talented food stylist, who has unlimited patience for the four women arguing around him; he produces the goods, shot after shot. Thanks to fabulous stylist Emma Knowles for pitching in so happily for our final shoot day. We are so thankful to the very clever Evi O and her talented team of Susan Le, Rosie Whelan, Nicole Ho and Joyce Cheng who have worked so hard to create beauty from cover to cover.

Behind the scenes, the hugest of thanks to Rachel Quintana in our test kitchen; she's an essential and much-loved part of the team. Thanks to Sally Montgomery, who came on board to help us get going on the huge task of collecting and writing stories.

Continuing thanks to our solicitors, Arnold Bloch Leibler, our accountants and auditors, MBP Advisory, and our accountant, Catherine Hunt of Dakota Corporation, for doing all the things needed to run a business that we *still* have no idea how to do. And for doing it all *pro bono*.

To the following wonderful cooks who gave us extra guidance with their recipes in our kitchen: Laura Gluckman, Elza Levin, Nilly Berger and Chef Riyad Seewan. Thanks to all those who helped us in our search for recipes across the globe, one of our most difficult tasks: Shoshanah Stein and Jacqui Sklenka from Canada, Susie Ivany and the ICJW, Myriam Macías Abady, Inbal Baum from Delicious Israel and to the many others who helped us along the way. And thanks to Rebecca Maher for reading our text with fresh eyes.

With love also to our extended sisterhood: Lynn Niselow, Lauren Fink and Paula Horwitz, who we miss having by our side in the kitchen.

Thanks to our beautiful families for all the years of love and encouragement, and for accepting that all we cooked for you during the last three years was sweet food.

Monday Morning Cooking Club is a not-for-profit company and 100 per cent of all our profits from the sales of our book go to charity. We appreciate our ongoing relationship with WIZO.

Visit mondaymorningcookingclub.com.au for a comprehensive list of the many charities we support.

313

Index

HarperCollins*Publishers*

First published in Australia in 2020
by HarperCollins*Publishers* Australia Pty Limited
ABN 36 009 913 517
harpercollins.com.au

HarperCollins*Publishers*
Level 13, 201 Elizabeth Street, Sydney NSW 2000, Australia
Unit D1, 63 Apollo Drive, Rosedale, Auckland 0632, New Zealand
A 53, Sector 57, Noida, UP, India
1 London Bridge Street, London, SE1 9GF, United Kingdom
Bay Adelaide Centre, East Tower, 22 Adelaide Street West,
    41st floor, Toronto, Ontario M5H 4E3, Canada
195 Broadway, New York NY 10007, USA

A catalogue record for this book is available
from the National Library of Australia

ISBN 978 1 4607 5167 1 (hardback)

Photography by Alan Benson
Design by Evi-O.Studio | Susan Le & Nicole Ho
Styling by David Morgan
Typeset in Cormorant Garamond by Evi-O.Studio | Nicole Ho & Rosie Whelan
Illustrations by Evi-O.Studio | Joyce Cheng

We gratefully acknowledge the permission granted by copyright holders
to reproduce the copyright material in this book. All reasonable attempts
have been made to contact the copyright holders; the publisher would be
interested to hear from anyone not acknowledged here,
or acknowledged incorrectly.

Colour reproduction by Splitting Image Colour Studio, Clayton VIC
Printed and bound in China by RR Donnelley

8 7 6 5 4 3 2   20 21 22 23

Visit us at mondaymorningcookingclub.com.au